The Augsburg

Confession

A Collection of Sources

J. M. Reu

REPRINTED BY PERMISSION.
CONCORDIA SEMINARY PRESS
WINTER, 1966

#9770

8. SCHWABACH ARTICLES, SUMMER, 1529

Article I. It is positively and unanimously [with great consent] taught that there is but one only true God, the Creator of Heaven and Earth; so that in the one, true divine essence, there are three distinct persons, namely, God the Father, God the Son, God the Holy Ghost. That the Son begotten of the Father from eternity to eternity, is with the Father, truly and by nature God; and the Holy Ghost, both of the Father and Son, is, with the Father and Son, truly by nature God, as all this can be clearly and effectually proved by Scripture, as John 1:1, 2: "In the beginning was the Word, and the Word was with God, and the Word was God. All things were made by Him." Matthew 28:19: "Go and teach all nations, baptizing them in the name of the Father, and of the Son, and of the Holy Ghost"; and other similar passages, especially in the Gospel of John.

Article II. That God's only Son became true man, having

been conceived of the Holy Ghost, born of the pure virgin Mary, complete in body and soul; and that not the Father or the Holy Ghost became man, as the Patripassian heretics have taught; also that the Son did not assume the body alone without the soul, as the Photinians have erroneously taught. For He Himself in the Gospel, very often speaks of His soul, as when He says: "My soul is exceeding sorrowful, even unto death" (Matthew 26:38). But that God the Son became man is manifest from John 1:14: "And the Word became flesh," etc., and Gal. 4:4: "When the fulness of the time was come," etc.

Article III. That this Son of God, true God and man, Jesus Christ, is one, indivisible person, who for us men suffered, was crucified, died, was buried, on the third day arose from the dead, ascended into Heaven, sitteth at the right hand of God, Lord over all creatures. So that no man can or should believe or teach that Jesus Christ has suffered for us [only *Latin*] as man or in His human nature; but because God and man are not here two persons, but an indivisible person, we should hold and teach that God and man, or God's Son, truly suffered for us; as Paul says, Rom. 8:32: "God spared not His own Son, but delivered Him up for us all." 1 Cor. 2:8: "Had they known it," etc., and more passages to the same effect.

ARTICLE IV. That original sin is properly and truly sin, and not only a weakness or defect. but such a sin as would condemn and eternally separate from God all men who come of Adam, if Jesus Christ had not interceded for us, and assumed this sin, together with all sins which proceed from it, and by His suffering made satisfaction for it, and thus entirely abolished and blotted it out in Himself; as in Ps. 50 and Rom. 5 it is clearly written concerning this sin.

Article V. Since, therefore, all men are sinners, subject to sin, and to death, besides to the devil, it is impossible that a man from his own strength, or by his good works, deliver himself thence, so that he may become again righteous or godly; yea, he cannot even prepare or dispose himself for righteousness, but the more he attempts to deliver himself, the worse it is for him. But that the only way to righteousness and to deliverance from sin and death is, if without all merits or works. we believe in the Son of God, who suffered for us, etc. As it is said, this faith is our righteousness; for God reckons and regards as righteous, godly and holy, and pre-

sents with the forgiveness of sin and life everlasting, all those who
have this faith in His Son: that, for His Son's sake, they are received into grace, and are His children in His kingdom; as St.
Paul and St. John in their writings richly teach us, Rom. 10:10:
"With the heart man believeth," John 3:15: That all who believe in
the Son, should not perish, but have eternal life."

Article VI. That this faith is not a human work, nor, of our
own powers, possible, but it is a work and gift of God, which the
Holy Ghost, given through Christ, works in us; and this faith, since
it is not a spurious fancy or presumption of the heart, as the hete-
rodox regard it, but an efficacious, new and living thing, produces
much fruit, is always doing what is good; towards God, by praise,
thanksgiving, prayer, preaching and teaching, and towards neighbors
by love, serving, aiding, counselling, giving and lending and by suffering every sort of evil, even unto death, etc.

Article VII. To obtain this faith, or to bestow it upon us
men God has instituted the ministry, or the oral word, viz., the
Gospel, by which He causes this faith and its power, use and fruit
to be proclaimed, and through the same, as a means, bestows faith
by His Holy Spirit, as and where He will; other than this there
is no means, mode or way to receive faith. For thoughts outside of
or before the oral word, however holy and good they appear, are
nevertheless nothing but lies and error.

Article VIII. With and besides this oral word, God has also
instituted external signs, which are called sacraments, viz., Baptism
and the Eucharist, through which, besides the Word, God offers and
gives also faith and His Spirit, and strengthens all who desire [Lat.
fleeing to] Him.

Article IX. That Baptism, the first sign or sacrament, consists of two parts, namely water and the Word of God, or that
men should be baptized with water, and God's Word be spoken. Nor
is it mere ordinary water, or pouring (as the blasphemers of Baptism,
at the present day, teach); but because God's Word is with it, and
it is founded upon God's Word, it is a holy, living, efficacious thing,
and as Paul says, Tit. 3:5 and Eph. 5:26, "a washing of regeneration
and renewal of the Holy Ghost." etc., and that this Baptism should
also be extended and administered to children. Moreover, God's
words upon which it is founded, are these: "Go ye, baptize in the
name of the Father, and of the Son, and of the Holy Ghost," Matt.

28:19; and Mark 16:16: "He that believeth," etc. Hence men must believe.

Article X. The Eucharist or Sacrament of the Altar also consists of two parts, viz., that there is truly present in the bread and in the wine, the true Body and Blood of Christ, according to the sound of the words: "This is my body, this is my blood;" and that it is not only bread and wine, as even now the other side asserts. These words require and also convey faith, and also exercise it in all those who desire this sacrament, and do not act against it; just as Baptism also brings and gives faith, if it be desired.

Article XI. That Private Confession should not be enforced by laws, just as Baptism, the Sacrament, the Gospel should not be forced, but be free; nevertheless that we should know how very consolatory and salutary, useful and good it is to consciences distressed or in error, because therein absolution—i.e., God's Word and judgment—is pronounced, whereby the conscience is freed from its sorrow and pacified; also that it is not necessary to enumerate all sins; but those may be indicated which torment and agitate the heart.

Article XII. That there is no doubt that there is and remains upon earth until the end of the world a holy Christian church, as Christ declares, Matt. 28:20: "Lo, I am with you alway, even unto the end of the world." This church is nothing else than believers in Christ, who hold, believe and teach the above-mentioned articles and parts, and for this suffer persecution and martyrdom in the world; for where the Gospel is preached and the Sacraments used aright, is the holy Christian church, and it is not bound by laws and outward pomp, to place and time, to persons and ceremonies.

Article XIII. That the Lord Jesus Christ will come at the last day to judge the quick and the dead, and to deliver those who believe in Him from all evil, and bring them to everlasting life; and to punish the unbelieving and godless, and to condemn them eternally, with the devil, in Hell.

Article XIV. That in the meantime, until the Lord come to judgment, and will do away with all power and rule, we should honor worldly magistrates and rulers, and be obedient to them, as to an estate ordained by God to defend the godly, and restrain the wicked. That a Christian who is regularly called thereto undoubtedly may administer such an estate, or attend upon it without injury and peril to his faith and his soul's salvation, Rom. 13; 1 Pet. 2.

Article XV. From all this it follows that the doctrine which prohibits marriage and ordinary food and drink to priests, together with monastic life and vows of every kind (because thereby grace and the salvation of the soul are sought for and intended and not left free), are nothing but damnable doctrines of devils, as St. Paul 1 Tim. 4:2, 3 calls them, since Christ alone is the only way to grace and the salvation of the soul

Article XVI. That before all abominations, the mass, which has hitherto been regarded an offering or good work, by which grace was to be obtained by one for another, is abolished; but instead of this mass, the divine ordinance should be observed, to distribute the holy sacrament of the Body and Blood of Christ in both forms to every one for his faith, and according to his own necessity.

Article XVII. That the ceremonies of the Church, which conflict with God's Word, are also abolished, but the rest are left free to be used or not, according to love, in order that offence may not without cause and thoughtlessly be given, or the common peace be unnecessarily disturbed, etc.

9. LUTHER'S STAND AT MARBURG, OCTOBER, 1529

a. Luther's Declaration on the Evening of October 3, 1529.[10] According to Oecolampadius' report Luther said: "We confess that by virtue of the words, 'This is my body. This is my blood,' the body and the blood of Christ are truly, (*hoc est*) *substantive et essentialiter, non autem quantitative vel qualitative vel localiter,* present and distributed in the holy supper. Now inasmuch as until now we were of the opinion that our dear sirs and brethren, Oecolampadius, Zwinglius, and their adherents totally rejected the true presence of the body and the blood, but in this friendly colloquy have found it to be otherwise, therefore we herewith declare and state that the *argumenta* and reasons found in our books concerning the sacrament are not directed against Oecolampadius, Zwinglius, and their adherents but against those who totally reject the presence of the body in the supper.

b. The Marburg Articles, October 4, 1529.[11] *First.* That we on both sides unanimously believe and hold that there is but one only true natural God, the Creator of all creatures, and this God is one in essence and nature, and triune in person, namely Father, Son and Holy Ghost, as it was decreed in the Council of

Nicaea, and is sung and read in the Nicene Creed by the entire Christian Church in the world.—*Secondly,* We believe that not the Father, nor the Holy Ghost, but the Son of God the Father, God by nature became man by the working of the Holy Ghost without the agency of virile seed; being born bodily of the pure virgin Mary, complete in body and soul, as another man; without all sin.— *Thirdly,* That this Son of God and Mary, an indivisible person, Jesus Christ, for us was crucified, died, was buried, arose from the dead, ascended into Heaven, sitteth at the right hand of God, Lord over all creatures, and will come to judge the quick and the dead.—*Fourthly.* We believe that original sin is innate and inherited from Adam, and is such a sin as to condemn all men; and if Jesus Christ had not come to our help by His death and life, we must on that account have died eternally, and could not have entered God's kingdom and salvation.—*Fifthly.* We believe that we are delivered from this sin, and all other sins. as well as from eternal death, if we believe in this Son of God, Jesus Christ, who died for us, and that without this faith we cannot be delivered from any sins by any works, station or order whatever.—*Sixthly.* That this faith is a gift of God which we can acquire by no preceding works or merit, nor obtain of our own powers, but the Holy Ghost gives and furnishes it as He will, to our hearts, when we hearken to the Gospel or word of Christ.—*Seventhly.* That this faith is our righteousness before God, since on account of this, God reckons and regards us righteous, godly and holy, without all works and merit, and thereby delivers us from sin, death, hell, receives us into grace and saves us, for the sake of His Son, in whom we accordingly believe, and thereby enjoy and partake of the righteousness, life and all possessions of His Son. Therefore all monastic life, and vows as necessary to salvation, are altogether condemned.— *Of the External Word. Eighthly,* That the Holy Ghost, to speak in proper order, gives this faith or His gift to no one, without preaching, or the oral word or the Gospel of Christ preceding, but, by and with this oral Word, works and furnishes faith, as and in whom He will, Rom. 10:17.—*Of Baptism. Ninthly,* That Holy Baptism is a sacrament, that has been instituted of God for this faith, and because God's command: "Go ye, baptize," Matt. 28:19, and God's promise: "He that believeth." Matt. 16:16, is therein, it is not a mere empty sign or symbol among Christians, but a sign and work of God, wherein our faith is required through which we are regenerated.—*Tenthly,* That by the efficacy of the Holy Ghost this faith, if we are thereby reckoned and become righteous and holy, exercises good works through us, namely, love towards one's neighbor, prayer to God, and suffering all persecution.—*Of Confession. Eleventhly,* That confession, or the seeking of counsel from one's pastor or neighbor, should indeed be unconstrained and free, but nevertheless is very useful to consciences distressed, troubled, or burdened with sins, or fallen into error, especially on account of the absolution, or consolation of the Gospel, which is the true absolution.—*Of the Magistracy. Twelfthly.* That all magistrates and worldly laws, courts and regulations, as they are, are a truly good estate, and are not forbidden, as some Papists and Anabaptists teach and hold. On the contrary, that a Christian who is called or born thereto, can certainly be saved through faith in Christ, just as in the estate of father and mother, husband and wife.—*Thirteenth,* That provided they do not conflict with God's Word, what are called traditions, or human regulations in spiritual or ecclesiastical matters, may be regarded or left free, according to the people with whom we have to do, in order in every way to avoid unnecessary offence, and to promote peace. Also that the doctrine which prohibits the marriage of priests is a doctrine of the devil, 1 Tim. 4:1, 2.—*Fourteenth,* That the baptism of children is right, and that they are thereby received into God's grace and Christendom.—*Of the Sacrament of the Body and Blood of Christ. Fifteenth.* We all believe and hold concerning the Supper of our dear, Lord Jesus Christ, that both forms should be used according to the institution; also that the mass is not a work, whereby one obtains grace for another, dead and living; also that the sacrament of the altar is a sacrament of the true Body and Blood of Jesus Christ, and that the spiritual partaking of this Body and Blood is specially necessary to every true Christian. In like manner, as to the use of the sacrament, that like the Word of God Almighty, it has been given and ordained, in order that weak consciences might be excited by the Holy Ghost to faith and love.

And although we are not at this time agreed, as to whether the true Body and Blood of Christ are bodily present in the bread and wine, nevertheless the one party should show to the other Christian love, so far as conscience can permit, and both should fervently pray God Almighty, that, by His Spirit, He would confirm us in the true understanding.

Martin Luther, Philip Melanchthon, Justus Jonas, Andrew Osiander, John Brentius, Stephan Agricola, John Oecolampadius, Ulric Zwingli, Martin Bucer, Caspar Hedio.

10. THE RECESS OF SCHWABACH, OCTOBER 16, 1529[12]

WHEREAS the counsellors of the worshipful and most worshipful, highborn, gracious and most gracious Princes and Lords, John, Duke of Saxony, Archmarshal of the Holy Roman Empire, Elector, etc., George, Margrave of Brandenburg, etc., and Philip, Landgrave of Hesse, etc., and the representatives of the city councils of the honorable, free and imperial cities of Strassburg, Nuremberg, and Ulm have convened here at Schwabach for the purpose of taking further and final action with reference to a secret agreement and alliance concerning which a preliminary understanding was reached at the Rotach conference; and WHEREAS only two of the above mentioned gracious and most gracious Lords, namely the Elector of Saxony and Margrave George of Brandenburg—in the conviction that said agreement pertains only to the question of how they may assist, succor, and help one another in keeping the one and only saving Word of God and a genuine, truly Christian faith and all that this implies in case one or more of the above mentioned Elector, Princes, or Estates should on account of the Word of God, the holy Gospel, our faith, or anything that is connected therewith, be unlawfully attacked, invaded, violated, or molested—have ordered their counsellors to formulate and present at this conference several articles of our holy religion which the members of this alliance should confess both individually and collectively, with the intention of arriving at an agreement on these points with the other above mentioned Estates, to the end that in the future all errors concerning the Word of God and our holy religion may be avoided; but WHEREAS the representatives of said honorable, free and imperial cities of Strassburg and Ulm (whose magistrates had not been informed of said summary of our religion) did not have instructions concerning the same and felt unauthorized to agree to these articles without their magistrates' and friends' knowledge and without orders from the same:

Therefore the counsellors of said Elector and Princes and the representatives of the honorable, free, and imperial cities, in view of the fact that the above mentioned alliance should rest solely on the

,agreement in our holy faith and in view of the imperative necessity of properly accepting these articles, have, for the time being, taken the following friendly and secret RECESS, to wit, THAT all representatives report to their respective superiors (without binding them as yet) what they have heard in regard to this matter; and, THAT all superiors send their counsellors and representatives to convene at Smalcald on the evening of December 15 next, that is the Wednesday after Lucia's Day, where, God willing, further profitable and necessary negotiations concerning the controversial articles and any others shall be conducted with a view toward establishing the proposed secret alliance.—Furthermore, like at the recent Rotach conference, the above mentioned counsellors and representatives have unanimously deemed it salutary and necessary that in case between today and the proposed date of meeting one or more of the Estates here represented should be attacked, violated, or molested on account of those matters which are mentioned in the agreement of Rotach, the party or parties so attacked shall inform the other members of this alliance and seek their comfort, counsel, and assistance in the firm assurance (for that is the purpose of our action) of obtaining from their faithful and sincere allies the same help that they themselves would offer if the case were reversed.

WHEREAS, moreover, it seems necessary and salutary from every point of view to keep this matter, especially the fact that no definite action has been taken and that no union has been formed as yet, positively secret in order that our adversaries may not hear of it and attempt to divide these Christian Estates or employ other tactics in trying to frustrate our union or at least rejoice because of the delay:—Therefore this transaction and this recess shall be kept most secret, and every party to this agreement shall in every way act as though the above mentioned Elector, Princes, and Estates were in all matters most perfectly, definitely, and absolutely united.

In witness whereof, this recess, made in six copies, has been signed by all representatives, one of each party receiving one copy. Done at Schwabach, Tuesday after St. Luke's Day, 1529.—Hans von Minckwitz, Knight, Georg Vogler, Chancellor, Wolf Christoph von Wiesentau, Sigmund von Boynebrockh, Mathis Pfarner, Christoph Fress, Ber Bessrer.

15. THE IMPERIAL SUMMONS TO THE DIET OF AUGSBURG, JANUARY 21, 1530[17]

To the most noble John, Duke of Saxony, Landgrave of Thuringia, Margrave of Meissen, archmarshal of the Holy Roman Empire, our dear uncle and Elector, Charles, by the grace of God, Roman Emperor, *semper Augustus*, etc.

Noble, dear Uncle and Elector! [The Emperor professes the greatest interest in the affairs of the Empire, explains his prolonged absence from Germany, asserts that he has concluded a somewhat unsatisfactory peace with his enemies, and states that he has consulted the Pope in the interest of securing peace and unity in the Holy German Empire. He then goes on:]

Soon after our arrival in Italy we received reports that the Turk, the traditional enemy of our holy Christian name and religion, with a large army had invaded the Christian Kingdom of Hungary and our fatherland the Archduchy of Austria, and was slaughtering and burning everything; and it was evident that the Holy Empire of the German Nation was in the greatest peril unless we should come to its assistance. So we changed our plans and decided to leave Italy, including our Kingdom of Naples (although it was greatly endangered by insurrection), and to avert, in person and with all our armies, this terrible calamity threatening the German Nation. We also petitioned His Holiness the Pope to confer with us at this city of Bologna on the pacification of the Italian countries on the unity of the Holy Roman Empire, and on the welfare of all Christendom in general, because the present need requires not only that the Turk be repulsed with the greatest possible force, but also that these

numerous varied and weighty opinions be judged with the greatest
care and wisdom. When His Holiness learned of our intentions, he
did not only very kindly grant us our petition but also travelled so
fast that he arrived here at Bologna before we did. He received
us with favor and kindness; and we found in him far more love and
eagerness to settle the affairs of the Holy Empire of the worthy
German Nation, to bring about peace and general agreement, and to
restore right and order in matters pertaining to the Christian religion
than we had dared to hope. When we had learned these things and
when we had received our Imperial crown, we intended to carry out
our original plan of continuing our journey to Germany; but just
at that time we were informed that the Turk had retreated so that
it was no longer so urgently necessary to travel with haste to Germany; we therefore decided that it was more expedient to carry out
our original purpose of first establishing order in these Italian regions
and to keep them firmly and faithfully aligned with the Holy Empire. We hope to complete this task shortly and leave nothing undone
that promises to be of help in the speedy adjustment of these difficulties.

In the meantime, however, we have not ignored the affairs of
the Holy Empire of the German Nation, especially since we learned
that the arrival of the troops which you, Well-beloved, and other
Estates of the Holy Empire, according to the recess of the Diet of
Speyer, resolved to send for the protection of the greatly exposed
Christian country of Hungary against the powerful advance of the
Turk, was delayed on account of another conference held at Ratisbon
to such an extent that it was impossible to stop the formidable Turkish
army and navy from crossing the Hungarian boundary lines and from
invading the kingdoms, duchies, and domains of the highborn Prince
Ferdinand, King of Hungary and Bohemia, Archduke of Austria, our
dearly beloved brother and personal representative in the Holy Empire. As a result, His Highness was unfortunately compelled inactively
to witness the capture of almost the entire Christian kingdom of
Hungary by the Turk, who at once proceeded to attack our Archduchy of Austria and grievously harassed, besieged, and distressed
its capital Vienna. And although the Turk, through the grace of the
Almighty and the dauntless and courageous resistance and defense
of the Christian army, had to give up his brutal designs, he has
nevertheless made so many forays, ravages, and inroads throughout
said duchy especially round about Vienna, as far as the river Enns,

and even into the Duchy of Styria, and shed so much innocent blood and caused such devastations by slaughtering many Christians and carrying them away and by burning their houses—as you, Well-beloved, undoubtedly know—that every Christian must be deeply grieved and moved to sincere sympathy with those who are so heavily afflicted. And since the Turk consistently and assiduously pursues all his aims, especially when he is victorious, as appears from his expedition against Hungary and more recently from his hundred-mile invasion of Austria where he devastated many fertile fields with fire, and since. even though he had to give up his plan temporarily, we may expect that he will seriously resume his brutal attacks upon all Christendom with still larger armies so as to carry out his intentions,

Therefore, We, as Roman Emperor and head of Christendom, who have always been solicitous of the welfare of the Holy Empire and have always been desirous of averting danger and defeat, have resolved, for the purpose of opposing, resisting, and repelling, the Turk, so far is it is humanly possible, and also for the purpose of settling in salutary and expedient manner other matters affecting the Holy Empire, to convoke a general diet and assembly, and, on the eighth day of April next ensuing, to hold the same in our Imperial City of Augsburg, by which time we hope that we shall have settled affairs in Italy so as to be present in person on that day, as we have been finally resolved to do. This day, then, we hereby announce to you, our Well-beloved, commanding you by the authority of our Roman Empire and by the duty wherewith you are bound to us and to the Empire, solemnly enjoining and ordering you to appear that day in person at Augsburg, and together with us and our other Imperial Electors, Princes, and Estates of the Holy Empire, whom we have summoned in like manner, to assist in undertaking, debating, resolving, and concluding how the proper provision may be made for the removal of the grievous burden and invasion into Christendom of the aforesaid Turk, with good deliverance, defence, and steady help according to need, in addition to the measure formerly taken in that behalf; and further, how in the matter of errors and divisions. concerning the holy faith and the Christian religion we may and should deal and resolve, and so bring it about, in better and sounder fashion that divisions may be allayed, antipathies set aside, all past errors left to the judgment of our Saviour, and every care taken to give a charitable hearing to every man's opinion, thoughts, and no-

tions, to understand them, to weigh them, to bring and reconcile men
to a unity in Christian truth, to dispose of everything that has not
been rightly explained or treated of on the one side or the other
to see to it that one single, true religion may be accepted and held
by us all, and that we all live in one common Church and in unity,
just as we all live and battle under the one Christ, and finally to
resolve, arrange, establish, and preserve good unity and peace throughout the Empire; also to decide on questions pertaining to coinage
and the public order and welfare of the Holy Empire . . . .

———————

18. DUKES WILLIAM IV AND LOUIS X OF BAVARIA TO THE THEOLOGICAL FACULTY OF INGOL-STADT UNIVERSITY, FEBRUARY 13, 1530[20]

By the grace of God, William and Louis, brothers, Dukes of Upper and Lower Bavaria, etc.—Greeting: Worthy, learned and devout, dear, faithful Ones! Since our most gracious lord and cousin, His Imperial Roman Majesty may upon his arrival in Germany be confidently expected to summon a general Diet at which the matters of our Christian religion and faith will be discussed first of all; and in order that this matter (as is proper) may be given the most thorough and careful treatment, and in order that the doctrines which Martin Luther and other new teachers during the past twelve years have set up in opposition to our Christian faith may be clearly shown to be erroneous and worthy of repudiation, therefore we order you at once to make a complete summary and catalogue of all such heresies, wrong doctrines, and slanderous statements, and to indicate how these views may be refuted so that we may obtain the list from you when we need it. This is our solemn order and command; and we will graciously acknowledge this service which you are bound to perform by virtue of your official position.

Given at Munich, Saturday, February 13, 1530.—Khoelner.

To the worthy, learned, dear, devout, and faithful dean and members of the theological faculty of our University at Ingolstadt.

19. THE TORGAU ARTICLES, MARCH, 1530[21]

Since some accuse my lord, although unjustly, that his Electoral Grace is dispensing with all divine service, and is introducing a heathenish, dissolute mode of life and insubordination, from which the distraction of all Christendom results, it is necessary for my lord first to show that his Electoral Grace, with the greatest earnest-ness, desires to introduce and promote the true, real divine service, and such as is pleasing to God, and that, to God's praise and glory, he is incurring danger, expense and trouble, which he would not do, if he did not think that he was thereby serving God. For it is well known how his Electoral Grace has always conducted his life, so that, thank God, he has always been inclined to peace, and has thus far, in these matters, often helped to maintain and make peace. To this effect it is well to place first a long and rhetorical preface.

Secondly, this is also manifest and clear, viz., that with the greatest earnestness, my lord is making provision that, in the territory of his Electoral Grace, the Holy Gospel be preached with all diligence, and that ceremonies be performed in accordance with it; and every one, even among the adversaries, must aknowledge that this doctrine, which is taught, and written, and treated is Christian and comforting, and that in it there is no error, although it be upbraided with being an innovation, without agreement with the councils. Because the adversaries themselves now confess that the doctrine is in itself right, my lord cannot be justly accused of dispensing with divine service, and tolerating unchristian doctrine or matters, etc. But his Electoral Grace knows and does not doubt that this is true, real divine service, and also, that the doctrine which your Electoral Grace has allowed in your lands, is Christian, and consolatory to all men, who fear God, and is salutary.

The present dissension now is especially concerning some abuses, which have been introduced by human doctrine and statutes, of which we will report in order, and indicate for what reasons, my lord is induced to cause certain abuses to be abated.

Of the Doctrines and Ordinances of Men. First. Although divine service does not consist in the doctrines of men, yet my lord, in the territories of his Electoral Grace, has caused the customary church ordinances, which are not contrary to the Holy Gospel, to be observed, and has caused it to be preached, and the people to be informed that such ordinances should be observed for the sake of peace; as is manifest and every one can see that, in the territory of his Electoral Grace, divine services are held with greater devotion, and earnestness, than with the adversaries.

Secondly. Moreover there are many human ordinances which cannot be observed without sin. To these my lord has neither wished, nor been said to have constrained any one by violence, contrary to God's command, for the reason that the Scriptures say, Acts 5:29: "We ought to obey God rather than men." This the canons also command, Dis. 8, viz., that every custom, however old it be, and however long it have continued, should yield to the Scriptures, and the truth, etc.

But since some, on the contrary, declare that no change should be made against the consent of the Church, or of the Pope; also that the sins which have originated from fictitious human doctrines are much more endurable, and less injurious than the schism which has now arisen by such alteration; also that as schismatics we are members cut off from the Church; and that with us the sacraments are invalid, etc.—charges that are made with great bitterness, etc.; It is therefore necessary to answer: "They may extol obedience as highly as they please, provided this declaration stand firm: "We ought to obey God rather than men." Also in Galatians: "Though an angel from heaven preach any other gospel unto you than that which we have preached unto you, let him be accursed." Hence it clearly follows that they are not accursed who abandon false doctrines and ordinances; but they are publicly condemned by St. Paul who observe false doctrines and ordinances, etc.

On that account, the unity of the Christian Church, consists not in external, human ordinances; and therefore we are not members cut off from the Church, if we observe dissimilar ordinances from one another; and, for this reason, the Holy Sacraments among us are not invalid. For dissimilarity in external human ordinances is not contrary to the unity of the Christian Church, as is clearly proved by the article which we confess in the Creed: "I believe the Holy Catholic Church." For since we are here commanded to believe that there is a Catholic Church, that is, the Church in the entire world and not bound to one place, but that wherever God's Word and ordinances are, there is a Church, and yet the external human ordinances are not alike, it follows that this dissimilarity is not contrary to the unity of the Church. Christ also says: "My sheep hear my voice" "And a stranger will they not follow; for they know not the voice of strangers." And "The kingdom of God cometh not with observation." "If any man shall say unto you, Lo here is Christ, or lo there." And Paul: "The kingdom of God is not meat and drink," etc. Augustine also writes expressly to Januarius that the unity of the Church does not consist in external human ordinances, and says that such ordinances should be free, and may or may not be observed. Also if it would be a schism to change external ordinances, they are more justly to be regarded as schismatics who, acting in opposition to the ordinances of all Christendom, and in opposition to the councils, make prohibitions, such as that of marriage, although the Council of Constantinople decreed that the priests should not be forbidden marriage. Also those who have introduced new divine services contrary to the usage and practice of the ancient Church, have sold masses, although the ancient Church knew nothing whatever of such marketable masses. Besides if citations be made from the fathers. continue to be forbidden, still worse will happen; for the longer the them, and the like, the schismatics mentioned by them are not those who practice dissimilarity in regard to external human ordinances, but those who abandon God's Word in an article, as Augustine expressly writes Against Cresconius, and Jerome: "It is no schism unless they devise some heresy."

Moreover what the human ordinances are that cannot be observed without sin we will hereafter enumerate. For it is necessary first to speak also of those ordinances which were observed as means, and from which also many errors, before this time, were preached and taught in the Church; as for example, of fasts, differences of food and dress, especially the observance of fasts, chants, pilgrimages, and the like, under the impression that all these are works whereby grace and the forgiveness of sins are obtained. Now it is manifest this is a pernicious, damnable error, as is acknowledged also by many among the adversaries. who have received consolation from the doctrine which teaches, on the contrary, that forgiveness of sins and grace are truly presented us through Christ out of grace, and that it is alone through faith in Christ, that we receive it, that for Christ's sake, and through Christ's merits, without our own merit, our sins are forgiven. Therefore if it be taught that through the above mentioned human ordinances, we receive grace and the forgiveness of sins, it is certainly manifest blasphemy, and directly contrary to the Holy Gospel. For Paul expressly teaches that if we would be justified and acquire grace through our own works, Christ has died for us in vain. Gal. 2, Rom. 3: "Knowing that a man is justified by faith without the deeds of the law." Also Ephesians 2: "By grace are ye saved through faith; and that not of yourselves: it is the gift of God; not of works." Therefore those who have taught that we obtain grace through our own self-chosen works, such as set fasts, or holidays or the like, have done Christ great dishonor, in ascribing the praise that belongs to Christ to their own self-chosen works; they have also thereby prevented Christ and his grace from being acknowledged, and that too when no higher honor can be rendered God than that Christ be acknowledged and heard; as it is written: "This is my beloved Son in whom I am well pleased; hear him."

Also Christ says: "In vain do they worship me with the commandments of men." There it is most assuredly declared that God does not regard human church ordinances as meriting the forgiveness of sins. Christ has also forbidden that sin and righteousness should be placed in a difference of food, and wishes this to be left free, as St. Paul says: "Let no man judge you in meat or in drink." But now those who do observe a distinction of food are reproached as heretics; and yet Paul calls such distinction a doctrine of devils.

Therefore if the true Christian doctrine concerning such ordinances, as are observed as means, be admitted, they may indeed be observed; as at first the church ordinance of holidays or fasts was established, not thereby to obtain grace, but that the people could learn and know when to come together, or might otherwise have bodily exercise that they might thereby become the better qualified to hear and learn God's Word. But if such ordinance be required as though it were servicable to obtain grace, or as though, without such work, no one could be a Christian, such an error should be resisted by doctrine and by example, as Paul would not circumcise Titus, in order to attest that such work would be neither necessary nor useful to acquire grace.

For this cause also my lord has constrained no one to observe distinction of food or set fasts, but has permitted such traditions to fall into disuse; for it is manifest that they were observed as works, whereby forgiveness of sins is obtained. In order that such errors should not be established, these ordinances should not be pressed upon men. The adversaries also proclaim that those persons are heretics, who do not observe the distinction of food, and thus make of it a work without which no one can be a Christian. Yet Christ says: "Food maketh not unclean" ("Not that which goeth into the mouth, defileth the man," Math. 15:11).

The ancient canons indicate what should be held concerning such human ordinances. Dist. 4. It is forbidden that the fasts which have fallen into disuse be again established. Now if such ordinance may be abandoned by custom, it follows that it is not necessary to the Christian life. Thus the penitential canons have become obsolete by custom, and yet no one regards it a sin to discontinue them. Thus many other ordinances and many ancient canons have ceased to be in force, as for example, in the decrees, the fasts on Wednesdays and Fridays. Nor has any one observed the entire fasts, as they have been commanded. It is also said in Dist. 12:5: "The Roman

Church knows that it is not detrimental to the salvation of the soul to change other ordinances with respect to times and places. Jerome and Augustine also write that of such ordinances a necessary thing should not be made.

Of the Marriage of Priests. These are the ordinances which cannot be observed without sin. First they forbid the priests marriage. This is contrary to God. For Paul writes: "It is better to marry than to burn." This is God's command, and can be abolished by no man. So also it is known that the Church thus held for a long time; and that the councils ordered that marriage should not be forbidden the priests. Likewise that to the observance of this prohibition, the priesthood in Germany has been with difficulty coerced by violence, and a bishop of Metz was almost killed when he published the Papal prohibition. What good results therefrom is easily seen, and there is ground for apprehension that if marriage continue to be forbidden, still worse will happen; for the longer the world lasts, the weaker it is.

Of Both Forms. This custom of receiving only one form of the sacrament is also one that cannot be observed without sin. For Christ commanded: "Drink ye all of this." So too it is known that the Church for a long time administered both forms to the laity, as may be found in Cyprian, and in the canons. But how it was changed, and who forbade both forms to be administered, is not known.

Of the Mass. It has hitherto been taught that the mass is a work, whereby he who administers it acquires grace not only for himself, but also for others; yea that it obtains grace for others, even though the priest be not godly. For this reason, many masses were instituted for the dead and the living, whereby to obtain things of every sort; that the merchant may succeed in his business, the hunter, in the chase, etc. For this purpose, masses are appointed, bought and sold, and are observed alone for the sake of base gain; so that many godly men before the present time have complained of this.

And although, at the present time, some wish to palliate their affairs, the mass should be observed as a memorial, and not that thereby grace may be acquired for the dead or the living. They may color the matter as they will, their books and writings are public, wherein it is to be seen how they have taught that the mass is an offering which merits grace and removes the sins of the dead and the living.

Moreover that this is an error may be proved by Paul, who in all places teaches us that we obtain grace and have consolation alone through Christ, when we believe that, for Christ's sake, God is gracious to us, and wishes to receive and help us. If now forgiveness of sins must, therefore, be obtained through faith, it cannot be merited for another by the work of the priest; and it is a great error thus to point men from faith to a strange work; and yet so much depends upon this faith, for it is the chief article of the Christian life to have true confidence to God, for Christ's sake, that he confers grace and will help in all need. Of this faith, they who sell masses do not speak, but they boast alone in their work, and wish by their work to save others; although Christ has done this once and for all, as Paul writes: "By one offering, he hath perfected for ever them that are sanctified."

Again, the words in the Holy Sacrament teach us the proper use: "This is the cup of the New Testament." Now the New Testament is not our work, but God's work, who offers and allots something, as is the custom in making a testament; and thus grace and the forgiveness of sins are offered and allotted. "If now this is promise," says Paul, "it must be received by faith." Therefore the mass is not a work that merits something for another, but he who uses it, to whom grace and the forgiveness of sins are here offered, receives them when he believes that he obtains this through Christ, and that it is determined that faith should be exercised and excited in those who use it. Nevertheless, the abuse is manifest that the majority of those who celebrate and say mass for the sake of base gain, do this with dislike and contempt of God. Therefore even though there were no other cause than the great excessive abuses, yet who would not change the present custom in all bishoprics? For Paul says: "Whosoever shall eat this bread, and drink this cup of the Lord unworthily, shall be guilty of the Body and Blood of the Lord."

On this account my lord has a pastor to celebrate mass in such a way that thereby other persons who are fit also use the sacrament; and this is a proper custom. For Christ has instituted it that it should be celebrated with one another in the churches, by those who are fit for it, as Paul also teaches the Corinthians that they should tarry for one another, and use it together—those, namely, who first so find their hearts in such a state that they do not dishonor the Lord's Body and Blood. And in order that no dishonor be done the Sacrament, the people should be often instructed why it should be used, and should be then admonished to use it.

The Zwinglian doctrine is also earnestly contended against, as the writings published concerning it in my lord's lands show; and the people are carefully instructed, that in the Supper the Body and Blood of Christ are present, and that they are given; for thereby faith is strengthened that consolation is received, that Christ wishes to be ours, to help, etc.

And my lord does not doubt that this mass is true and Christian divine service, especially since, even to the times of Jerome and Augustine, there were only such masses, and it is not known whence the mercenary masses came, or when private masses began.

Of Confession. Confession is not abolished; but is maintained with such great earnestness, that the pastors are enjoined not to communicate the Holy Sacrament to any one who has not previously been examined and sought absolution. For the absolution is very needful and consolatory, because we know that to forgive sins is Christ's command, and that he wishes this declaration of the priest, whereby sins are forgiven, to be regarded as though it were his voice and verdict from heaven. And men are taught with the greatest diligence concerning the efficacy of the absolution, and the faith that belongs thereto, so that they know how highly consolatory are confession and absolution. Yet previously the monks said nothing of faith and absolution. They only tortured poor consciences with the enunmeration of sins, which, however, is possible to no man on earth. On this account, the people are not compelled to enumerate their sins; for the command to enumerate sins is not to be found in the Scriptures, which is also not possible, as the Psalmist says: "Who can understand his errors?"

Again, the command concerning confession, on this account, has been thus given, viz. that the priests are charged to communicate the Sacrament to no one who has not sought of them absolution. Otherwise no time and measure are prescribed to men, when they should confess; for such a command would produce a certain abuse of the Sacrament, as it occurred, in former times, that men who were unwilling to cease from sins, were forced to the Sacrament, whereby the Sacrament was greatly dishonored. For absolution is a consolation to alarmed consciences. This consolation is mocked at, if one should ask for it, who, nevertheless, does not desire it; besides if one should fix time and measure when men are to go to the Sacrament, it would follow, contrary to the rule of St. Paul, that many would be compelled thereto, who would then receive unworthily the Body and Blood of Christ. Of such dishonor to the Sacrament do they become guilty who have compelled such persons to the Sacrament.

Besides, the people are earnestly admonished by God's Word, and it is held up to them, that he who wishes to be a Christian is, in duty bound to use the Sacrament; he also who never uses it shows that he does not wish to be a Christian, as the canon made in the Council of Toledo, *Si qui intrant,* Dis. 2, *de Consecr.,* also declares.

Of Jurisdiction. Of the Jurisdiction and Sovereignty of Bishops. My Lord has taken no jurisdiction or sovereignty from the bishops, but since men would no longer seek the spiritual tribunal, and the clergy in many places abused their power and the ban, my lord, in his capacity as prince, has been compelled to harken to and to interest himself in the matters pertaining to his Electoral Grace; as the administration of ecclesiastical law is also entrusted to sovereigns, in dealing with such matters, if the clergy abuse their jurisdiction.—Secondly, it is the chief part of ecclesiastical jurisdiction to reprove erroneous doctrines; for this is commanded the bishops in the Scriptures and the canons. Now before this time, they have never exercised this jurisdiction, but have allowed all sorts of errors to be preached. If they now wish, under the pretext of their jurisdiction. to suppress the true doctrine, their jurisdiction in this respect cannot be approved. For if the bishops would, in a regular and Christian way, have examined in time these matters, whence the present dissension has originated, much displeasure would have been avoided.—Thirdly, if my lord is not in duty bound to aid the bishops in seizing the priests who have been married, and in thereby maintaining allegiance to them, my lord could not then help them with a good conscience. Besides every patron is rather in duty bound, according to ecclesiastical law, to protect the ministers of his churches against the unjust power of ecclesiastical prelates, especially if the patron be not subject to the same prelates; for the patron has even the power to appoint a capable priest to a parish, against the will of a prelate who has made an unsuitable appointment. *C. Decernimus,* 16, 9. 7.—Fourthly, if, in regard to ecclesiastical tribunals, complaint is made, concerning many matters pertaining to marriage, that they necessarily require an appeal to other tribunals (and the cases are these, viz., that a secret marriage vow is confirmed, even

if a child be taken by theft from a reputable man; also that spiritual
paternity breaks marriage vows; also, that after divorce, the innocent
part is not to marry again, a point directly contrary to God's Word;
nor is it needful to mention further the abuses that have occurred
therefrom), for this reason, their sovereignty and jurisdiction cannot, in this respect, be conceded. It is also worthy of consideration
that, even though one might wish to establish such sovereignty against
the whole world, yet it is not possible; for men cannot be forced to
seek such a tribunal with the burdens upon their conscience.

Of Ordination. Likewise because the bishops burden the priests
with such oaths, as they cannot observe without sin, viz. not to
preach this doctrine and not to be married, ordination cannot be
sought from them; for such an oath is contrary to God, and we
must obey God rather than men, as also the canons prescribe that
the bishops are to be deserted who compel men to act contrary to
God. Here there are many disputations which it is not needful
to ponder, viz. whether the priests must be ordained by bishops,
whether the office of priest be appointed for doctrine, or to make
an offering for others, whereby grace is acquired for others.

Also concerning the ceremonies of ordination, the advice moreover is indeed given to yield somewhat, if there is unanimity concerning the chief article, so that the bishops acquiesce therein. For if
they would make peace, we would do right in giving up everything
that could be yielded, with a good conscience, for the sake of peace
which is higher and more worthy of regard, than all the outward freedom that can be imagined. If indeed these matters pertained alone
to our persons, and not to the government, country and people, we
would, at our own peril, treat the adversaries for ourselves with still
greater rigor. But this has been divulged, and much mischief has
been practised by the populace in this rupture, and the government
has been usurped by its aid; for what pernicious and horrible offences originate from such ruptures, can easily be conjectured. Be
sides what might occur in the future, is to be considered. It is to
be apprehended that not many Dr. Martins will come after this time,
who would control these important matters with such grace, and
would avoid false doctrine and war. If now the discord continue,
and indiscreet and wicked persons interfere still more in the future.
O God, what will they prepare? God grant grace that the nobles
may exercise their office for both sides, and besides may consider
their most dear children, whom they can have instructed in nothing

better than the true religion and a good government. But that hitherto some indifferent ordinances have been abandoned, has occurred because they condemned the doctrine; if then the doctrine be allowed us and be cordially received, they might be recalled and would be regarded by us in no way otherwise than had we recalled them, and thus to please them we would observe certain customs, provided the doctrine would receive no injury.

Of Vows. Of Monastic Life. This subject of monastic life does not concern my lord, for his Electoral Grace has ordered the monks neither to go out of, nor to go into monasteries, but it is proper to ask of them themselves the reason why this has happened. It is a private matter, and does not pertain to the Church at large. Nevertheless the reasons are recounted why my lord has not again founded monasteries, and why his Electoral Grace has tolerated the persons who have abandoned them.

There are especially three reasons why the monastic life, as it has hitherto been conducted, is wrong and contrary to God. The first is, that this life is entered with the imagination that thereby satisfaction is made for sin, and grace is merited, as Thomas in express words held that monastic life is equal to baptism, and says that to become a monk takes away sin just as baptism. What else is this than to give human and self-devised works the honor of divine service, which belongs to Christ? Christ has purchased grace which we obtain through faith in his merit, Eph. 2. Therefore it is a great blasphemy to wish by means of monastic life, to merit grace, and settle for sins. Baptism has God's word and institution, and is God's work; and for this reason, removes sin. But monasticism has not God's word; for it rests upon mere human commands, of which Christ says: "In vain do they worship me with the commandments of men;" whence it is certain that monasticism cannot remove sins, and that the commands of men wherein monasticism is entirely comprised are a vain service. Since now the monastic vow is an ungodly vow, if any one imagine by such work to merit grace, it is in vain, and of no avail. — The second reason is, that it is also contrary to God's command to make a vow not to marry. To those who suffer from concupiscence, Paul says: "It is better to marry than to burn." Because also such a vow is contrary to creation and the nature of man, it is also impossible. Because now it is contrary to God's command, and besides impossible, it follows that it is not a vow, and that those who need married life, should and must leave the monasteries. On this account the ancient canons permitted young persons to leave the monasteries. 20.41. Besides Augustine writes that even though they who leave the monasteries, and marry, sin, it is a true marriage, and should not be sundered. — The third reason is, that those who have hitherto been in monasteries, even though they would and could live in marriage, were nevertheless compelled to observe the abuse of the mass for the dead, and other unrighteous services, as the invocation of saints, etc. Therefore they have just cause to flee from such an unchristian mode of life, where, under ,God's name, base gain is served, and to avoid it as a sin against the Second Commandment.

Of the Worship of Saints. Touching the saints, it is taught that the example of their faith is useful to us; also that their good works are serviceable to us for instruction, to do the like, each one according to his calling. But to pray the saints for anything, and through their merit to procure anything, is an honor that belongs alone to God and our Lord Christ. Therefore the saints are not to be invoked as intercessors; for Christ has commanded us to adhere to him as the one intercessor and mediator. As Paul says: "To us Christ is Mediator"; and Christ says: "Come unto me, all ye that labor and are heavy laden." And to the illustration, that a good advocate at court is useful, it is easy to answer that such an advocate would do injury, if the prince had given an order that the petition was to be presented by the person himself.

Of German Singing. What in general is to be held concerning indifferent ceremonies, has been said above, viz. that if they are required not for doctrine, but that, by these works, sins might be removed, such service is wrong and is contrary to the Gospel. Since now ceremonies ought to be of service for doctrine, some have adopted German singing, that by this practice men might learn something, as Paul also teaches, 1 Cor. 14, that in the Church nothing unintelligible should be spoken or sung. Yet no command to that effect is made, and Latin also is always sung for the practice of the young. The things thus far stated are concerning external ordinances and customs.

If in addition there should be a desire to know what else my lord causes to be preached, articles may be given in answer wherein the entire Christian doctrine is set forth in order. that it may be seen that my Lord has allowed no heretical doctrine, but has had the Holy Gospel of our Lord Christ preached in the purest way; for even many of the adversaries must acknowledge that they have been better instructed, concerning many sublime and important subjects, by this doctrine which is preached in my lord's lands, than they previously were taught by the sententiarists and summists; as for example, concerning obtaining the forgiveness of sins through faith; also, how to use the sacraments; concerning the distinction between the civil magistracy, and the office of bishop; also, worldly human Church ordinances are to be regarded, whereof there is no end in the summists.

20. THE FIRST DRAFT OF MELANCHTHON'S PRE-FACE TO THE CONFESSION, APRIL, 1530[22]

Whereas the Imperial Majesty, our most gracious Lord, in the recent summons of Your Majesty to this appointed general Reichstag has graciously offered to the Electors, Princes and other Estates of the Empire, to hear, in gracious affection, their individual judgments, opinions, and beliefs concerning the Christian religion, in each other's presence may Your Majesty graciously hear and give audience to the obedient report concerning the doctrine, and church usages that are observed and maintained in the lands of the Elector of Saxony and also the circumstances in general which are the reason for the aforementioned doctrine and church usages.

For thus, in ancient times, preceding Roman Emperors, like Constantine, Theodosius, Charlemagne and Henry II, have acted in similar matters relating to religion and the Christian faith, and on all occasions have graciously heard the transactions and agreements, as far as was necessary, so that in such matters, concerning the soul and conscience they might not strive against God.

So likewise the Holy Ghost, in the Second Psalm, admonishes the Kings, Princes, Potentates and Rulers of the earth, and directs them all to Christ the only supreme King, and to the hearing of the Gospel, and such admonition, which will be clearly manifested at the Last Day, should be accepted with genuine seriousness, for the Psalm speaketh thus: Be wise now therefore, O ye kings; be instructed ye judges of the earth that ye hearken to Christ, to the Gospel, etc. Furthermore, the Forty-seventh Psalm says: The princes of the nations are gathered together, even the people of the God of Abraham, when the shields of the earth turn unto God. Thus the prophet indicates that the real honor of God, and the real and genuine service of God would be increased and preserved when kings and princes piously maintain true and pure Christian doctrine in the Church. Therefore they are called the shields of the earth because God has laid on them the responsibility of faithfully protecting the pious and godly.

Now as the Imperial Majesty is one of the most mighty among the emperors that has ever ruled the Roman Empire, and is of most noble imperial excellence, of laudable name and reputation, not less renowned than Constantine, Theodosius, Charlemagne and Henry II, Your Majesty will act in a very praiseworthy, Christian, and imperial manner if you will endeavor kindly and graciously to promote unity in such matters pertaining to the Christian religion, according to the terms of your summons.

So that all matters of religion may be deduced and investigated according to the divine Scriptures, and the truths of the Christian Religion may be derived therefrom, and not from human propositions, ancient traditions, usages or customs, which though they may have legal validity in worldly business, temporal possessions and the like, may not be advanced nor maintained in matters of faith, as the words of Augustine and Gregory, quoted in Decretum VIII diss. in c. *veritate manifestata* and c. s. *consuetudinem*, likewise indicate. There they testify that in such matters of faith, when the truth has been revealed, all usages that might conflict with it must be relinquished, no matter how ancient or how long their duration, and Gregory proves this by the saying in John XIV; when He says, I am the way, the truth, and the life, He does not (says Gregory) state, I am a custom, but the truth. So it is quite evident, from their statements, that in the days of these fathers abuses contrary to the Scriptures had taken root in the Church. For if such customs and ancient prerogatives against which they desired to quote these words had not been rooted in the Church they would not have dared to argue against them or attack them with such words and similar statements. And since the enemy of the truth, from the very earliest days, did not rest, but sowed such seed of abuses as the statement of the above mentioned fathers, and especially that of the most excellent and learned bishop and martyr Cyprian, whom Gregory also quotes in this passage, proves, how much more is it to be considered that he did not rest nor refrain from sowing such evil seed of abuses in these latter perilous days, in which St. Paul the holy Apostle clearly predicted perverse men would arise, who put their trust in so many and such varied orders, sects and schisms. Afterwards St. Bernard, in his day, as he surveyed the character and customs of the Church, deplored and complained, warned and was apprehensive least finally out of these abuses would come the abomination Christ predicted.

So, likewise, Pope Innocent the third, ordered the prelates that they should not allow the people who frequented their churches to be betrayed with many fictions, fabrications and false teachings, as (he says) was being done in many places for profit or gain, from which testimony of Pope Innocent it is clearly evident with what deception and false teaching the. devil operated in those days and how he ventured to introduce them into worship and teaching.

In addition the Imperial Majesty will graciously recall how numerous and varied were the abuses that by Your Majesty's gracious permission were recounted and presented at the first Reichstag held by Your Majesty at Worms.

Likewise Pope Hadrian recently, through a legate, at the previous Reichstag at Nurnberg (1522-1523) acknowledged such abuses and promised, with the help of God to change and amend them.

These things are humbly brought to the recollection of the Imperial Majesty so that Your Majesty might not be persuaded or influenced by any one (as you doubtless would not be) to believe that there are no abuses contrary to God and the Scriptures in the teachings and ceremonies of the Church.

And though it would be possible to indicate and enumerate to the Imperial Majesty such abuses one after the other, nevertheless we contemplate passing them by, so that the Imperial Majesty may afterwards specifically perceive and see what is taught and preached in the Electorate of Saxony and also the usages that are observed in ceremonies and sacraments. From these Your Imperial Majesty, and each and every one to whose attention these transactions may come, can easily understand what opposite abuses have been removed and omitted.

However, that the Imperial Majesty may be informed concerning the origin of the teaching that is held in the lands of the Elector of Saxony, and how the removal of ceremonial abuses necessarily followed, we recall, what is a matter of common knowledge, particularly in the German nation, that almost everywhere little was preached or taught concerning the chief articles of the Christian faith, and that many harmful and unnecessary teachings were propounded to the people in place of God's Word. This was especially true in the matter of the indulgences, concerning which the Questors, who were

appointed for that purpose, spoke to the people in such exceedingly
ungodly and unbecoming ways, that occasion was given to exhort
and dispute concerning these and similar false teachings which were
being inculcated for the deception of the people. For, among other
impudent assertions, some ventured to declare openly and proclaim
from the pulpits that when the money dropped into the basin, the
soul for which the money was given immediately flew up to heaven.
Therefore it was fitting that the people should be given Christian
instruction in such matters, for if the deception of the simple people
had been allowed to continue in silence any longer such open blasphemies would of necessity have brought the true Christian religion
itself into contempt, had not God in His grace and compassion restored the true and genuine doctrine. But when certain persons,
under the compulsion of their conscience, set themselves against unbecoming and blasphemous preaching and proclaiming of indulgences,
the opponents and their adherents who promoted such an unfounded
and blasphemous teaching concerning indulgences as has been de-
scribed above attempted, as is known to everyone in the empire,
most violently to justify and defend these teachings, both by their
writings and with tirades from the pulpits and ventured to add still
more unfounded declarations to their previous impudent assertions,
so that on our part it became an unavoidable necessity to publish the
Christian teaching opposed to such false teaching and to instruct the
people against it by proofs drawn solely from the divine Holy Scriptures, show them how grace and the forgiveness of sins are to be
obtained and consciences consoled by faith in Christ, as it is most
needful for all Christians to know. From this had to follow, because
it was necessary to speak of the basis of their unseemly teaching,
through the demonstration of established truth that one abuse after
the other had to be abolished, and as one was removed for an indis-
putable reason another and still another, involved with it, had to be
removed, just as in a building whose foundation is not solid nor firm.
The prelates allowed these loutish sermons and writings to go on un-
checked and did not perceive, as they should properly have done, how
the matter was being carried so far, in various publications, that many
honest and learned persons, who had read and weighed the controversial writings published by both parties, had to approve our party
and its teaching, regarding and judging it good and Christian, especially perceiving that in the part which relates how grace and the
forgiveness of sins is to be obtained, we have taught rightly, and

that our opponents have made assertions that are unfounded and untrue, yea, that were fabricated in contradiction to the clear divine Scriptures. So the Imperial Majesty may also graciously consider that it would not have been fitting for those to whom God has given grace to understand divine Scripture to keep silence continuously, to have allowed Christian people to be deceived continually by such fictions and offensive teachings and to have concealed or kept silent the testimony of acknowledged truth. For as St. Chrysostom says (XI. q. IIIC) the word, *nolite timere*, may be summed up: No one shall refrain from openly confessing the truth because of the fear of men. For not only is he a false witness who speaks lies in the place of the truth but likewise the one who does not openly confess the truth or does not defend it is a false witness. This is proved by the statement of St. Paul to the Romans. With the heart man believeth unto righteousness and with the mouth confession is made unto salvation. In addition no offence has appeared or been manifest of such nature that on its account the truth should not openly be spoken against manifest falsehood. For the Imperial Majesty knows that in matters of faith it is more profitable to allow offences to arise and increase, than to keep silent or suppress the truth for the sake of avoiding the offence.

Since the opponents desire to make this teaching and its preachers responsible for the supposed destruction and abolition of all good order, ceremonies, pious and useful Church usages, just as they presume to say, without the possibility of proof, that it forbids good works, so the Imperial Majesty will perceive, from the following accounts, exactly how the Church usages, ceremonies and other matters are conducted in the lands of the Elector of Saxony and also what is there everywhere taught, likewise whether or not upright Christian works and order, or anything that is godly, is omitted, rejected or destroyed, and that what is published by our antagonists is an unnecessary, unprovable and unjust accusation, for our teaching is not directed in any way to such an end.

21. CHANGES OF AND SUPPLEMENTS TO THE FIRST DRAFT, APRIL, 1530[23]

It is widely known that many great and destructive abuses affecting Christian doctrine and other spiritual matters have existed in the Church for a long time. Many eminent persons and those of high rank have complained about this condition in previous times as the Imperial Majesty will graciously recall that in Worms at the Reichstag held by Your Majesty many such abuses were enumerated and were presented to Your Majesty by the Estates. Subsequently Pope Hadrian through a legate acknowledged the same to the Estates of the Empire at Nurnberg and assured them that the specified abuses would be changed and amended as far as possible.

And among other abuses the most conspicuous was this that in almost all the schools, cloisters, and churches little was preached or taught concerning the chief articles of the Christian faith, while much harmful teaching concerning the false service of God was presented, by which consciences were heavily burdened and human institutions, orders, devotions to saints, pilgrimages, indulgences and other unnecessary and useless matters were more frequently and zealously considered, to the destruction of souls, than what the Gospel teaches for the consolation of consciences. In addition new abuses were daily devised for the sake of gain, new institutions, new misuses of the mass, new saints and other fictions,* while the monks practiced such tyranny that not only the common people but even the bishops and other prelates had to remain silent, and for this reason great indignation was aroused among large numbers, particularly against the monks. It is well known how the affair of the indulgences began, which gave occasion to speak of all kinds of abuses, for when such unchristian assertions are made as this, that "when the money drops into the basin the soul flies up to heaven," and many other unseemly statements which are not only contrary to the divine Word but even to papal law, it became the duty of pastors and preachers to instruct the people in these matters, for, if there had been no further Christian instruction such manifest lies would have been exposed and the true Christian religion itself would have been brought into contempt if God had not provided true and certain teaching as a defense against them. When Luther, as was his duty, attacked these unseemly sermons and proclamations concerning indulgences in a short Latin sermon, throughout which he carefully spared the papal authority, the opponents attacked him so fiercely in Latin and German libelous writings that he was compelled to state the basis and reason for his opinion. He then gave such statements of many great and weighty matters, particularly of how consciences were to be consoled by faith in Christ that many

---

* Melanchthon wrote on the margin but later crossed out: so that the Christian religion, with such a multitude of saints, divinities and belly gods, hardly differed from heathen religion.

learned and honest persons were convinced that his teaching was both Christian and necessary, and that much false and erroneous doctrine had previously been preached and written on this point as to how grace and forgiveness might be attained, although the grace of Christ should be the chief subject of preaching and teaching in all Christendom. At first, indeed, Luther did not refer to any other abuses but was only concerned about the chief article of faith, which it is most necessary for all Christians to know. But the opponents did not cease and continued to attack Luther again and again with citations, banns and unseemly writings, and created many more abuses and through their own improprieties aroused such dissent that changes followed in many places. In these situations Luther strenuously opposed harmful teachings and unnecessary changes. Before Luther's time others attacked not only the lives of the clergy, but also many doctrines, from which far greater discontent would have resulted if Luther had not averted it.

22. DR. ECK'S 404 ARTICLES, MARCH, 1530[24]

a. The unpublished Dedication of the Book to the Emperor: To our glorious Lord and Imperial Majesty, Charles V., Emperor of Rome, Catholic King of Spain, Germany, Naples, and Sicily, the God-fearing, happy, and renowned victor and conqueror: prosperity and victory over the enemies of the faith!

All Catholics believe that, in the midst of these numerous tumults of wars and afflictions of Christianity, you, most worshipful Emperor, are the divinely appointed, chosen, and consecrated instrument for stopping the decline of the Catholic faith, for helping the afflicted Church and the oppressed ecclesiastics, for saving the Christian empire from Soliman the Turk, the bloodthirsty tyrant; in short, they believe that the Lord would work the salvation of the Christian world through your hand. But Martin Luther, the Church's enemy within the Church, has refused to heed the high admonitions addressed to him by your Majesty and hurled himself into a veritable whirlpool of godlessness: he calls· the Pope of Rome the "anti-Christ", the Church a "harlot", the bishops "worms and idols", the schools of theology (studia generalia) "synagogues of Satan"; monasteries he calls "brothels", theologians "bats" (vespertiliones), secular princes "louse's eggs, fools, insane drunkards worse than the Turks"; moreover, he does not even refrain from injuring your majesty's sacred shoulders and holy arm but attacks the Anointed of God, and defiles the imperial orders with his filthy, derisive, and contemptuous glosses. He has fallen into a deep pit of despair; he blasphemes God; he has no reverence for saints or sacraments and no respect for ecclesiastical or secular magistrates; he is contumelious and rebellious; he slanders all good men but extols and praises only the heretics and schismatics; he kindles the fires of sedition throughout the empire; he is making ardent preparations for a deluge of Christian blood; he is arming the hands of the Germans in order that they may bathe in the blood of Pope and Cardinals. Thus he has produced a vast offspring, much worse than himself, bringing forth broods of vipers. We must acknowledge as Luther's sons the iconoclasts, the sacramentarians, the Capernaites, the neo-Hussites and their descendants, the anabaptists, the neo-Epicureans who declare the soul to be mortal, the enthusiasts, also the neo-Cerinthians who deny the deity of Christ. Above all, they lacerate our most pitiable German land with these ugly and terrible things; they destroy the churches, demolish the altars, and trample upon the most holy Eucharist; they burn the images of Christ and the saints, exstinguish the worship of God, cast the relics of the saints into the dirt; they steal the church's treasures, gold and silver; they rob the churches and monasteries of their rents and revenues; they invalidate the testaments, bequests, and last wills of the dead. In short, in their insane rage against everything pertaining to the Christian religion they even go so far as to use persuasion, intimidation, threats, and violence so as to drive out of the monasteries the virgins who have been consecrated to God. Nevertheless most of them now have the audacity openly to glory in all their dreadfully execrable crimes and to fling out the boast that they can shield themselves behind the recess of the Diet of Speyer and that they can defend their actions before God and your most venerable Majesty; they allege, as it were, that the most worshipful and venerable ruler of the world is the defender of their ungodliness, slander, thievery, sacrilege, and sedition; and they hope that the Emperor's extreme justice will vindicate their own extreme injustice. While they are not unaware of the fact that it is forbidden under pain of punishment to recommence disputation concerning matters which have once been properly adjudged and settled by a council, they actually revive ancient heresies condemned a thousand or more years ago; they follow teachers who have been burned at the stake and other men held in wretched remembrance, and they deceive the plain people by posing as adherents to the gospel, the Bible, and the Word of God.

For the purpose of stamping out their deceitful vaunts, I present myself before your most worshipful Majesty, ready to perform the same service that I performed at Leipzig against Luther and at Baden against Oecolampadius, namely to defend all the ordinances, usages, doctrines, and ceremonies of our Catholic religion and faith and to attack the arguments of the antagonists. Let them come on, these enemies of the church, these instruments of godlessness, these advocates of heresies, and vessels of iniquity; let them fulfill the proud and insolent boasts which they have broadcast among the people, and let them give an account concerning the faith before the power which is of God, before the servant of God, the defender of the church, the protector of the faith! Farewell, father of our land, most worshipful conqueror! May our blessed and mighty God protect and guide you; may He grant you victories over the Turks and the enemies of the faith, and may He still further increase and extend your dominion! Ingolstadt, Bavaria, March 14, in the year of grace 1530.—Your most worshipful and Catholic Majesty's obedient servant John Eck.

b. *The Title and the Preface of the Printed Edition.* The *title:* Sub Domini JESV et MARIAE patrocinio articulos 404, partim at disputationes Lipsicam, Badensem et Bernensem attinentes, partim vero ex scriptis pacem ecclesiae perturbantium extractos, coram divo Caesare Carolo V., Romanorum imperatore semper augusto, ac proceribus imperii Ioannes Eckius, minimus ecclesiae minister, offert se disputaturum Augustae Vindelicorum die et hora consensu Caesaris posterius publicandis.—*The preface:* Inasmuch as for a number of years false prophets have been rising up and attempting to tear away the people from the unity of the Catholic Faith, corrupting all Germany with errors, impieties, and blasphemies, so that what was formerly regarded most Christian has now become the cesspool of all errors, in behalf of the faith and for the Church I have hastily gathered these few out of their infinite errors. And since the enemies of the faith are making a parade of their writings and are offering in secret to dispute concerning them before the people, I offer, according to the judgment and disposition of our Most Glorious Prince and Lord, Charles V., perpetual Emperor of Spain, Germany, Sicily, a Catholic King, and our most clement Master, and of that of all the Princes of the Roman Empire, especially of our Most Serene Prince and Lord, Ferdinand, King of Hungary and Bavaria, and Archduke of Austria, and of our Most Illustrious Princes of the renowned House of Bavaria, to discuss in public the points below noted against any assailant of the Catholic truth; so as to establish our dogmas and overthrow the false dogmas of the adversaries, to the praise of God, the increase of faith and the strengthening of the weak. To God alone the glory.

c. The 404 Articles of Luther and Others.

First Eck gives 41 articles of Luther condemned by the papal bull, June 15, 1520; then the *conclusiones Eckii Lipsiae* 42-54; then the *conclusiones Eckii* in Baden [in Switzerland, May 26, 1526], 55-61; finally the *conclusiones Eckii in Bern* [Jan. 6, 1528], 62-65. Now under the heading *Errores novi et veteres iam ventilati* the new part of Eck's book begins, 66-404.

New and Old Errors now Stirred Up

Concerning Christ: 66. Christ experienced terrors of soul even to despair (Bugenhagen, Psalmorum 34).—67. Christ in despair cried out, My God, why hast Thou forsaken me (Praemonstratensis, in the disputation at Magdeburg).—68. The greatest cause of the fear of Christ was the sense of desertion and of divine wrath, by which Christ wavered between hell and life. In this fear, there was a desolation of the divine gifts in Christ; for in this affliction and anguish, there was a despoliation of love, because the divinity withdrawing itself, love did not glow (Melanchthon, Super Matth. 5).—69. After the death of Christ, his soul ought to suffer in hell, and in martyrdom be attacked by demons (Antonius Zimmermann, in proprio libello).—70. Christ complained that he was deserted of God, i. e., that he was bereft of life and blessedness and all good (Idem).—71. Christ is finite according to his humanity; therefore, he truly grew in wisdom and grace (Zwingli, Bernae, 153).—72. Christ as a man, is the adoptive Son of God (Bugenhagen, Ad Ephes. 4).—73. Christ merited nothing for himself, but for us (Luther, In maligno iudicio, 155).—74. Christ rose not from a closed sepulchre, neither did he enter into the company of his disciples, while the doors were shut (Bucer, Bernae, fol. 160).—75. Christ is not Head of the Church according to his human nature (Haller, Bernae, fol 64). 76. Christ no longer prays to God for us (Zwingli, Bernae, fol. 206).— 77. Christ did not appear personally to St. Paul, but only through angels (Zwingli, Bernae, fol. 164).—78. In Christ, the two natures, human and divine, are mixed (Burgauer, Bernae, 119. Eutyces).—79. Christ did not have an intellectual soul, but in place of his soul had divinity (Lutheranus, in libro *Der einfaltig Glaub*, fol. 3, Spelt. Apollinaris).— 80. Christ Jesus, according to his divine nature, is, properly speaking, the essence of all things (Zwingli, Bernae, 66. Almaricus).—81. The humanity of Christ is not to be adored; hence, the Eucharist is not to be adored (Zwingli, De eucharistia comment. 278).—82. My soul hates the word "homoousion," i. e., the Father and the Son are of the same essence (Luther, Contra Latomum. Arius).—*Against the Holy Spirit:* 83. Since the death of Christ, the Holy Spirit is his Vicar (Bucer, Bernae, 8. Macedonius).—84. Reason pretends to give Christ honor by reflecting and meditating upon his death, but this is nothing to Christ

(Melanchthon, Super Ioan. 142).—*Against the Sepulchre of Christ:*
85. The sepulchre of Christ's body, which the Saracens hold is no more
a matter of care to God, than, according to the teaching of Paul, oxen
are (Luther, De abroganda missa, 41.—*Against God:* 86. The opinion is
certain that all things are done by God, both good and evil, not only
permissively but properly, as the adultery of David, etc. Accordingly the
betrayal of Judas no less than the call of Paul is His proper work, i. e.,
God wills sin (Melanchthon, Super epistola ad Rom. 29. 31. Floriani).
—87. God wanted himself regarded foolish by means of folly; a
spiritual man by means of folly recognizes God (Melanchthon, 1 Cor.
3).—*Against the Cross of Christ:* 88. It would be much better were the
Cross lost than found, humbled than exalted. And it is an abuse for
churches to be built and founded in honor of the wood, upon which
God hung (Luther, In sermon 36 de cruce et passione hominis Christi-
ani, Erphurdiae, in fine, et in sermone 24 de reliquiis et ornamentis,
sanctae crucis exaltatione).—89. It is a silly play and an idolatrous error
to inclose a portion of the Cross in gold, carry it about the church, and
offer it to the people to be kissed; hence were I to own a portion of the
Cross, I would burn it to ashes. In the world there are so many pieces
of the wood of the Cross, that a house could be built out of them.
Would that no crown of thorns, yea, no holy cross had ever come to
light (Luther, ibidem).—90. It was a singular and horrible festival that
was instituted in honor of the tunic of Christ at Treves (Luther,
ibidem).

Against Mary: 91. Christ said to Mary: "What have I to do
with thee!" meaning: Because you are my mother you think that some
special favor will be shown you by me on the ground of a merit of
prerogative. Understand, however, that you have no more influence
with me than the woman who was a sinner, or the Syrophenician (Melanchthon, Super Ioan. 28).—92. Christ permitted Mary to err. And
Joseph wanted to desert her under the suspicion of adultery (Luther,
Tomo 4. Dominica post Epiphaniae).—93. When Christ preached, the
centurion had greater faith than Mary; for while Christ gave his
mother great faith at the conception and nativity, afterwards it was not,
or only rarely, so great, and meanwhile he permitted it to waver (Luther, In postilla, dominica 3. post Epiphaniae).—94. The contradictory
of the statements that the Blessed Virgin was conceived without original
sin has not been censured (Luther. . . .).—95. We certainly are just as
holy as Mary. On this account, we are unwilling to have her as an advocate (Luther, Sermo 12 de nativitate Mariae, art. 149 and 162).—96.
That on the day of the nativity of Mary we use the Epistle concerning

the wisdom of God, and the Gospel concerning the nativity of Christ, is a falsehood and blasphemy (Luther, ibidem, art. 145; the first printed edition adds: Nuernbergenses).—97. The "salve regina," "regina coeli" are improper, and do a wrong to Christ, since they ascribe to a creature what belongs to God (Luther, ibidem, art. 157; Heyden, in libello; Freissleben, [pastor] at Weiden).—98. Thy prayer, says Luther, is just as precious as that of Mary, because thou canst aid me just as much as she (Luther, ibidem, artic. 160).—99. Christ was unwilling to comply with the curiosity of Mary, when she asked for a miracle when the wine failed (Zwingli, Bernae, 209; Luther, In postilla).—100. Claustra virginitatis Mariae in partu fuerunt aperta et dimota (Luther, In postilla dominica post Epiphaniae prima).—101. I hate no festival more than that of the Conception of Mary, and that of Corpus Christi (Luther, In sermone de festo corporis Christi, art. 427).—*Against the Apostles:* 102. The Council of the Apostles erred in commanding those converted from the Gentiles to abstain from blood and from what was strangled, and, accordingly they were corrected by Paul to the Colossians: "Let no man judge you, etc." (Quidam [Erasmus] in suo consilio: meminit Schatzger contra Schwartzenbergium).—103. In the time of the Apostles the Gospel was not preached as clearly and purely as by me. Hence I was one whom they call Elias, Daniel, and a Man of God (Luther).—104. The Apostles were not believers when they were baptized. For this reason, Christ willed that the Apostles should first baptize men, and then teach what should be done and left undone (Nuremberg preachers). —*Against St. Paul:* 105. Paul wanted to be damned for his brethren (Melanchthon). So Moses was willing to be led to the devil and to be condemned in soul and body for the people (Melanchthon, Ad Rom. 30; Luther, Sermo 10: nisi abundaverit, art. 112).—106. Many, with much probability, have asserted that this epistle was not written by the apostle James, and that it is not worthy of an apostolic spirit (Luther, In captivitate Babylonica, 40).—*Against the Gospels:* 107. The Evangelists wrote contradictions. This is so evident in many passages, that they cannot be harmonized. Moreover we believe that all the Apostles could err (Brunfels, In libro de evangeliorum ratione).—108. The opinion ought to be abrogated that there are only four Gospels and four Evangelists (Idem).—109. We are compelled to assert that there is no Scripture that can be proved to be such, except the Old Testament (Idem).— 110. Unless the Apostles had explained the Gospel in their Epistles, we would have nothing but trifles, and stupid and lifeless narration. To the Apostles, Peter, Paul, James, and John, and not to the Evangelists, is due the credit of handing down whatever we have that is pure with respect to the use and form of the Gospel (Idem).—111. The New Testament has lost its power as well as the Old. Accordingly, we are to adhere to no Scripture, but only to the Spirit, according to the Eternal Gospel (Pneumatici and other Zwickauer according to Emser).—*Against the Saints*: 112. That those worshipping the Saints for temporal advantages, are little better than those who for money make a covenant with the devil (Luther, De decem praeceptis 167). —113. Prayers to the Saints for avoiding any temporal evil are to be shunned, since they cannot aid us (Melanchthon, Super Exod. 3).— 114. Only through Christ, do we have access to God; accordingly confidence in the Saints falls (Luther. In sermone de nativitate Joannis baptistae art. 204 et ubique).—115. Christ alone, and not the Saints, has been given as an example of a holy life (Zwingli, In actis primis 21).—116. The worship of Saints has reached such a pass that it were better that there were no festivals of Saints and that their names were unknown (Luther, De decem praeceptis. 174).— 117. The resorting of men to the churches of Saints is a work of the devil (Luther, ibidem 176 et sermo 18: De fide et operibus, art. 243).—118. God cannot suffer that any one should say: St. Peter is my Apostle (Luther, In sermone 3: Sic Deus dilexit mundum, art. 29).—119. One cannot tell whether it be St. James or a dead dog or horse that is buried at Compostella or Toulouse (Luther, In sermone in die Jacobi, art. 78).—120. The first Christopher who is portrayed as such was not a Saint. A ridiculous story! Every learned man laughs (Pillicanus, Noerdlingensis, in libello de S. Christophero).— 121. Everything is a matter of suspicion that the church of priests reads today concerning Christopher, and not concerning him alone but also concerning Gregory and others [Margareta] (Idem).— 122. The Saints are to be honored more on account of their doctrine than on account of their life (Luther, In sermone 16 in die S. Johannis, art. 197).—123. Since the ascension of Christ no one has gone to heaven or will go until the end of the world (Luther, In sermone de divite epulone, art. 300).—124. Through Christ I have the same access to the Father as Peter and Paul (Luther, In sermone de S. Johanne baptista, art. 202).—125. Great idolatry has resulted from the worship of Saints (Luther, Zileysen [Glaib] Stifelin, and [Lonicerus] in libello, art. 205).—126. I would not give a farthing for the merits of St. Peter, so far as aiding me is concerned. He cannot help himself. Any beggar will be more useful to me than St. Peter, for what can St. Peter have more than you and I? (Luther, In sermone dominica X post octavam pentecostes, 457).—127. The names of the Saints ought not to be placed in the Canon of the Mass, but only devils, since they are also devils (Luther). He also calls the Church of All Saints, the church of devils; and St. Benno he calls the devil of Meissen.*— *Against Relics*: 128. The Relics of the Saints are nothing but an imposition on the people; on this account, they should be entirely buried in the ground (Luther).—129. The Blessed are no members of the Body of Christ (Zwingli).—*Against Miracles:* 130. Miracles do not prove that Saints are to be invoked; the devil assumes masks (Oecolampadius, Zwingli).—131. Miracles have not been given to confirm faith (Zwingli).—*Against Jerome:* 132. The Commentaries of Jerome and Origen are mere trifles and foolishness, if compared with those of Melanchthon. They teach their own rather than Pauline and Christian doctrine; but Melanchthon is next to Paul (Luther).—133. Jerome superstitiously extols virginity in opposition to Jovinian. There are in Jerome many such things, superstitious rather than godly (Melanchthon).—134. Jerome did not write in a proper way against Jovinian. He seeks to prevail by assertion rather than by erudition. He also does violence to passages of Scripture, not to say corrupts them. Who knows whether Jerome may not have been one of those of whom it is said by Ezekiel that when a prophet has erred and spoken a falsehood, "I the Lord have deceived that prophet!"—135. If a book of Vigilantes were extant concerning the Relics of Saints, as there is one of Jerome. I think that the former would have written in a far more Christian way than the latter (Luther). For he is a singular, immodest, vain caviller (Zwingli).—136. Books should be edited by Christians having the sense of Christ. It is on account of this defect that many interpreters of Scripture, even Jerome, have erred in many passages (Luther). Holy Scripture does not admit of several meanings, as they dream of a literal, an allegorical, etc. But there is one most simple meaning of Scripture (Luther).—*Against Gregory:* 137. Jerome and Gregory erred when they took from us the right to judge concerning every doctrine (Luther).—138. Jerome erred when he forbade circumcision (Melanchthon). And he is a hundred thousand miles off from the opinion of St. Paul (Luther).—*Against Augustine:* 139. Augustine thinks that man is the image of God, because there are in the soul intelligence, memory, and will; but this figment has been

---

* For lack of space we omit the particulars about the books from which Eck took his citations in what follows, and refer to Gussniann's edition.

fabricated not only without the authority of Holy Scripture, but even without reason (Melanchthon).—*Against St. Thomas:* 140. A dove is painted at the ear of St. Thomas; I think it should have been a young devil in order that he might be adored (Luther).—*Against St. Francis:* 141. St. Francis erred stupidly and fell, and included himself and his brethren in his poverty; and thus drew the Gospel into the external sphere, into temporal poverty, against Christ (Luther).—*Against Bernard:* 142. Bernard, Francis, Dominic remained in great errors with the godless; for in their ignorance, they worshipped the Pope, believing that all that pertains to him is of God and right, which is directly contrary to the Gospel (Luther).—143. Francis, in founding his order, erred as a man. What if all the Fathers erred when they made vows? (Luther). For it was with a pious error that they fell when they vowed; and God tolerated that folly in his elect (Luther).—*Against Benedict:* 144. Benedict boasts with impious hypocrisy and perverse emulation of men (Luther).—*Against the Council of Nice:* 145. In the Council of Nice certain forms of penance were appointed. I do not declare in what spirit the decree was made by the Fathers. A good part of the Gospel, I see, yea, the true sense of the Gospel was obscured by this tradition (Melanchthon).—146. In the Holy Council of Nice, faith and the Gospel were lacking, and human traditions gained the upper hand (Luther).—*Against Noah:* 147. Although Noah was subject to judgment, and hearing the Word of God and sentence of condemnation would be judged, nevertheless he was taken away by the mercy of God (Melanchthon). 148. Noah's flood is the same as that concerning which the heathen have written as the flood of Deucalion (Zwingli).—*Against the Limbus Patrum:* 149. Christ descended ad inferos, not to a *limbus patrum*, a term unknown in Holy Scripture, but truly to hell, in order to see all places full of despair. On this account Christ praises God, that He has freed him from the hell, in whose chains he would have been eternally lost, unless the hand of the Lord had been present (Bugenhagen).—150. That the Fathers in the Old Testament descended into the "limbus" is fictitious (Haller). 151. Abraham's bosom is nothing but the Word of God (Luther).

Against the Old Testament: 152. I wish the Mosaic Law would be adopted in place of the foolish and Gentile laws, i.e., in place of the Civil Law (Melanchthon).—153. The part of the Law which has the Decalogue or Moral Precepts, has been antiquated in the New Testament (Melanchthon). Of the Decalogue, Luther makes eight and Zwingli eleven commandments.—154. The Old Testament may be observed or omitted today. Hence Jerome erred asserting that it was abrogated (Luther).—155. They do not sin who are circumcised, or who omit circumcision (Melanchthon).—156 The reason why the Mosaic Law was abrogated is that it was impossible for it to be kept (Melanchthon).—157. Christ, by his death, confirmed the Old Testament (Weidensee).—158. The Old Testament is not a covenant, but a type of covenant (Melanchthon).—*Against the New Testament:* 159. The New Testament is nothing else than a promise of all good things without law, no respect being had to our righteousness, because good things are promised us without condition, since nothing is required in return from us (Melanchthon).—160. Whatever is done under constraint of the Law is sin; hence in the New Testament there are not precepts that force, but only exhortations and entreaties (Luther).—161. Christ did not come to make a people or to impose a law (Melanchthon).—*Against the Gospel.* 162. The Gospel commands nothing whatever (Melanchthon), neither does it prohibit (Luther). —163. The testament of Christ is confirmed by faith by which we believe his death (Eberhard Weidensee).—164. Christ bore every penalty in the New Testament, and only permitted his Word to act (Luther).—165. The Gospel is nothing else but the message of the resurrection of Christ, because here all works are eliminated (Luther) : —166. Scripture does not distinguish Law and Gospel, so that you would think only that to be Gospel which Matthew, Mark, Luke and John wrote, and the books of Moses to be nothing but law, but the doctrine of the Gospel is scattered through the books of the Old and New Testament (Melanchthon).—167. Just as circumcision is nothing, so also baptism and the partaking of the Lord's Supper (Melanchthon).—*Against Angels:* 168. The wicked do not have angels of their own appointed for their guardianship; this pertains only to the elect (Bugenhagen).

Against the Church: 169. Only the predestinated are in the Church, but the wicked or reprobate are not of the Church (Bucer).—170. Whoever is in the Church cannot be damned (Zwingli). —*In Regard to Contingency:* 171. All things that occur, occur according to divine predestination; hence our will has no freedom. For according to His predestination all things occur to all creatures necessarily (Melanchthon).—172. All things occur by absolute necessity (Luther). —*In Regard to Evangelical Counsels:* 173. Between the Commandments and the Evangelical Counsels, there is no distinction (Melanchthon).

—174. There is but one Evangelical Counsel viz., virginity; although this is not praised in Scripture (Luther).—175. It is impossible for an Evangelical Counsel to become a commandment (Luther).—*Against the Commandments:* 176. The commandments of God are impossible (Melanchthon). You are doing very wrong in denying that our Saviour commanded impossibilities (Luther).—*Against the Lord's Day:* 177. The Sabbath does not signify the religion of the seventh day; and since the abrogation of the Law, all days are equal (Melanchthon).—178. There are some who think that the Sabbath ought still to be observed, since we have Scripture for this, and not for the Lord's Day (Balthaser Hubmaier).—179. The Lord's Day was instituted only that men might meet to hear the Word of God, not that they might rest from work (Glaib; Carlstadt, Bucer und Zwingli).—*Against Sin:* 180. The "fomes" is truly actual sin, and actual privation of that which ought to be present, a thing that is alive and that daily excites to sin (Luther, Rieger [= Urbanus Rhegius]).—181. Every sin is ignorance (Melanchthon). And invincible ignorance does not excuse sin (Luther).—182. The distinction made today between venial and mortal sin is wrong, since every affection of concupiscence is mortal sin (Melanchthon). Every sin according to its nature, is mortal, but it is venial to those who are in Christ (Lutheranus, Der einfaeltig Glaub).—183. Original Sin is no sin, but a natural defect, like stammering (Zwingli).—184. Original Sin is an actual wicked desire; hence Scripture does not distinguish between Actual and Original Sin (Melanchthon).—185. Original Sin always remains (Luther).—*Against Faith:* 186. Faith alone justifies, not works, because faith and works directly antagonize; hence works cannot be taught without injuring faith (Luther). 187. An error in faith does not hurt, provided only one believe that Christ, our Lord, has saved and redeemed us (Bucer).—188. There are no works so wicked as to be able to accuse and condemn believers in Christ; where there is faith, no sin injures (Luther).—189. He who has once believed that Jesus Christ has redeemed him, has the seal of the Holy Spirit, and can never sin unto death (Bucer). 190. Christ has ordained that there should be no sin but unbelief, and no righteousness but faith (Luther).—191. It is necessary to elevate faith above all virtues; but it is extinguished by any crime (Idem).—192. We have no doubt whatever that we are saved when we are baptized; since the promise there made is not mutable with respect to any sins. Hence one baptized, even though

he so will, cannot lose salvation, because no sin but unbelief can
condemn him. All others are swallowed up by faith in a moment
(Luther).—193. Faith alone is necessary; all other things are most
free, neither commanded nor prohibited (Luther). 194. Love does
not justify, but faith which is preferred to love. Moreover, it justifies with respect to no works, whether good or bad (Melanchthon)
—195. Only unbelievers are wicked (Zwingli), because it is with God,
not with men that they deal by means of works.—196. Faith never
respects past. but only future things (Luther).—197. Acquired "fides
informis" is a dream, a matter unknown to Holy Scripture, taught
by the prostitutes of the Pope (Luther); an insanity (Melanchthon.)—
Against Works: 198. All the works of man, however praiseworthy
in appearance, are altogether vicious and are sins worthy of death
(Melanchthon).—199. Wicked deeds do not make a wicked man
(Luther).—200. The commandments are necessarily fulfilled prior to
all works (Luther).—201. We are, we have been, we always remain
equals before God (Luther).—202. God cares not for our works;
or if they be anything before Him, nevertheless all are equal as to
merit.—*Against Merits:* 203. Paul dissipates the dreams of theologians
who have invented "meritum congrui et digni" to obtain grace
(Luther; Rieger).—204. To say that our works are meritorious is to
detract from the honor and merit of Christ (Haller), because there
is no merit in man whatsover (Zwingli).—205. The grace of God is
not a quality in us (Melanchthon). He who believes, loves (Nuremberg provosts).—*Against Love:* 206. All the commandments of God are
to be observed in love; for one not killing, sins, if this be not in love
(Luther). So one in sin giving alms or doing any other good work,
sins (Luther).—207. Love does not abide in the eternal home
(Zwingli). 208. The Christian is on his guard lest he ever be uncertain as to whether he be in the grace of God, or whether his works
please God; for he who doubts as to this, sins, and loses all his
works (Luther). 209. The statement is most certain, that we are
always most certain of the remission of sin. The saints know that
they are in grace, and their sins are forgiven (Melanchthon).—
210. Acts of hope and of faith are not distinguished in Scripture
(ib).—211. I regard it a human fancy that a habit is one thing. and an
act, another. Faith, accordingly, is nothing but a movement of the
heart and means "to believe" (Luther).—212. The freedom of the Gospel consists in the fact that all power of accusing has been wrested from

the law, as well as of condemning us; i. e., if you have sinned, you cannot be damned (Melanchthon).

Against the Sacraments: 213. The invention of sacraments is a recent thing (Luther), and there are only three Sacraments, viz., Baptism, Penance, and the Holy Supper (Luther); elsewhere he states but two (Luther; Glaib).—214. The Sacraments of the New do not differ from those of the Old Testament, so far as efficacy or significance is concerned (Luther, Bucer).—*Against Baptism:* 215. Baptism neither justifies nor profits any one, but it is only faith in the word of promise, to which Baptism is added, that accomplishes this (Luther, Melanchthon).—216. Baptism, even so far as the sign is concerned, is not a momentary, but a permanent matter (Luther).—217. To baptize is incomparably greater than to consecrate bread and wine (Luther).—218. For this reason Baptism cannot be administered except by a priest (Luther) —219. Baptism pertains no less to the second than to the first forgiveness (Melanchthon).—220. Penitence has no other sacramental sign than Baptism (Melanchthon).—221. It is pernicious to believe that so far as a son of light is concerned, the force of Baptism is lost by sin (Luther).—222. Baptism has respect to the entire course of our life (Luther).—223. The Baptism of Christ and that of John is the same. Accordingly, John the Baptist preached the Gospel before Christ (Zwingli).—224. The form of Baptism is not "in the Name of the Father," but "I baptize thee in the Names of the Father and of the Son," etc. (Zwingli).—225. The water of Baptism is not to be blessed, neither is exorcism to precede Baptism; but, all ceremonies being excluded, we are to use Baptism in the most simple way, as Christ instituted it (Jo. Landtsperger).—226. Infants are not to be baptized; but when those baptized have attained the use of reason, they are to be rebaptized (Balthasar [Hubmaier] and all the Anabaptists).—227. Baptism does not profit an infant, unless it have a faith of its own (Luther, Rieger, Weidensee, Landtsperger). But infused faith is a fictitious thing (Osvaldus, Glaib).—228. It is not the laver of Baptism, but only the Blood of Christ, that removes Original Sin (Luther).— *Infants:* 229. Infants of Christians, who die before Baptism, I believe are not condemned (Zwingli).—230. A child must not be hurried to Baptism; for even God cannot give faith to it, when baptized, and it is lost; and he can give faith to an unbaptized child, who is to be saved (Weidensee).—231. It is not certain, then, that a child departing after Baptism, is saved (Weidensee). One, then, is ignorant concerning a child departing without Baptism (Landtsperger).—232. If one would bring up hundred children, and know that all are eternally lost, he should not be grieved on this account nor once lament (Weidensee).—*Against the "Character": 233.* The "character" impressed in Baptism or in Ordination, is a fictitious matter, and without Scriptural authority (Luther, Melanchthon, Rieger, Zwingli).—*Against Confirmation: 234.* Confirmation and Extreme Unction are not sacraments instituted by Christ (Luther and all others. The Albigenses, the Heracleanitae).—*Against the Eucharist: 235.* In the Eucharist, the substance of bread and wine remains; because transubstantiation is a figment of sophists and Romanists (Pirkheimer, Melanchthon, Luther).—*236.* I firmly believe not only that the Body of Christ is in the bread, but also that the bread is the Body of Christ (Luther, Wicleff).—*237.* As the Body of Christ is in the bread, where there is neither blood nor soul, so the Blood of Christ in the wine is without body and soul (Luther).—*238.* In the Eucharist, the true Body of Christ is not really, but figuratively only and as in a sign (Zwingli, Oecolampadius, Capito, Keller, Rottenacker, Bucer, Blarer). —*239.* I do not know whether is was a greater abomination to worship the golden calf in Dan, or that bread (Zwingli).—*240.* The Eucharist is the idol of Moazim, which, according to Daniel, we have worshipped in the Holy Place, and is true idolatry (Zwingli).—*241.* The Body of Christ can be only in one place; hence if it is to be received by us, it must leave the Right Hand of the Father (Zwingli).—*242.* The miracles wrought in the Eucharist have Satan as their author and are from the father of lies (Oecolampadius).—*243.* There is much danger in the adoration of the Eucharist; for this reason, it would be better not to adore it, for such was the practice of the Apostles. Neither is Christ there in order to be adored (Luther).—*Against Processions: 245.* Where the Eucharist enclosed in gold and silver is carried about with pomp and external adoration in a procession, this is nothing else than to make sport of God (Pirkheimer, Lang, Strauss, Luther).—*245.* Therefore that the Eucharist should be made a show of or be carried about, or be laid aside in an ark, are abuses of the Eucharist; but that it should be imprisoned is a sport of demons (Pirkheimer, Glaib, Balthasar [Hubmaier]).—*Against Communion: 246.* That no one should receive the Eucharist except fasting, is a madness madder than any madness; so it is ridiculous that a layman should not handle the Eucharist, the Cup, since he can communicate himself (Luther). Afterwards, however, he [Luther] prohibited this.—*247.* They only commune worthily whose consciences are afflicted, confused, and erroneous, and burdened with sins (Luther).—*248.* The greatest sins are committed at Easter on account of the impious requirement of the Pope requiring men to commune, even more than at the Carnival (Luther).—*249.* It is my faithful

advice that a Christian in Lent and at Easter, should neither confess
nor come to the communion, and that he should think: For this very
reason I will not do what that man, the Pope, here commands, but I
would do it if he had not commanded it (Luther).—*Both Kinds:* 250.
To deny both kinds to the laity is godless and tyrannical, and bishops
sin, who give one kind alone (Luther, Osiander).—251. The Greeks and
others are not to be accounted heretics or schismatics on account of
both kinds, but the Romans are rather to be so accounted (Luther).—
252. It would be better to receive neither part than one alone, since it
is a snare most harmful to souls to commune once a year under one
form (Luther, Zwingli).—253. A layman, without the desire to receive
the other form, is godless and denies Christ (Luther).—*Against Confessions:* 254. Confession made into the ear, cannot be approved by
divine law, neither was this done orginally, but then it was public
(Luther, Zwingli, Oecolampadius).—255. That secret sins pertain to
sacramental confession can be proved in no way, by reason or from the
Scriptures; I suspect that this was an invention either of the avaricious
or the curious or the tyrants of souls (Luther, Oecolampadius, Rieger,
Strauss).—256. A priest ought to absolve a penitent from punishment
and guilt, or he sins; a superior likewise sins in reserving cases to himself (Luther).—257. Circumstances are to be entirely disregarded; the
observance of places, times, persons, is of no account, and should it be
made it is another superstitious assumption (Luther, Carlstadt).—*Penitence:* 258. Penitence lacks any sign divinely instituted; accordingly,
it is not properly a sacrament, but a way and return to baptism (Luther,
Melanchthon).—259. If St. John had taught that fear is the beginning
of penitence, it, nevertheless, would not follow that penitence begins in
fear (Luther).—260. It is false and dangerous to think that penance is
"the second raft after shipwreck" (Luther, Carlstadt, Melanchthon).—
Against the Keys: 261. The keys are not given except to one who is
righteous and holy in spirit (Luther, Oecolampadius, Bucer).—262. To
bind and to loose is nothing else than to preach the Gospel (Luther,
Zwingli).—263. The laws concerning Satisfactions, by which we are
taught to blot out sins by our works, are impious. Here we see that the
whole Canonical Law and the Kingdom of the Pope, being contrary to
Christ, is condemned (Luther).—*Satisfaction:* 264. No satisfaction is
required for sins, except the death of Christ (Luther, Melanchthon,
Bucer, Zwingli) —265. The Sacrament of Penance has been abolished
by prelates in the Church (Luther, Melanchthon).—266. Any one can
absolve any one; accordingly the freest authority of hearing confessions is to be conceded to all brethren and sisters (Luther).—*Ordina-*

tion: 267. The Church of Christ ignores the sacrament of Ordination (Luther). But it is a figment invented by men (Zwingli, Rieger, Amsterodamus).—268. As many of us as have been baptized are all equally priests; and any layman can consecrate churches, confirm children, etc. (Luther and all others).—*The Mass:* 269. The Gospel does not allow the Mass as a sacrifice, because to retain the use of masses under the name of sacrifices is to deny Christ (Luther, Rieger).—270. At any hour and as often as one wishes, one can celebrate Mass (Luther). None can offer for another as he can drink for him (Zwingli).—271. They lie who say that the Mass of a wicked priest is useful *ex opere operato* (Luther). Although the name "Mass" is here improperly applied (Luther, Zwingli, Rieger).—272. The office of the Mass is not satisfactory, as offered for the dead, the troubled, or as applied for another (Luther, Rieger).—273. The Mass has been changed into a sacrifice of Satan, and that by a common error; but this is the very worst idolatry and a more than a heathen infidelity (Luther, Rieger).—274. We condemn and despise the Canon of the Mass, by the authority of the Gospel (Luther); because it is false and has nothing solid in it (Zwingli and Melhofer [the Nuremberg preachers]).—275. Today the celebrants of the Mass are idolaters, and commit idolatry as often as they sacrifice (Luther, Oecolampadius).—276. All private masses are to be abrogated; but on every Lord's Day, and then only, the Eucharist alone is to be consecrated (Luther).—277. Nay, all masses, both public and private, are to be abrogated (Zwingli, Bucer, Capito and all the others [Haller, Blarer, Rottenacker]).—278. Water is not to be put into the Cup in the Mass; because it is a wicked and unfavorable sign (Luther, Zwingli and others [Carlstadt]).—*Canonical Hours:* 279. I believe that they sin more who read the hours coldly, than they who omit them; for they are hypocrites. There is scarcely greater sin than this laborious worship of God which is rendered by crying out through those Canonical Hours (Luther). Accordingly the provosts at Nuremberg have dispensed with Matins and Completorium.

Matrimony: 280. Matrimony is not a sacrament divinely instituted, but one invented by men in the Church (Luther). —281. The conjugal debt is a sin, and according to Ps. 50, altogether mad (Luther). Yea, it is never paid without sin (ib).—282. Priests ought to ratify all marriages that have no other impediment than that of the Papal, but not of the Divine Law. Every priest, yea every brother, or any one can make a dispensation for himself with regard to impediments decreed by the Church (Luther, Zwingli).—283. It is lawful to marry the daughter of one's sister, or niece; likewise the children of two brothers or sisters may marry; or one may marry the sister of his wife or connection by marriage; also no spiritual relationship hinders matrimony (Luther, Zwingli).—284. Marriages of children contracted against the will of their parents are invalid; hence the title "De Clandestina Desponsione" is from Satan (Luther).—285. If those contracting marriage have not completed nineteen years, the marriage is invalid (Consistory of Zurich).—286. If any one violate a virgin, he will not be obliged to give her anything except a pair of shoes. A new Zurich law that fell from heaven.* (Turicenses in edicto. Similiter Nerobergenses [Nurenbergenses, or Neuenburgenses?]).—Divorce: 287. When a man is impotent, let the wife seek a divorce; but if he be unwilling, let her, with the consent of her husband, have intercourse with another, or the brother of her husband in secret marriage, and let the offspring be accounted those of the reputed father. The woman is safe in a state of safety (Luther).—288. For I prefer bigamy to divorce, (as the Lutheran monks have shown effectually) (Luther).—289. If a wife do not obey her husband when he asks for the conjugal debt, let him call in a servant girl. Yea, on this account, he can ask for a divorce (Luther).—290. Divorce occurs not only on account of adultery, but for other more grave reasons. Suppose a husband be under sentence of death, a madman, quarrelsome, withdrawing from his wife without her consent and long absent. (Zuricher statute, Luther).—291. When the divorce has been decreed it is allowable for the innocent party to marry; only the guilty party should be hindered (Luther, Melanchthon).—292. It is an error to assume that the marriage is broken if, before it has been consummated, one of the couple enter a monastery or convent (Luther).—293. Former betrothals are not broken if one have afterwards known a second spouse (Luther).—Celibacy: 295. Ordination does not hinder marriage or break the contract, but celibacy has been introduced by the devil (Luther, Bugenhagen).—295. By virtue of the words of Paul, I absolve all priests from celibacy; for between a priest and a true wife, there is a true and inseparable marriage, approved by the commandments of God. This the godless forbid from pure tyranny (Luther, Zwingli, [Zell], Blarer, Stoerer).—296. The Nicene Council concedes marriage to priests (Zwingli, Spengler [of Nuremberg], Rieger).—297. In the time of Augustine, no one opposed the marriage of priests (Zwingli [in] Ad Sacerdotes Suiceros).—298. It is allowable for a priest, for a bishop not only to marry, but to marry the second, third, and fourth time, whether

---

*Compare Gussmann, 180. The statutes speak of married men who beside the recompense mentioned were to be punished as adulterers.

bride be a virgin or one who has been corrupted (Luther).—*Vows: 299.* Would that I were able to persuade all persons either to abolish altogether or avoid all vows (Luther, Lambertus Avinionensis).—*300.* If a vow be dispensable, any brother can make such dispensation for his neighbor, or he can dispense himself; if a neighbor cannot so dispense, there is then no law by which the Pope can do it (Luther, Jonas, Carlstadt [Eberlein]).—*301.* The mode of life proceeding from a vow is without a precedent in the Scriptures (Luther, Blarer [Kettenbach], Lambertus).—*302.* Parents have the right to remove children from monasteries, who have entered without their consent. If the Pope say the contrary, he lies (Luther).—*303.* Religious vows conflict directly with the Gospel of Christ [and Baptism] and are opposed to faith and the Word of God (Luther, Lambertus).—*304.* To become a monk is to apostatize from the faith, to deny Christ, and to become a Jew; their vows, accordingly, are worthless (Luther).—*305.* For a man to be continent is an impossibility; but just as it is necessary for man to eat and drink, and to sleep, so also is it to have sexual intercourse. Hence no man can be without a woman, nor any woman without a man (Luther). —*306.* The state of virginity is beneath the marriage estate, than which there is none better on earth (Luther). If Jerome had known that marriage would be one of the seven sacraments of the Church, he would have praised virginity less, and would have spoken more reverently concerning marriage (Luther).—*307.* All vows are temporary and mutable (Luther [Lambert]).—*308.* No monk or priest can be a Christian (Luther [Zwingli]).—*309.* Castigations voluntarily assumed by men, like voluntary fastings, are repudiated by Paul (Bucer).—*310.* We properly think that all monasteries and cathedral churches and like abominations, should be entirely abolished (Luther to the Duke of Savoy).— *311.* I discourage all from entering any religious order, unless they know that the works of the members of these orders however arduous and holy, in God's eyes are no better than the works of farmers laboring in the fields (Luther).—*312.* Whatever is promised men in secular matters is to be fulfilled, but in matters of conscience, if anything be promised God, it is not to be kept (Zwingli).—*313.* No saint became a saint through Monasticism (Luther).—*Poverty: 314.* Evangelical poverty is exacted of men by divine right, accordingly no vow should be made (Melanchthon).—*315.* To establish a mode of life for begging likewise conflicts with the Gospel (Melanchthon, Luther).—*316.* Monasticism is of the devil (Zwingli, Lambert).—*317.* Would that all monks and nuns would flee from the cloisters, and that all cloisters throughout the whole world were to be abolished (Luther) —*318.* All Carthusians, all monks and nuns depart from that which has been ordained by God and from liberty, when they imagine that they are polluted by eating meat (Luther, Lambert).—319. Put before your eyes the infinite crowd of priests and nuns, with their masses, sacrifices, laws, doctrines, and all their works; and you will see nothing but a theater of Satan, godless people of perdition, reserved for the wrath of God forever (Luther).— 320. Church ceremonies always obscure liberty and the force of the Gospel; hence it is profitable to disregard them (Melanchthon, Nuremberg preachers).—321. Unctions, tonsures, ceremonial vestments, benedictions of water, salt, palms, candles, herbs, consecrations of churches, altars, vases, men, etc., are human inventions (Zwingli, Luther, Oecolampadius, Melanchthon, Balthasar, Glaib, [Lambert, Bucer, preachers of Nuremberg]).—*Against Purgatory:* 322. There is no purgatory after this life (Capito, Zwingli, Osiander, Haller, Oecolampadius, Rieger, [Bucer, Lambertus, Rottenacker]).—323. It would be safer to deny all purgatory than to believe Gregory in his Dialogues (Luther).—324. Here sink anniversaries, vigils for the dead, depositions, the seventh, the thirtieth, fraternities, oblations, and other inventions of man (Zwingli). Chanting, organs, candles, ornaments, vestments, chrism disappear (Luther, Zwingli, [Lambertus, Balthasar]).—325. We have no command to pray for the dead; you may, therefore, pray once or twice or thrice for a dead person, but afterwards cease lest you tempt God or distrust Him (Luther).—326. Moreover, that perpetual masses are founded upon this, and that, every year, the cry ascends as though God had not heard before that year, is death and the devil, unbelief, makes sport of God, and such prayer is mere blasphemy (Luther).—327. The office for the dead is of about as much service to deceased Christians as it is to dead cattle (The unhappy provost of Nuremberg).—328. No Christian implicates himself in masses and prayers for the dead, unless he be willing to deny Christ, to repudiate Baptism, and to act in opposition to the whole Bible (The provosts of Nuremberg).—329. If you have in your house a spirit who when adjured seeks for aid by means of masses and prayers, account him without any hesitation as the devil; because from the beginning of the world until now no soul has appeared, neither does God so permit (Luther).—*Contra imagines:* 330. No images are to be kept in the church, but rather to be destroyed and burned; nay, neither publicly nor privately are they to be retained, or to be painted or carved; for they are relics of the old idolatry contrary to the Second Commandment (Zwingli, Haller, Bucer, Carlstadt).—*In liberum arbitrium:* 331. It is under the tutelage of Satan that the term "Free Will" has entered, and that, with the purpose of seducing men from the way of right; for it is a mere figment, since the will contributes nothing towards its own willing, and that it has any activity in good works is erroneous (Luther, Carlstadt, Rieger).

Contra obedientiam et principes: 332. The name fraternity forbids one from being superior to another, and, especially in spiritual things from having more right and inheritance than his brother (Luther).—333. We Christians are free, exempt from all the laws of men, liberated through Baptism (Luther). —334. No laws can be imposed with any right upon Christians, whether by men or by angels, unless so far as they be willing (Luther).—335. Subjects neither can, nor will, nor ought to endure your tyranny any longer (Luther to the Princes).—336. The Emperor and the Princes deal in manifest falsehoods and publish contradictory commandments (Luther).—337. That the Pope has transferred the power from the Greeks to the Germans is the chief or greatest and most deceptive mark of Antichrist (Luther).—338. I regret that I submitted to the Emperor at Worms and let them be judges of my doctrine for it is of no account with tyrants (Luther).—339. There is no more excellent secular law than that of the Turk, as he has no canonical and civil law (Luther). —340. The secular Princes are stupid, and according to their stupid brain they want to lead the Holy Spirit into the schools and publish directions, and if the Emperor would give a command, they want to appear as though they were seriously doing what was commanded (Luther).—341. The madness of foolish men is directed to the extinction of the faith, because they want to force men to believe (Luther). —*Seditiosa:* 342. God has delivered the Princes up to a reprobate mind, and he wants to put an end to them just as to ecclesiastical houses (Luther).—343. The secular government is at just as low a stage as that of the ecclesiastical tyrants, so that the one will not perish without the other (Luther).—344. Princes prohibiting Luther's New Testament act like murderers of Christ, such as Herod; but these tyrants act as the secular Princes are accustomed to do, in order to satisfy their titles (Luther).—345. Ever since the beginning of the world, a wise prince has been a most rare bird; for generally they are either the greatest fools or the very worst rascals; for they are God's policemen and executioners (Luther).—346. The common people have now become intelligent and wise; a blow to Princes is clearly impending from the side of the people and rabble. I fear that it cannot be prevented (Luther).— 347. The Turk is ten times as wise and just as our Princes; how then could such fools be prospered against the Turk (Luther).—348. In the halls of Princes, the devil sits in the highest place, and has there his chief throne (Luther).—*In regem Franciae:* 349. The kingdom of France, from its impious service to Antichrist, on account of the blood it has shed, has been impiously called most Christian (Luther). He also has treated the Most Noble King of England with the greatest insults, wrongs and reproaches (Luther).—*In nobiles:* 350. The sin of robbery is now an honor and title of the nobility (Luther).—351. If the peasants prevail, the devil is abbot; if the Princes prevail, his mother will be an abbess (Luther).—*In papam:* 352. The kingdom of the Pope is nothing but tyranny, the realm of Antichrist with his faces (Luther). Yea, he is Antichrist himself, the son of perdition (Luther [Lambertus]).—353. The name of Pope is recent, unheard of in the time of [Pope] Nicholas [I.], or of Augustine (Zwingli, Balthasar).—*Contra ecclesiasticos:* 354. Bishops ought to be grave men, married, laymen, advanced in years (Luther and all).—355. It is not allowable for a bishop to do aught except to teach the Word of God. Preaching the Gospel is so peculiarly the prerogative of a bishop, that it is not proper to substitute another for him, to teach in his place. If, therefore, he do not teach, he is not a bishop (Melanchthon).—356. There is no ecclesiastical authority over men (Bucer). Hence the bishops have usurped the jurisdiction which belongs to the secular princes (Bucer, Luther, Zwingli, Blarer, Rieger).—357. Ecclesiastical power is not of God (Luther).—358. Christ subjected himself and his Church to secular power (Haller). This immunity of churches and freedom of the clergy have ceased (Haller, Luther).—359. The civil, but not the ecclesiastical power, has the authority to make and ordain laws (Melanchthon).—360. To impose law upon Christians is to tempt the devil (Zwingli).—*Constitution:* 361. Neither the Constitution of the Church nor the Ordinances of the Apostles put the conscience under any obligation (Bucer).—362. We are, therefore, under no obligation to celebrate the festivals of the saints, to fast in Lent and on other days, to abstain from flesh on six festival days, or to obey other human precepts (Luther, Osiander, Rieger, Zwingli).—363. No prelate, but only the Church, can excommunicate (Zwingli, Haller).—364. We confess that the world has been miserably led astray by Popes, Councils, decrees of Fathers, with these traditions, or more properly, snares of the devil (Luther).—365. No Pope or bishop nor any other man has the right of imposing a single syllable upon any [Christian] man (Luther).—*Against Councils:* 366. After one has been justified, no laws or ordinances bind him (Melanchthon).—367. That was an erroneous decision by the Council that essence neither begets nor is begotten; also that the intellectual soul is man's substantial form (Luther).—368. Openly heretical is the resolution of

the Council referring to the extinction of the heretics (Melanchthon).*
—369. I declare that all the Articles of Huss at Constance were most
Christian and were condemned by Antichrist and his disciples in a synagogue of Satan collected from the most worthless sophists (Luther).
    Here notice, O Emperor, that the calumniator of the most holy and
    free Council of Constance is now making an appeal to a future Council!
—370. Huss and Jerome were burned in violation of faith publicly
pledged, because it was concluded in the Council that a safe conduct
with heretics ought not to be kept; hence our Germans have learned
from the Romans to break faith and promises (Capito).—371. The
Princes of Germany once had the highest reputation for their faithful-
ness, but they have learned in obedience to the idol at Rome and to the
perpetual ignominy of the nation, to despise nothing more than faith-
fulness (Luther).—372. When I was called I went to Worms, even
though I knew that the promise of safe-conduct given to me would be
violated by the Emperor (Luther.)—373. In those things that pertain
to faith, every Christian is Pope and Church to himself (Luther).—374.
Every Christian is allowed to judge concerning every doctrine, for we
are not bound to believe Councils and Popes (Luther, [Blarer]).—Seditiosa: 375. It is only a matter that should be laughed at, if a great
sedition should arise against bishops and their rule: because those exposing their fortunes and bodies to such an emergency are sons of God,
true Christians; and in a short time matters will come to such a pass
that there will be no bishop, no prince under the sun, no cathedral
church, no monastery (Luther).—376. Nothing is to be received except
what is expressly taught in Holy Scripture (Zwingli, [Bucer], Blarer,
Berner, Memminger).—377. I will not permit you to ascribe more than
one sense to the Holy Scriptures. For Scripture does not admit of a
number of meanings, "literal, allegorical," etc. (Luther, Zwingli).—378.
The literal meaning of the creation of the world Gen. 1 is hypocrisy,
and a carnal opinion concerning the condition of nature (Melanchthon).
—379. The Apocalypse was not written by John the Evangelist. The books
of Baruch and Maccabees are not to be received (Luther, Zwingli).
—Contra jura: 380. For the Gospel to share authority with the Canon
Law, is an impossibility (Luther).—381. I know that no state is successfully administered by means of laws (Luther).—382. It is impossible at
the same time to observe the Gospel and human laws; accordingly, it
is impossible to keep the peace and at the same time the laws (Luther).
—383. There is no hope of a remedy, unless, all the laws of all men being

*Melanchthon refers to the Council of Verona, 1184, that condemned all who
teach differently of the sacraments than the church.

once anulled; we ought judge and rule all things according to the Gospel (Luther).—*An iurandum:* 384. We must not swear for temporal things; for he who requires an oath of another, or himself swears, must be of a malicious and trifling mind, not regarding the truth (Melanchthon). —385. It is not allowable for a Christian for any cause to take an oath (Anabaptists). For it is unjust and contrary to the Holy Scriptures to demand an oath for an other one (Luther, Anabaptists and Enthusiasts).—386. All are heathen who contend in court for property or reputation (Luther).—*Bellare:* 387. If anything be taken from us we ought not to demand it back in court or by war (Luther).—388. It is a doctrine of devils that it is allowable for a Christian to wage war; for all who go to war are accursed children of Cain (Oecolampadius). —*Emere:* 389. To buy and sell are purely heathen matters (Luther). —390. Business contracts even for godly purposes, as churches, benefices, etc., are usurious (Straus); or at least, unjust (Luther).—*Communio:* 391. A community of all things is commanded in the New Testament (Melanchthon).—392. Altars are to be abolished in the New Testament, because Christ is there crucified, divided, buried, and bitten with the teeth; for the Lord's Supper, a table answers the purpose (Osvaldus Glaib, Balthasar [Hubmaier]).—393. One should not care to be buried in a cemetery, or consecrated place, because it is certain that all blessed by man is cursed by God (Osvald Glaib).—394. Wicked spirits will hereafter be saved together with the damned (John Denk).—395. They blaspheme who rave that the Turks or heretics should be attacked not with the Word of God, of which they are ignorant, but with war and worldly tumult, or with the din of censorships (Luther).—396. The word of Christ that many false prophets shall arise and deceive many, I verily think was spoken with reference to the public universities (Melanchthon).—397. The doctrine of all the schools, speculative as well as practical, has been condemned (Luther).—398. All moral virtues and speculative branches of knowledge are not true virtues and sciences, but sins and errors (Luther).—399. I doubt whether the Creed was handed down in writing by the Apostles, although I do not doubt that it was composed by Apostolic men, and yet, I doubt so far as to wish that it could be proved. Neither, unless I am mistaken, did Augustine believe this. But it was an abuse of the common people, not indeed with a godless opinion. And before: That good and, in his Christian simplicity, exceedingly credulous man erred (Erasmus [in the printed edition: Quidam]).—400. Pilate was not free to acquit Christ, since his power was compelled to serve the madness of the Jews. The same says it is the veriest trifle what Beda says about the humility of

Mary, namely, that she by her humility merited to become the Mother of God (Quidam. Erasmus [in the printed edition: Quidam]).—401. It is not entirely clear to me whether in the time of Christ's infancy, it was clearly revealed to the Virgin Mary that he was God and Man. If Mary and Joseph had known that the child Jesus was God and Man, and would suffer nothing but that which was necessary, why would they have feared and grieved for him? (Quidam. Erasmus [the printed edition has no equivalent]).—402. Jesus wished his death not to be mournful, but glorious; not to be deplored, but adored; for he was to be extolled for his victory (Quidam [Erasmus]).—403. It is proper and in accord with God's word to excite seditions and tumults; hence there is no better proof that my doctrine is of God, than that it excites discords, seditions, and tumults (Luther). Many of them, therefore, have often publicly testified to the common people: "The Gospel wants blood" (Zwingli).—404. Among Christians, there should be no superiority, no courts, nothing fenced up or closed, no "meum" or "teum," no restraint or excommunication; and this they want to be practiced more and more (Anabaptists).

❖   ❖   ❖

But, who is Luther? From the following we learn it; for he wants to be heard. "I was the very first whom God put into the field." "Surely, I never did wrong." "Had I been disposed to proceed impulsively, I could have caused great shedding of blood in Germany." "Aye, I could have begun a game at Worms, that the Emperor had not been safe." "I am also the one to whom God first revealed this, that I might proclaim these words to you." "You know not how much labor it is to contend with the devil; but I know him well, and he knows me well; for I have already eaten with him one or two bits of salt, and I would have perished had there not been a confession, etc."

All the articles above noted, both those of Luther himself, as clearly a man familiar with the devil, and those of his followers who, being infatuated with his errors, have so degenerated as to become deaf to the truth, we reject and anathematize each of them as heretical, or scandalous, false, and offensive to godly ears, and misleading the simple, or entirely seditious and disturbing the public peace. With respect to this, I am ready to give an account in a public disputation, at the pleasure of the Most Revered Emperor, God aiding me, and the Virgin Mary and all Saints supporting me with their intercessions.— To God alone the glory.—The day and hour of the disputation Eck will publish at the pleasure of the Emperor.—Ingolstadt, 1530.

While in order that Thy Holy Majesty and the Christian world

may see and judge the impieties of the adversaries, I have gathered a
very few out of their infinite errors, nevertheless I have guarded them
from head to foot with my assertions, and offer to reply as to all in
behalf of the faith and the Church.

The Assertion of Eck. I assert with entire confidence given by the
Holy Spirit that the Articles of Luther concerning this shameful matter
condemned by Pope Leo X. were legitimately condemned as heretical,
erroneous, and scandalous. I anathematize and condemn them, and
freely declare that they who agree with the Bull are Christian men, but
that they who oppose it are enemies of the faith, who ought to be regarded as heathen and publicans. Hence we introduce here all these
XLI. Articles, ready to receive the attacks of any opponent, and to take
the part of the Church.

23. CAMPEGIUS' INSTRUCTION TO THE EMPEROR, MAY 9, 1530[25]

See at the end of the book.

24. THE ELECTOR'S LETTER TO LUTHER ACCOMPANIED BY THE FIRST DRAFT OF THE AUGSBURG CONFESSION, MAY 11, 1530[26]

First of all our Greeting, Honorable, Learned and Devout
[Friend].—After you and our other learned men at Wittenberg had,
at our gracious thought and desire, made a draft of the Articles of
Religion which are now in dispute, it is our wish to let you know that
Melanchthon has further revised the same and drawn them up in a
Form, which we are sending you herewith. And it is our gracious
desire that you would feel free to further consider and revise these
Articles, and where you deem it wise and well to take away or to
add anything, please do so in the margin. Send back the same carefully secured and sealed without delay that we may be ready and prepared for the arrival of his Imperial Majesty, whom we expect in a
short time —We also desire you to know that our representatives at
the Imperial court at Innsbruck have written that it is the plan to
deal with us on the arrival of his Imperial Majesty, that we should
not permit preaching in the churches, as we have begun it. This you

will infer from the enclosed statement. And although I have drawn up an opinion on this subject, yet I wish your further opinion, that we may do right in the sight of God and our conscience. In this you will do our gracious pleasure.—Augsburg, Wednesday after Jubilate, A. D. 1530.—To Dr. Martin.

25. MELANCHTHON'S LETTER TO LUTHER, MAY 11, 1530[27]

To D. Martin Luther, his very dear Father:—Greeting. Our Apology is being sent you, but in truth it is rather a Confession. For the Emperor has not time to listen to lengthy disputations. Yet I have said that which I believed most useful or proper. On this ground I have succinctly given nearly all the Articles of Faith, since Eck has circulated the most Satanic slanders against us. Over against these, I wished to oppose a remedy. Please give judgment on the whole writing according to your spirit.—Duke George and Margrave Joachim have gone on to meet the Emperor. Now a Diet will be held *ueber unseren Hals.* Therefore pray God to bring to naught the counsel of the nations that want war.—A question is being referred to you, to which I greatly desire an answer from you. There is no doubt the Emperor will prohibit the Zwinglian sermons. We judge from this, that under this pretence our sermons will also be forbidden, for Eisleben is already preaching publicly in a church. Now what is your opinion? Is not the preaching in a public place to be given up, in case the Emperor desires this; if he should wish this in order that the Zwinglian preaching might also be prevented without disturbance? I have answered: one must yield to the will of the Emperor, in whose city we now are guests. But our old man [= Dr. Brueck] is difficult to soften. What therefore you think. I beg that you will write it in German on separate paper. Please answer concerning this matter.—We reckon that the Emperor cannot arrive within fourteen days. Now the Austrian estates are assembled at Hall [in the neighborhood of Innsbruck]. Other news we have not. In such a great divergency of opinions it is not possible to judge what can be hoped for from the deliberations of the Emperor, but we await help from Christ. Farewell. Wednesday after Jubilate. Eisleben sends greetings.—Philippus.

26. LUTHER'S ANSWER TO THE ELECTOR, MAY 15, 1530[28]

To the most worshipful, highborn Prince and Lord, John Duke of Saxony, Elector, Landgrave of Thuringia, Margrave of Meissen, my most gracious Lord.—Grace and peace in Christ our Lord.— Most worshipful, highborn Duke, most gracious Lord! I have perused Magister Philip's *Apologia,* which pleases me very greatly. I see no need of changing or amending any part of it; nor should I know how to improve it, for I cannot tread so gently. May Christ our Lord cause it to bear much good fruit as we hope and pray. Amen.

In Reply to the Question, what should be Your Honor's attitude in case His Imperial Majesty commands Your Electoral Honor to stop the preaching of the Gospel, I answer now as I did before that the Emperor is our lord; the city and everything else belongs to him— just as no one has a right to interfere with any of the orders which you give your city of Torgau. I should indeed prefer, if it is possible, that a wise and appropriate attempt be made at changing His Imperial Majesty's intention in this respect and that His Imperial Majesty be humbly petitioned not to prohibit our preaching without any investigation but rather to order someone to listen to our preachers. His Imperial Majesty should not prohibit the pure and unadulterated preaching of the Scriptures; our men do not preach enthusiastic or rebellious sermons. But if that is of no avail, we will have to suffer this injustice. We have done what we could and are absolved from blame.

This is my answer to Your Electoral Honor's question. The God of mercy comfort Your Electoral Honor through His Holy Spirit.— Cantate Sunday, A. D. 1530.—Your Electoral Honor's obedient Martin Luther.

27. MELANCHTHON'S FIRST DRAFT OF THE 28th ARTICLE, MAY 11, 1530 (?)[29]

Of the Power of the Keys. Concerning this, it was formerly held that the power of the keys is the ecclesiastical and the civil governments, and that, by the keys, the Pope has received the power to appoint and remove kings, and that, without the confirmation of the Pope, there can be no king. This error was so insisted upon, that those who have held otherwise were condemned as heretics. But now all our adversaries proclaim that this is a pernicious, un-Christian error, viz., that the Pope, by the power of the Keys and the Gospel, usurps the civil power and appoints and removes kings.

But we teach how the power of the keys is to be used, namely, that the power of the keys is the command to preach the Gospel, and to reprove and forgive sinners in the name and on behalf of Christ. Thus the power of the keys is now only spiritual government, the preaching of the Gospel, the reproof and forgiveness of sins, and the administration of the sacraments. This alone is to be the office of bishops or priests, and, according to the Gospel, the establishment and regulation of the civil government, and appointment and removal of kings, do not belong to this office; for Christ says in express words that he would give Peter the keys of "the kingdom of heaven." Thereby the ecclesiastical is separated from the civil government. So too, John 20: "As my Father hath sent me, even so send I you. Receive ye the Holy Ghost; whosoever sins ye remit, they are remitted unto them; and whosoever sins ye retain, they are retained." From these words it is manifest that the Apostles had no command concerning civil government, but only concerning doctrine and preaching and the administration of the sacraments, whereby the forgiveness of sins is bestowed. Again, Christ forbids the Apostles to undertake civil government, when he says: "The kings of the Gentiles exercise lordship; but ye shall not be so." Again, Matt. 5: "Resist not evil;" now punishment and resistance of evil always belong to the civil government. Again, Christ would not interfere in the government of the Romans; for to one who asked him to divide an inheritance, he said: "Who made me a judge or a divider over you?" Again: "My kingdom is not of this world."

From these and many other passages, it is clear that the keys are not civil government or civil polity. But if something besides is conceded to the Pope by the Emperor it does not pertain to the keys, but is a human donation which we do not accept. For this doctrine of the Gospel lets lord be lord, and deals alone with the conscience and heart, as to its present relation with God, and how it should harmonize with Him. Often before this time, ecclesiastical abuses have been punished; but our predecessors have always acted in a seditious manner, and wished to deprive the bishops of their property. But we now have the office of the ministry and the civil government so distinguished, that what pertains to conscience, and what respect should be shown property and external dignitaries, is readily shown.

Since now the power of the keys is the preaching of the Gospel and the administration of the sacraments, it also follows that, in virtue of the keys, the Pope has no power to arrange new divine services contrary to the Gospel, or to bind consciences by laws. And if the Pope makes a law, he does this, not in virtue of the keys, but as any other civil ruler, for which he nevertheless has no command, and when he issues dispensations, they are again repealed, just as a ruler may set free a thief. If now these laws and dispensations are contrary to God's Word, we are in duty bound to obey God rather than man, as has been indicated above. Also, since the keys are nothing else than the preaching of the Gospel and the administration of the sacraments, the Pope has no more power in the use of the keys than every pastor; as the canons themselves indicate, for they concede that in the article of death a pastor may absolve all reserved cases.

Of Excommunication. Christ has taught how excommunication should be inflicted, Matt. 18, and Paul, 1 Cor. 15, that those who are in open crimes, and, after admonition, will not reform, should be excluded from the Church, and the sacraments should not be administered to them. And in such cases excommunication may be conceded to the bishops, if they will not antagonize the doctrine of the Gospel, as above presented. But in matters that pertain to the civil tribunal, they should not have power to excommunicate. The pastors also might be commanded to report those who persist in open crimes, when the bishops visit the pastors, as they are in duty bound. A like rule might be observed with respect to those who have not communed for a year or more, that they be admonished by the pastors, and if they will not commune, they be reported as others who live in open crimes.

Of Degrees of Consanguinity, etc. Matrimonial cases abound in details, and, if jurisdiction is to be exercised, it is necessary to discuss, with reference to them, not only the question of degrees, but also many points. Besides, it is our judgment that the subject of degrees be committed to the jurists, and those to whom the jurisdiction is entrusted. For the civil power may make laws, for reasonable causes, not only to forbid future marriages, but also to dissolve those which have been solemnized contrary to such power. But that sponsorship should hinder marriage has no ground or cause, and is a law which serves the more to perplex consciences. The Pope also has no power to make such a law. Again, the Pope has no power to make dispensations in regard to cases that are forbidden by divine law. In regard to many cases that are not forbidden by divine law, the conscience is not bound, and if, then, against this decree, a man marry a woman, and live with her, and be not forced from her by the magistrates, this is regarded as a valid marriage. Therefore the law of the Popes must be censured, which gave men scruples as though all cases were contrary to God; but these cases are trivial.

31. FINAL FORM OF MELANCHTHON'S PREFACE TO THE CONFESSION, MAY, 1530[313]

Since there has been much and all kinds of talk about the Elector of Saxony because his grace has permitted and suffered the change of some few abuses in the order of the Church, his Elec. Gr. has placed his highest hope and trust next to God in the clemency and goodness of Y. Imp. Maj., which is as famous and glorious with every one as the powerful conquest of your enemies. And although in former ages no emperor achieved as much against his enemies, there is nothing more glorious and laudable than that Y. Maj. has done in this nothing else than seek the peace of all Europe. Besides, no pride, insolence or cruelty has been noticeable in this conduct. Also that Y. Maj. in the odious actions, which arose from a difference in common religion and faith, has shown your clemency so manifestly, that you have been willing to consent to graciously hear such dissension. Hence no cruelty may be ascribed to Y. Imp. Maj., since you have so graciously permitted us to come to such a hearing of the case, contrary to the opinion of some.

Hence it is the submissive request of the Elector of Saxony that
Y. Imp. Maj. would, in the first place, not suffer yourself to be
moved to any disfavor or suspicion against him, and secondly, to
hear and consider the case in such a way that thereby the glory of
God may be furthered and common peace be preserved and maintained,
which the Elector of Saxony desires, not only in view of his age;
but also on account of the danger which every one may expect in
it. May God help Y. Imp. Maj. to further the unity of Christendom
with the same grace as has been done in other matters, since Y. Maj.
could perform nothing more well-pleasing to God, nor more glorious
or honorable to yourself forever, than to use your power and might
for the inquiry into this case and the unification of Christendom.

Therefore, Y. Maj. should also endeavor to follow the example
of the most famous emperors, Theodosius, Charlemagne and Henry
the Second, who rightly considered it to be a duty of their office
to weigh the dissensions of faith and to bring about the preaching
of pure doctrine in Christendom, as the Holy Ghost specially admonishes princes to defend the faith, when he says in the second
Psalm, "Now, therefore, be wise, oh ye kings; be instructed, ye
judges of the earth," and elsewhere: "The princes of the peoples
gather themselves together unto the God of Abraham." When the
princes of the land gather unto God, God is praised gloriously.
With such words the prophet would indicate that God's honor is
furthered when the people are induced by the piety of the princes,
and the princes maintain God-fearing preachers. Therefore, He also
calls the princes the protectors of the land, since they are to protect
and defend the righteous and the God-fearing with their power.

Since Y. Imp. Maj. is endowed with no fewer virtues and fear
of God than above-mentioned Theodosius, Charlemagne and Henry,
yea, far transcends several of them in power and glory, it would not
ill become Y. Maj. to examine into the affairs of Christendom and
bring about a union. The Apostles have prophesied that Christendom
in these last times would have much adversity, wherefore it would
be quite necessary to mark the present evils in such a manner that
things may not become worse and more dangerous.

But, later on, we will indicate what the doctrine is that is taught
in the Electorate of Saxony. At present we will briefly show of
what mind the Elector of Saxony is in this matter, so that it might

not be thought that he would further and abet this new doctrine out of evil purpose.

The honorable Electors of Saxony, Duke Frederick and Duke Hans, brothers, have always been of such an honorable and brave nature that they have never been known or suspected of any evil. It is also manifest how kind and gracious they have always been toward everyone, no matter of what estate; moreover how much they have always inclined to the Christian religion and faith, is attested publicly, not only by their whole life, but also the institutions and churches which they have in part, at their own expense, built from the foundation, and in part adorned and endowed. Thus they have also shown their faith and allegiance to the Roman Emperors in such a manner as became honorable electors. In all affairs of the empire they have never fallen short in furnishing money or sending stately well-armed auxiliaries. With foreign nations or enemies of the empire they have never had any understanding or treaty. For the peace and unity of a common Germany they have been so inclined that they neither ever gave any one occasion for disturbance; but, though they were highly tempted, they have shown patience for the sake of common peace, so that the disturbance did not become greater. They have also more than once, when others were already arrayed in arms, by their diligence and care brought them to peace and quiet.

And though such things as told above are more than sufficient, more and more praiseworthy things may yet be shown from which the faith and good-will of above-mentioned Electors of Saxony may be seen to greater evidence.

Who would imagine that the Elector of Saxony, without notable and honorable reason, would imperil his honor, children and grand-children to such an extent? Or what advantage might accrue to him from this miserable discord and dissension, that could be compared with this danger which he undergoes and sees before his eyes daily? From this it may well be concluded that if his conscience had not driven him, he would not have undertaken to represent these matters, for it was not hidden from him what a burden he would thus load upon himself, although the matter did not originate with the Elector, but with others.

In the first place, many pious and learned people took pleasure in this doctrine, since all upright men were desirous of a pure doctrine, and bore it grievously that the Christian doctrine was oppressed and darkened with the teachings of men and with useless talk. Every one complained of the abuses that increased daily; all teaching in the schools was corrupted; some showed and praised their philosophy; some exalted human teachings. But the things that were given us through Christ, of repentance, of forgiveness of sins that is given us not for the sake of our merit, but through faith in Christ,—of all this no one could speak, although among Christians, above all things, the righteousness ought to be preached that comes from faith, the forgiveness of sins from faith, etc. Every day new forms of worship were invented in the Church that brought revenue, new ways of selling the mass, new saints, new ceremonies, indulgences without number, new monkery, and the consciences of the simple were daily burdened with new commandments.

But there was no one who informed or comforted the consciences with the gospel. This was the complaint, not only of the common man, but also of the bishops, though in secret, for nobody could speak against these things publicly, since the monks ruled so powerfully in Christendom, even over the bishops. But it happened that the indulgence and letters of remission were preached in Saxon lands and exalted unduly. This Martinus Luther contradicted by means of several smaller treatises, scholastically and not before the people, and also without abusing or maligning the Pope. But his adversaries quickly kindled a great controversy and published many malicious books in both languages, and soon, before the case was heard, brought up the ban and condemnation of the doctrine. Through such unjust action its respect was somewhat dimmed, and a change took place in many locations.

Nevertheless, Luther was importuned to answer, and many pious and learned people took pleasure in his answer, not because he rejected the indulgence, but on account of the salutary and comforting doctrine of repentance and the righteousness that follows from faith. Thus this doctrine was adopted by many pious people, so that it would have been difficult for the Elector of Saxony to proceed in any wise against the originator of this doctrine on account of so many brave and learned people that clung to it, and on account of his own conscience. This was especially the case, since those whose duty it was did not wish to undertake the matter and the change of religion was already at hand, and would only have become greater and worse, if the learned preachers had been put away. For before Luther had written anything, all sorts of erroneous and scandalous doctrine had already arisen, which would have caused much grievous change and oppression in Christendom if Luther had not prevented it.

And the adversaries, if they have any sense at all, cannot deny that much that is salutary and useful to the salvation of the soul is contained in this doctrine, which they themselves accept and allow. For it has brought this about that the preachers now teach much more thoughtfully of the power of the keys, of forgiveness of sins, of work-righteousness, of the use of the sacraments, of evangelical counsels, of worldly statutes, of the merit of monastic life and such like human doctrine, of the worship of saints, after such things have been brought to light by us. They also dispute more sharply with us, and even endeavor to slay us with our own sword.

And, as can be proved, more than one heresy has thereby been allayed, which had arisen with new and unchristian writings against the holy sacraments. The Anabaptists had spread a seductive and seditious doctrine against the possession of temporal property, against the courts, against the power of the magistrates, against all civil order, against preaching, against the Holy Sacrament, all of which would have been spread much further had not the hearts of men been warned and strengthened by this teaching, whereby authority and civil order are well maintained, and the righteousness of faith is so bravely defended against the hypocrisy of the Anabaptists and their imagined angelic holiness. Hence it is not denied by any upright, honest man, that in these schisms much has been brought to light that is absolutely essential to know. It is also entirely unfounded to say that the Anabaptists of their ilk have originated from Luther's doctrine, for such things have occurred before Luther, and most of all in such places where there was a lack of skilful pastors who ought to have strengthened and warned the consciences of men against false doctrine.

This cause was made specially odious on account of the general rumor spread by our adversaries that we had done away with all ceremonies, and were destroying all spiritual order and rule. With how much reason such things are attributed to us the facts will show. For this doctrine is not directed to the end that ceremonies be done away with but rather that they should be preserved with true fear of God, and we can say with truth, that in all Germany the mass is not celebrated with greater fear of God and greater participation of the people than with us. It is also celebrated according to common custom, except that along with the Latin singing we also use German, so that the people may have something which they can understand and learn.

The Sacrament is received by the people with greater reverence and oftener than before; and every one is previously examined and instructed, a thing which formerly could not easily be done, as at such a time a whole crowd was accustomed to go together.

Confession is likewise still observed, and the power of the keys is ofttimes praised in preaching and the people admonished what a great power there is in absolution.

The sermons are pure and sensible, which beyond doubt is the most acceptable sacrifice unto God.

Psalms and the litany are also chanted at the proper time, not for lucre or money, but by the pupils and the congregation of people. Thereby the unskilled are practiced and earnestly urged through the Word of God to pray. For this reason the ceremonies must be observed in the churches.

The holy days are still observed, with the exception of a few more recent ones, which have long been displeasing to well-informed men, for which reason the bishops and princes have often counselled how they might abolish some.

Besides all this a very useful ceremony is also observed, which formerly was used with great diligence in Christendom, but afterward fell into desuetude owing to negligence of the pastors and the people, namely, the catechism and instruction of the young. For this the boys and girls are asked to come together to the churches, where one of the preachers delivers to them the beginning and foundation of Christian doctrine, as the Creed, the Ten Commandments, the Lord's Prayer, several portions of the Gospel on the remission of sins, of repentance, of faith in Christ, of good works, of the cross, of Baptism and the Sacrament of the Altar. Afterward every one is examined as to what it has retained. Thus the children advance exceedingly in Christian knowledge, which formerly was lacking even to the older ones on account of much useless disputation and talk.

The schools are maintained with great diligence and at great expense to the authorities.

This is the order of the churches in the Electorate of Saxony, mostly in accordance with ancient custom and usage of the Roman Church, according to the instruction of holy teachers, and we desire nothing more than that such should also be acceptable to the bishops;

but they are a little too hard on us, because they persecute us on account of the marriage of priests and such like things.

But if they were inclined toward us with somewhat more grace, no one would need to complain that the order of the Church is being broken. For the matter of which many accuse us, as if this doctrine had the sole tendency to break up the power of the clergy, is altogether without foundation. For they would lose nothing of their power and magnificence if they would only cease some new and improper abuses. They would also not need entertain any fear for their possessions, although many others more than once before us have endeavored, under the semblance of a reformation, to take away the possessions of the clergy.

The Bohemians at the Council of Basel, among other things, have also postulated that the servants of the Church should have no private property; but our teaching is entirely different, namely, that as it is permissible to every Christian to use other external things, just so every Christian, whether he be a bishop or a pastor, may legally have and possess his own property. For even if bishops should become poor and lose their properties, that would not help other Christians. But it would help them, if the bishops would provide for the preaching of the pure and unadulterated Word. These seditious propositions to take from the clergy what belongs to it have nothing to do with our doctrine, which demands only that Christendom be instructed in the pure teaching, and the consciences be unburdened from unchristian commandments, for the Christian Church is born and maintained solely from the Word as it is written: He has begotten us through the Word of truth. Thus we teach that all civil laws and ordinances under spiritual and secular power are to be observed as an order of God for the sake of peace and unity. Never has a reformation been undertaken so entirely without violence as this one, as it is evident that through our adherence others have been brought to peace who were already arrayed in arms.

Up to this point we have shown that this controversy arose not without cause, and that it was not tolerated by the Elector of Saxony from a malicious purpose. Now we speak of the doctrine, and first of all enumerate the principal articles of faith from which Y. Imp. Maj. may learn that the Elector of Saxony does not tolerate any unchristian teaching in his territory, but has given all diligence to the universal Christian faith.

32. MELANCHTHON'S DRAFT OF THE CONCLUSION TO THE CONFESSION, MAY-JUNE, 1530[34]

Since the Imperial Majesty, as a most renowned Christian Emperor, has learned herewith the basis of the doctrine that is taught and preached in the principality, lands and territories of the aforesaid Elector of Saxony, and especially what constitutes the justification of men, and where a man is to seek and where not to seek the forgiveness of his sins and the attainment of God's grace. Also which are the Christian and pious ceremonies, for what they are profitable and useful, and how they are to be observed, and likewise which ceremonies are offensive, and, furthermore, how the people are taught and instructed that they are in duty bound to be obedient to the government with submissive homage (so long as they are not compelled to commit sin or to act against God). So may the Almighty and Merciful God grant your Majesty grace and imperial courage, in accord with the Imperial Majesty's gracious summons, to act in these most important and weighty matters in such manner that after having heard the opinion and judgment of each party in love and graciousness, everything that is found contrary to the clear and plain divine Scriptures, and therefore is wrongly held by this or that party, may be turned to the one and only Christian truth, which God Himself has revealed to the world through His Word alone, and in Christ has shown what is His divine will and what He requires of men whom he would justify and cause to be saved, that all divisions and misunderstandings of Scripture may be done away since on Scripture the unity and oneness of Christianity alone shall rest and stand as on the right foundation and so the one true Christian religion may be accepted and held by all estates. In this way the dangerous and lamentable dissension which is now found in churches and congregations may be put down and removed. For if this be not done, in the manner the Imperial Majesty, in your previously mentioned summons, has indicated as a gracious and Christian way, the result can only be that daily new and dangerous schisms, separation, dissent and disorder will result in the Church. As, unfortunately is very evident, there are many forward persons in the German nation who only to gain notoriety for themselves, begin many disputes and put forward all kinds of harmful and dangerous doctrines attacking the Christian Sacrament, that was instituted by God. And further, as is manifest, they would venture to meddle with other

articles of doctrine, especially should they find support and opportunity, as might easily happen, then if those of our party, who up
to this time through the teaching of the truth have most vigorously
opposed such things and strenuously contended against such heresies,
were banished or driven away, because they were not present, these
others would no longer hesitate and would add still more dangerous
errors to their previous heresies which they have invented concerning
the Sacrament.

Therefore may the Roman Imperial Majesty tread in the foot-
steps of the pious kings, who ruled over the Jewish people, who
had no higher concern than to remove and destroy everything set
up as a religious observance among the people that was contrary
to the commandment and decree of God. They were most highly
praised by the prophets of their day, because in these matters involv-
ing God's honor and service they heeded His command and decree
more than the inventions of men, but the others, who did not do
so and failed to destroy and forbid false worship were severely
punished. Therefore may you consider all Christendom and the
salvation of men's souls and act in these affairs for the true glory
of Almighty God and the peace of the German Nation, for the improvement of the people and the maintenance of the preaching of
the Holy Gospel and God's Word, that the youth may be faithfully
instructed therein and the true Christian doctrine may be transmitted to following generations, for which it is the duty of all men
to provide. Without doubt this will be the most exalted and praiseworthy imperial work that Your Imperial Majesty, in your eminence,
can ever perform. For Your Imperial Majesty can graciously perceive that these matters do not concern temporal possessions, lands
or nations, but that they involve the eternal salvation or injury
of souls and consciences, and that at the Last Judgment God will
demand an accounting concerning those matters that have herein
been discussed. God grant Your Imperial Majesty grace and safety
for this undertaking. Amen.

so that he summoned the emperor from Spain, (Who could see through
the trickery?) and then crowns him in the absence of the German
princes, as the Bull testifies. I am no prophet but I beseech all you
gentlemen to observe carefully for yourselves and not to imagine
that you are dealing only with men when you are dealing with the
pope and his party, but with sheer devils. For I know that back
of all are the devices of the devil. May the Almighty God so aid
you that all may make for peace. Amen.

Herewith I commend Your Grace to the grace of God, and in
so far as I can aid with my prayers I will serve you truly. May
Your Grace regard this epistle favorably. I cannot refrain; I must
care for poor, miserable, forsaken, despised, beguiled and betrayed
Germany, for which I seek no ill but only good, as a debt which
I owe to my dear fatherland.—Ex Erimo, Feria 4, post Visitationis,
anno 1530.—Your Grace's Obedient, Martin Luther.

---

45. FIRST DRAFT OF THE CONFUTATION, JULY 8, 1530[47]

*Catholic and, so to say, extemporaneous answer concerning some
articles proffered to the Catholic Imperial Spanish Majesty a few days
ago at the Imperial Diet at Augsburg by the most illustrious men, the
Elector of Saxony and some other Princes and two Cities.—MDXXX.*

Paul in his first Epistle to Timothy, 3rd Chapter, The Church
is the Pillar and Ground of Truth.

Most Serene, Most Invincible, and most August Emperor. Some
days ago a certain confession concerning our Catholic faith and religion was presented to Your Imperial Majesty by the Elector of
Saxony and certain other princes and two cities. It has pleased
Your Majesty that the most Reverend Father and Lord in Christ,
Lorenzo, the Holy Roman Church's Cardinal of the title
of St. Mary beyond the Tiber, Legate of the Apostolic See, should
deliver the proferred writing to several doctors expert in the study
of sacred literature, and enjoin them carefully to read and examine
the confession which was presented and approve what to them would
seem right, pious, and orthodox, and to reduce to writing whatever
would differ from the Catholic Truth and the true religion. The appointed doctors have most humbly done this work.

And in the first place of all, they find that in this same writing
there are certain articles which are not incompatible with our most

holy religion; but neither the Elector, nor the princes, nor the cities have invented them. Indeed, even from the very beginning of our faith the universal Church of the faithful as well as the pious and holy doctors of our orthodox faith have continually believed them and have proved this by illustrious literary productions and by their works and deeds, even in the most holy manner by their blood. In this respect, therefore, those men have certainly addduced nothing new, but only what from olden times has been observed, written, and preached. All these matters Your Holy Imperial Majesty may graciously accept from the Elector, the princes, and the cities; and Your Imperial Majesty may exhort the said Elector, the Prince of Saxony, and the rest that they themselves, together with their doctors and preachers, faithfully persevere in the same confession and doctrine and by no means depart from it.

Secondly, There appear in the aforenamed confession certain articles through which, incessantly, during the last ten years conflicting and contrary things have been publicly disseminated and divulged among the inexperienced multitude by the preacher's in many pamphlets and sermons, which fact is made manifest by the books that they have broadcast far and wide. In order that these things no longer cause the wretched common people to vacillate in doubt and to be involved in inextricable errors, the best thing to do would seem to be that pamphlets and books of that kind would be destroyed and abolished by an imperial edict, especially also since the preachers have of their own accord renounced their errors here and in part at a visitation in Saxony.

Thirdly, A good many articles emerge in that same confession which neither agree with the Holy Scriptures nor with the doctrines of those doctors whom the Church has sanctioned, and which therefore several centuries ago have been held to be heretical and erroneous and have been condemned by the holy Councils. Concerning these articles it seems worth the trouble that Your Imperial Majesty should deign graciously to take action with the Elector, the princes, and the cities in order that this schism no longer continue in the Church of God, that the same princes renounce their heresies and errors, and consent with the Catholic Church which truly is the pillar and ground of the truth, and also the Bride of Christ, and governed forever by the Holy Spirit, and that they do not separate and divide themselves in the Christian faith from the other Catholic nations, kingdoms, and potentates, and even from the greater part of Germans themselves.

Fourthly, It is evident that, besides the proffered articles, part of which are clearly shown to be erroneous, many other heresies and- doctrines invented to raise tumults are left in the writings, books, and pamphlets published within several years, Luther being the primary author and source of them all; for he has thought out some new and unheard of heresies, and resuscitated and restored some views which had been examined in regular Councils of the holy and most learned men by mature counsel and had been condemned as wicked and heretical, and had been entirely forgotten. Therefore, in order that at last the peace and harmony of Germany be reestablished and religion be restored to its former high level, it seems best to advise Your Imperial Majesty to inform the Elector, the princes, and the cities that—since in the books of Luther and the preachers there are contained until now very many matters alien to the truth, yet not mentioned in the proffered articles—Your Imperial Majesty must insist on receiving definite assurance that the princes and preachers have silently retracted, revoked, or condemned whatever other heresies and errors may have existed. For, Most Clement Emperor, it would be a small thing to keep peace in this or that matter, while in others, and indeed the gravest, there is no peace.

Fifthly, It is admitted that besides innumerable errors which through Luther and the doctrine of his followers and accomplices have afflicted Germany, there exist unheard-of, foreign, wicked, criminal, and absolutely intolerable heresies and sects, suddenly sprung up and born by the recent discord and internal war among the Lutherans. Such are the Capernaites, who rail against the Sacrament of the Eucharist; the Anabaptists, who oppose the baptism of children, besides many others so that now nearly every single house and almost every single mortal person invents his own new religion.

And although the princes themselves and the preachers detest these heresies and hostile sects, and do not in the least approve of them, yet it is apparent that the fountainhead and origin of them all is Luther and his wicked, frivolous, and self-contradictory doctrine. Therefore it seems advisable for Your Imperial Majesty to direct your eyes and your mind to distinguishing these things to the glory of the Highest God and the tranquility of the Roman Empire's subjects, and to weed out by their deepest roots and to extirpate radically and as fast as possible such abominable heresies of unheard-of wickedness, and the discords, and inner wars and tumults, and to see to it that neither the princes nor the two cities in their provinces and places tolerate these sects and their instigators nor allow new ones to crop up, but that they hasten to embrace again the old Catholic religion.

And how Your Most Holy Imperial Majesty may be enabled to understand the meaning and tendency of the proffered articles and in what respects they are contrary to what formerly was preached and inculcated in the simple people by the preachers of the princes, will appear more fully from the confutations and answers here following.

First Article of Faith Offered by the Princes and Preachers. Our churches with great consent are teaching that the decree of the Synod of Nicaea concerning the unity of the Divine Essence and concerning the Three Persons is to be believed truly and without any doubt; that is to say, there is one Divine Essence, etc.—*Answer:* Correctly they here agree with the norm of faith and concur with the Roman Church. However, since the princes have signed that confession for themselves and for the preachers, they are not without cause confronted with the objection why Luther, the principal preacher and the instigator of these dissensions, writes to Latomus, "My soul hates this word 'homusion'," since it was precisely this word which the Council of Nicaea has formed against the Arians. Whence also the Christians adhering to the Sacred Council mockingly were called "Homusiani," which name migrated also to Africa and Spain. For Hunaricus, King of the Vandals, who was infected with the Arian heresy, passed a law to persecute the Homusiani. Why, then, does Luther hate this word "homusion," when it signifies nothing else but what they here confess, namely the same essence in three persons? For "homusios" means in Latin "co-essential." Moreover, at this time we might ask these preachers, who have often testified that they would accept nothing except what is given by the Holy Scriptures, why they here say, "three persons," when this word or expression, "person," is not found in this sense in the Scriptures, although we Catholics most firmly confess three persons in the deity. Moreover, what does this mean that at the beginning they put forward the Nicene Council (indeed, the most holy one), that with it they begin their confession of faith which they want us to regard as a most sincere one, while Melanchthon, among those dogmatists by no means the least, has written so spitefully about the Nicene

Council? For he speaks thus, "Let us call to mind a few examples of church traditions from which one may see that nothing is so subversive of piety as are man-made doctrines. At the Synod of Nicaea certain forms of penitence have been appointed. I do not judge in what spirit the fathers have decreed them, but I see that a good part of the gospel, in fact the real power of the gospel, has been obscured by that same tradition. For there the satisfactions originated, which in the beginning, perhaps, were tolerable because up to that time the understanding of the gospel was purer in the Church, but soon afterwards—what torture of consciences has resulted from the satisfactions! Grace was obscured, and what the gospel had attributed to faith began to be ascribed to satisfaction. What is more wicked and more pernicious? And to these evils surely the Synod of Nicaea gave occasion." It is therefore a great surprise that the princes think so highly of the Nicene Synod while Melanchthon attributes to it godlessness and even obscuration of the gospel. Also Luther says, "At the Synod of Nicaea faith as well as the gospel waned and the traditions grew stronger."

Appendix to the First Article. They condemn all heresies which have sprung up against this article, as the Manichaeans, Valentinians, Arians, Eunomians, Mahommedans, Samosatenes, etc.—*Answer:* Also here the princes act correctly in that they reject the heretics who were condemned by the Church, the Councils, and the fathers. But we would ask them always to do what they do here, viz., never to permit their preachers to resuscitate the doctrines of heretics long ago condemned and buried.

Second Article. They teach that since the fall of Adam, all men begotten according to nature, are born with sin, that is without the fear of God, without trust in God, and with concupiscence; and that this disease, or vice of origin, is truly sin, even now condemning and bringing eternal death upon those not born again through baptism and the Holy Ghost.—*Answer:* Correctly do the princes here add an article on original sin; but we are afraid that here some things which pollute this article were smuggled in by the preachers. For, in the first place, they do not correctly explain original sin when they say that a child is born without fear of God, without trust, etc. This is indeed incorrectly stated. For to be without the fear of God, without trust in God, is rather "actual" sin of an adult person than the original sin of a child. Moreover, what sane person can say that a child is sinning because he does not fear God, does not trust in God while he is lacking the use of his reason! Therefore, that explanation of original sin is worthless. But the preachers give themselves away when they add, "with concupiscence," for here they repeat what Luther has so stubbornly asserted, viz., that concupiscence truly is sin, and that therefore, sin truly remains in a child after baptism. For he says that grace is withheld according to the measure of concupiscence. But to say this, means to cancel the efficacy and power of baptism, and it is certainly more execrable to say that baptized children are still in sin than to say that the children of Christians are saved without baptism, as other Catabaptists and previously also Zwingli have said. For if that vice (concupiscence) warrants eternal death, and remains in the child, it will follow logically that a baptized child is damned in eternity, as Luther's disciple Eberhardus Widensee of Magdeburg has publicly taught.

Appendix to the Second Article. They condemn the Pelagians and others who deny that the vice of origin is sin, and who, to obscure the glory of Christ's merits and benefits, argue that man can be justified before God by his own strength or reason.—*Answer:* Also here the princes correctly reject the Pelagians who were condemned at the Councils of Milevitanum and Rome, because on the one hand they denied sin in children, and on the other hand attributed justification to our own powers. But here the sacred Emperor sees how one sect destroys the other. For, since they condemn the Pelagians and "others", who are those others if not the preachers of Strassburg, Basle, Constance, Zuerich, Memmingen and the like. because Zwingli writes more than once that original sin is not sin, but a natural defect like stammering. Bucer also teaches the same thing and thus retracts what he had only recently subscribed to at Marburg in the Landgraviate of Hesse at a certain convention. But why do they not condemn Melanchthon for saying that the Scripture does not make any distinction between actual and original sin, and for writing that original sin is a certain actual evil lust? Why do they not condemn Luther, the author of this disturbance, because he has stated that original sin always remains? For, if they wanted to walk in purity with the Church, then also those heresies should have been put away.

Third Article. Also they teach that the Word, that is the Son of God, did take man's nature in the womb of the blessed Virgin Mary, so that there are two natures, the divine and the human, inseparably conjoined in the unity of the Person, one Christ, true God

and true man. born of the Virgin Mary, who truly suffered, was crucified, dead, buried, etc., according to the Symbol of the apostles.—
Answer: Also here the princes and their preachers do not differ
from the rule of faith. But one must marvel that the preachers,
contrary to their most established principle not to accept anything
but what may be proved by clear and plain Scriptures, here again act
far differently. For, in the first place, when they attribute this article
to the Symbol of the apostles, let them show us the Scripture that
the apostles have framed something of this kind (a symbol); for we
find some who have had their secret doubts about it: they say, We
do not know whether the Symbol which is called "apostolic" has
been delivered by the apostles themselves or not. It is therefore
evident that the princes and preachers, after rejecting the authority
of the Church and the fathers, find themselves in a precarious condition. But we Catholics follow our Mother, the Church, and do
not have any doubt about that Symbol of the apostles. Beyond this,
we may note that the preachers confess that the two natures are
inseparably conjoined in the unity of the person. For that is very
true as the Catholic faith shows us.

But again the preachers are urgently asked to tell, since they
will not receive anything but explicit Scriptures, why they confess
something which plain Scripture nowhere asserts. For the word
"person," as we have said. is unknown to Scripture in this meaning.
Furthermore, that that blessed union is inseparable, we acknowledge
with Damascenus. But where will they adduce Scriptures, especially
since the Lutherans are in that nefarious and wicked error that in
the Eucharist. where they confess the union of bread and Christ,
the Body and Blood of Christ are present only as long as and while
they are offered for the use of communing, but that when they are
not destined for the use of communing nothing of Christ is present?
We would wish that they would show us from plain Scriptures why
they affirm the inseparability of the one but deny it of the other.—
Nor is their confession of Christ as true God and true man unas-
sailable in all respects. For if they would believe this as firmly
with the heart as they claim to do with boastful words, they would
not permit their preachers to blaspheme and dishonor our Saviour.
Yea, indeed, because Bugenhagen the Pomeranian, has fallen into this
ungodly error he could write, "Christ has experienced the terrors of
the soul even to despair." Melanchthon wrote "The highest cause
of Christ's fear was the feeling of being deserted and of the divine

wrath; while Christ hovered between hell and life. In this terror Christ was deprived of His gifts. For in this desolation and anxiety a certain deprivation of charity was made in such manner that while the divinity withdrew, charity did not glow forth." Antonius Zimmermann, also a Lutheran, wrote even worse things, "Christ complained that he was forsaken of God, i.e., that he was abandoned by life and blessedness and all good things." We pass by a Lutheran who edited an anonymous book entitled "On the Simplicity of Faith," in which he denies that Christ had an intelligent soul, and asserts, like Apollinaris the heretic, that the divinity stood in the place of the soul. Therefore, as long as the princes are Catholic-minded in this article, they must be warned to induce their preachers to recant such wicked and godless statements about Christ our Saviour.

Fourth Article. Also they teach that men cannot be justified before God by their own strength, merits, or works, but are freely justified for Christ's sake, through faith.—*Answer:* About faith and works we shall speak later; now we shall treat only of merits. Firstly, no one of all Catholics has ever thought that we might attain to blessedness by our merits without grace. For grace must precede, accompany, and follow, even as our mother Church has taught us to pray, "We beseech Thee, O Lord, that in all our actions the gift of Thy grace may go before and its assistance follow after us." We know that John has said, "Men cannot receive anything except it be given him from heaven," John 3; and James says, ch. 1, that every best and every perfect gift is from above, coming down from the father of lights. We know that all our sufficiency is from God, 2 Cor. 3, and that Paul says, "What hast thou that thou didst not receive?" 1 Cor. 4. And Christ says, "No man cometh to Me except the Father Who sent Me, have drawn him," John 6. And Augustine says, "When God rewards our merits He crowns His gifts." Let no one, therefore, think that he is able by his own strength to merit or to do anything good without the grace of God, as the Pelagians, the enemies of grace, have said. But, grace precedes the will, moves the will, perfects the will so that the works which otherwise would be nothing, by the assistance of the grace of God are something, and are meritorious.

This is the way in which the Catholics whom the new dogmatists condemn, think and speak about merits, and the preachers of the princes here obscure everything. But that our merits are something by the grace of God and by the merits of Christ's passion, is proved 2 Tim. 4, "I have fought a good fight, I have finished my course,

I have kept the faith; henceforth is laid up for me a crown of righteousness which the Lord, the righteous Judge, shall give me at that
day." Thus Christ has promised blessedness to those who do good
works, Matt. 5. And Paul has said, "We must appear before the
judgment seat of Christ, that everyone may receive the things done
in his body according to that he has done good or bad," 2 Cor. 5.
And Christ Himself bears witness, Matt. 25. Unto Abraham God said,
"Fear not, I am thy protector and thy very great reward," Gen. 15.
And Isaiah says, "Behold, his reward is with him and his work
before him," Is. 40. God said to Cain. "If thou hast done well, wilt
thou not be accepted?" Gen. 4. God has led us into the vineyard and
has agreed with us on a denarius a day, Matt. 20. Paul says, 1 Cor. 3,
"Everyone will receive his own reward according to his labor." And
innumerable words of that kind we read in the Scriptures, testifying
that our merits and works are to be rewarded by God, the highest
Good. But, the sacred writings do not attach the same value to all
merits, for some are the result of divine influence and prevenient
grace; but this is not the grace making the doer worthy of eternal
life. Thus Cornelius the centurion merited by his alms and prayers
that an angel told him, "Thy prayers and alms have come up as a
memorial before God." Acts 10. Other people, however, do good
works by which they become worthy of eternal life, not in regard
to the works in themselves, because we know this word of Christ,
"If you shall have done all those things which you are commanded
to do, say, We are unprofitable servants, we have done that which it
was our duty to do," Luke 17. But those merits are worthy through the
grace of God. In this way righteous men render themselves worthy
of eternal life by their good works. Thus John says, "They will
walk with me in white robes because they are worthy," Rev. 3. And
Paul, Col. 1, says, "With joy giving thanks to the Father Who hath
made us worthy to have a part of the lot of the saints in the light." We
would make these brief statements concerning merits over against the
preachers of the princes and all who contrary to express Scriptures
deny our merits. Consequently Luther errs wickedly, and Rieger errs,
who presumptuously have said that Paul destroys all the theologians'
fanciful notions about the "meritum congrui" and "condigni." Zwingli
and others err wickedly who deny every merit. On the other hand,
when they say that we are justified by faith this is the great and
principal error of the preachers. For to faith alone they ascribe
that which is proper to charity and to the grace of God. This they

have impressed upon the people. And Luther has dared to falsify the Scripture by adding to Romans 3 this word, "Sola," which is found neither in the Greek nor in the Latin copies. For, that faith alone does not justify, Paul expressly testifies, 1 Cor. 13, "If I should have all faith so as to move mountains, but should not have charity, I am nothing." Here the apostle, the teacher of the Gentiles, knocks to pieces all statements of the adversaries because faith alone does not justify. Wickedly, therefore, has Melanchthon spoken and stamped his foot on Paul, the chosen vessel, when he writes that charity does not justify, but faith which is preferred to charity. This proposition is iniquitous not only because he denies that charity justifies, but much more also in this respect that he prefers faith to charity, while St. Paul says, "Faith, hope, charity, these three, but the greatest of these is charity." The same wickedness did Luther add when he said, "We ought to elevate faith above all virtues," as if Paul had not said, "But above all things put on charity," Col. 3. And he turns Paul, who teaches, Gal. 5, "Faith which worketh by love," upside down by saying, "Love which worketh by faith." We shall repeat these statements later. Nor does the holy Paul espouse their cause when he says somewhere that faith is ours, and that it justifies, because Paul does not speak about faith as those preachers think who thrust the "sola fide" upon the simple people, but he speaks, as he himself says, of faith which works through love, Gal. 5. Hence they should have learned from that word of the apostle the meaning of his other statements. And we see that it is true when St. Augustine says that this heresy has arisen from a misinterpretation of the words of Paul. However, we shall say more about this matter later. At present, Your Holy Imperial Majesty may at least recognize this much that in the days of Augustine this heresy which the preachers of the princes have raised up again from the ashes, was condemned, as St. James destroyed this error in his epistle, also St. Peter according to the essence of the same holy Aurelius Augustine.

Fifth Article. That we obtain this faith, the office of teaching the Gospel and administering the Sacraments was instituted. For through the Word and the Sacraments, as through instruments, the Holy Ghost is given who works faith, etc.—*Answer:* The princes here speak correctly of the office of teaching the Gospel and administering the Sacraments, but their preachers have planted many tares to lead the people away from the true faith. For in the first place, they

confess that through the Sacraments, as through instruments, the
Holy Ghost is given; but Luther has more than once stated and
taught the opposite. Therefore, Pope Leo X of blessed memory has
condemned this article of Luther: "It is a heretical though familiar
doctrine that the Sacraments of the New Law grant justifying faith
to them who interpose no obstacle." Hence, what Luther called
heretical, this the preachers now confess as Catholic; so nicely they
fight against each other!

Secondly, although the preachers oftentimes mention the Sacraments, they nowhere explain what they think about the Sacraments,
they nowhere explain what they think about the Sacraments and
their number, as they should have done if they really wanted to give
an account of their faith. For Luther has taught wickedly that the
Sacraments had been only recently invented. In some places he states
that there are three Sacraments, in some that there are only two.
There is also a passage where he mentions only one Sacrament
and two sacramental signs, an error which the Anabaptist Oswald
Glaib eagerly imbibed. He has also declared more than once that
the Sacraments of the New Law do not differ from the Sacraments
of the Old Law so far as their efficacy and meaning are concerned.

Thirdly, in reference to their assertion that faith is produced
by the Sacraments and the Word, it has been stated in the former
article that faith does not justify without charity, as Paul testifies,
although in baptism, according to the dotrine of the Catholics, faith
is infused together with hope and charity. Moreover, we have discussed in the preceding article the precise meaning of the Catholic
doctrine that merits contribute to our justification and to the growth
of grace, also in what respect this is to be denied over against the
Pelagians. And as far as Paul's words in praise of faith are concerned; Gal. 3, they must be understood of faith which works through
charity, Gal. 5. This faith the theologians have correctly named
"fides formata," because it is clothed with grace and charity, acceptable to God, etc.

Appendix to the Fifth Article. They condemn the Anabaptists and
others who think that the Holy Ghost is given to men without the
external Word, through their own preparations and works.—*Answer:*
All those are here correctly condemned who are not willing to be
taught by a man. But here they do not condemn only the Anabaptists
and Zwingli (who wished to be taught by God and not by men, who
also writes somewhere that he is sure he was instructed by God, for

he felt it), but also a great part of the Lutherans who have supported their views by what the prophets have written, "And they shall all be taught of God," John 6. They have also brought forward that statement, 1 John 2, "Ye need not that any man teach you, but as his anointing teaches you concerning all things, and is truth and is no lie." They have therefore wished that we be taught of God. Aside from this we cannot understand why Luther and Melanchthon have been so malign towards the universities except because they have desired to have the Holy Spirit as the teacher. For Luther says, "Both, speculative as well as practical learning of all schools is condemned." Melanchthon says, "Christ's word, 'Many false prophets shall arise and deceive many,' plainly was spoken of the studies of the universities." Luther has said that the universities are the twelfth face of Antichrist, the most noxious of all, in Daniel, and that the universities are prefigured by the idol Moloch, and that the doctors are the locusts. Melanchthon said since the academies of the general studies had been founded they had never found anything either more pernicious or more godless. "I see," he says, "they do not belong to the bishops but to Satan himself." How often does Luther call the school "brothels and houses of lewness"! By such terrible invectives they have emptied all schools, even the common schools, so that there is already a very great lack of priests and learned men, able to teach, which want will be much greater in the future; and the ministry of the Word which they here advocate will suffer the loss, and in the course of time the kings and princes and all public business will feel the scarcity of learned men unless a remedy is soon found against this evil.

Sixth Article. They also teach that this faith is bound to bring forth good fruits, and that it is necessary to do good works commanded by God, because of God's will.—*Answer:* Here the princes show a little more understanding of the matter than their preachers; therefore your Imperial Majesty and the princes themselves must induce their preachers publicly to recant and revoke their errors because they have preached most scandalously against good works, so that many simple people thought they would commit a mortal sin by doing a good work. But to show that the present confession contradicts their public utterances and writings, Most August Emperor, we shall quote directly from their innumerable writings, but only from a few of them in order that Your Imperial Majesty may not be nauseated. Luther says, "Faith and works absolutely contradict each other, therefore works cannot be taught without damaging faith."

Pomeranus writes, "Two men exist between whom there is never peace, namely faith and works." Melanchthon says, "All works of men, however laudable in appearance, are thoroughly corrupt; they are sins worthy of death." Luther says, "God pays no attention to our works, or if they are anything before Him, yet they are all equal as far as merit is concerned." In this sentence he, firstly, contradicts himself because he affirms merit. Secondly, he raises up a condemned heresy of Jovinian which has been condemned by the Church and St. Jerome, namely, that merits are equal. And thirdly, he asserts the wicked and blasphemous doctrine that God pays no attention to our works, when as a matter of fact did look on the alms of Cornelius; He did see the affliction of Hagar; He did see that Abraham would direct his children and his household after him, etc., Gen. 18. And, "By myself have I sworn," says the Lord, "because thou hast done this thing," Gen. 22. And the whole Scripture affirms the con trary, and testifies that God considered good works, the sacrifice of Abel, the righteousness of Noah, the tasting of the Ninivites, the tears of Hezekiah, etc. Therefore it is an erroneous doctrine of Zwingli that "only the unbelievers are evil, because before God we do not need works, but only toward men." And lest the preachers evade the question under the pretext that they need not answer for Zwingli, let them answer for themselves. Luther wrote, "Christ has ordained that there is no sin except unbelief, and no righteousness except faith." But why then has Paul said, "Manifest are the works of the flesh, which are fornication, uncleanliness, etc." Gal. 5? Luther has said, "if one believes in Christ, there are no evil works which could accuse and damn him." This is the reason he gives: "Where there is faith, no sin is doing any harm. This again agrees with the heresy of Eunomius who asserted that no sin is imputed unto him who remains in faith. This also was the opinion of Arius the heretic. Was not also the following statement by Luther injurious to good works: "Let us never doubt that we are saved, after we have been baptized, because the promise given us there is not changed by any sins; hence a baptized person even though he wanted to, cannot lose his salvation, because no sins can condemn him except unbelief; all other sins are blotted out by faith in a moment." Who of the common people will do good works when he hears this? And in another place he says, "Faith alone is necessary, all other things are entirely free and neither commanded nor prohibited." Here the princes may see how their preachers agree with the present confession "that faith must bring forth good fruits!" How could Luther become so insane as to write what neither Turk nor Tartar nor Persian would ever believe, viz.. that evil works do not make an evil man, as though Christ had erred when He said, "By their fruits ye shall know them," Matt. 7. St. John has taught us to shun such heresies, 1 John 3, "Little children, let no one lead you astray, he that doeth righteousness is righteous." By those wicked doctrines it has come to pass that Germany which erstwhile was the most Christian country, has, wherever Lutheranism prevails, totally fallen away from those Christian works and devotions.

Furthermore, the confession of that article has been badly stained by the preachers when they attribute justification to faith alone. We attribute this to faith, as a foundation and beginning, because without faith it is impossible to please God, Heb. 11. But charity makes it perfect, for charity is active in conformity with the divine will, because "glory and honor and peace (are due) to every man working good," Rom. 2. And Christ has shown that works are necessary when He says. "If thou wilt enter into life keep the commandments," Matt. 19. Again, the word of Christ testifies that faith is not sufficient: "Not everyone that says unto me, Lord, Lord. shall enter into the kingdom of heaven, but he that doeth the will of my Father," Matt. 7. Hence believers who are not doing good works, are not friends of God, for Christ has said, "You are my friends, if you have done what I command you," John 15. From this we return to Augustine, "On the Christian Life." But the preachers of the princes quote the word of Christ, Luke 17, "If you have done all those things, etc." Whoever adduced this text must have been half asleep; the text is distorted in favor of faith against works, whereas in that very message the preceding verses treat chiefly of faith when the disciples asked the Lord, "Lord. increase our faith." And .in order to overthrow by one single word the whole foundation in which the adversaries glory, let us say this : if a man does not merit his justification by good works he will much less merit it by faith, because he is justified alone by the mercy of God, and faith and good works are gifts of God, as will be explained later. Therefore the Catholics confess, "If we have done all things", and, we may add, "and if we have believed all things out of humility, let us say that we are unprofitable servants." For our works are not useful to God but only to us; the works are useful to us because Paul says, Col. 3, "And whatsoever ye do, do it heartily as to the Lord, and not unto men, knowing that of the

Lord ye shall receive the reward of inheritance." We, therefore, firmly confess that our works, compared with the divine, do not deserve a reward. as Paul teaches us, "I reckon that the sufferings of the present time are not worthy of the future glory shall be revealed in us," Rom. 8.

They claim that the ancient ecclesiastical writers teach the same thing; however they misuse the fathers as deceitfully as they do the Scriptures. For, when Ambrose is brought in, it is evident that everywhere he speaks about the works of the Law without which indeed faith justifies. For in Rom. 3 it is written, "But now without the Law the righteousness of God, etc." It is evident that the righteousness of God has been manifested without the Law, that is to say, without the law of the Sabbath and circumcision and the new moon and vengeance. Ambrose pursues this subject in chapter 4 where he speaks about Abraham, who without the Law and without the works of the Law, believed God, even before circumcision. However, St. James repudiates the notion that Abraham was justified without any work, saying, "Abraham, our father, was justified by works when he offered Isaac, his son, upon the altar. Thou seest how faith wrought with his works, and by works was faith made perfect." and later, "You see that by works man is justified, and not by faith only." Let the princes rather believe this apostle than the preachers who wrest the Holy Scriptures and the statements of the fathers.

* * * * *

Since then among these few articles of their confession so many thoroughly reprehensible articles are found, as we have shown above, faithfully and obediently, without intention of injury or offense, what may we expect to discover if all their articles, of which there is an endless number in the books of their preachers, should be discussed more exactly and examined precisely according to the standard of faith?

Therefore we humbly ask, Your Imperial Majesty rather to advise them that, mindful of their faith and their salvation, and avoiding endless wrangling about their rather tedious confession, they would simply say with us, with one heart and one voice, "We believe one holy Catholic and Apostolic Church," of which Luther himself very often has written and publicly confessed that it cannot err, because Christ has given it the spirit of truth to teach and suggest to it all things, and to abide with it forever.

It has easily been proved conclusively, Your Imperial Majesty, both by this our answer and by the deeds and fruits of this new gospel of their preachers, that their confession is not the true gospel of Christ. It leaves no room for the reward of our good works which Christ has so liberally, frequently, and so clearly promised in his gospel; it declares that no one is entitled to rewards on account of his merits, as if Christ were the most unjust judge who indeed threatens with hell-fire those who merit evil, but decides that those who have merited well need not be requited—a view which flatly contradicts Christ Himself, Who most plainly, everywhere, and according to all the evangelists, teaches that we should pray and do alms, not in order that they may be seen by men from whom we could receive the reward of vainglory but "in secret that the Heavenly Father Who seeth in secret may reward you," and that we should invite to the banquet not the friends, the kinsmen, the neighbors, or the rich, lest perhaps we may be repaid by them; but the poor, the sick, the lame, and the blind who do not have whereby they may requite us, and He promises us that we shall be blessed by that which will be given to us in the resurrection. But the confession of the preachers, in accordance with Luther's doctrine that faith alone justifies, leaves no repayment or reward of good works which, although they may have been done in the best manner, Luther holds to be sin. Thus it has come to pass that the people are very torpid to do good works since they have ever so often heard from those preachers that we merit nothing by good works.

Although they everywhere make much ado about the Word of God, yet their doctrine, so far, is very unstable and self-contradictory.

Therefore it cannot by any means be the Word of God; for it does not "remain forever," but changes like the moon from day to day; it is not the word of peace, but of confusion, a thing which we have indeed experienced only too much ere this, and Luther himself admits that there must be confusion wherever his gospel is being preached. And how can the Holy Spirit be in this cause when Luther dares to write that it was begun from envy and that by necessity it must end in violence; and when he does away with all authority among the Christians, what else does he scheme to do but to destroy, under the guise of his gospel, all government?

Let Your Imperial Majesty, therefore, mercifully consider by your innate prudence and the singular grace granted you from the Most High, what a dangerous thing it would be to permit those dissensions about our faith and religion to exist any longer, and to

defer action until some future Church Council; how many and terrible
things could be attempted by the tyrant of the Turks, this most fright-
ful foe of the Cross and the Name of Christ; that most of these
heresies have been dashed to pieces long ago in very many councils; moreover, it is not fitting, yea it is quite contrary to the public
laws of the Christian emperor when matters which have once been
settled by a Council, are called again into question and subjected to
renewed discussion, otherwise there would never be an end of councils and debates and it would be necessary to convoke a council
every single month whenever some freakish apostate has a new dream
or some stubborn foolish notion. Furthermore, it is well known what
those preachers have chiefly written and taught about the Councils;
but they appeal to a future council: not indeed because they wish
with all their heart a decision by which they do not intend to abide
anyway, but rather because they wish to disseminate their errors
in the meantime more freely and widely among the people. For
Luther has written openly, "If once a council would decide that the
Holy Sacrament should be given the laity in both kinds, then the
people ought, in defiance, not to take both kinds, but either the one
or the other." We do not, therefore, believe that the preachers seriously
want any council.

Finally, O Most Glorious Emperor, these very wicked and absurd
doctrines of the new sects cannot be placed before the other nations,
in a council without exposing a prominent nation to the greatest
dishonor and more appalling disgrace. For who would, without
blushing and shame, debate in the presence of so many great
prelates and illustrious representatives of the other nations,
whether there are seven Sacraments, whether baptism takes sin
away in children, whether by the words of consecration the substance
of the bread is really changed into the Body of Christ, etc.? All
these matters have been decided long ago. What would meanwhile
become of the miserably oppressed and distressed Catholics? With
how many tears and prayers, with what deep sighs and groanings have
so many holy virgins been praying incessantly to God for your Majesty's happy return from Spain—virgins who either have already
been driven out of their homes, or are constantly in fear of being
driven out soon, unless Your Imperial Majesty will come shortly!
How many miserable old men, most of whom have served God in
monasteries night and day for forty or fifty years, have been crying
with continuous petitions to God for the advent of Your Majesty—

like Simeon in the temple, who prayed for the redemption of Israel—
that they might be able to pay their vows' to God until the end!
Lastly, how many Catholic people of both sexes are there, here and
there·in all the states who, because Lutherans and other sects are
prevalent, are hindered from the accustomed worship of God and
who desire to be restored by Your Majesty's presence to the former
liberty of serving God! These heresies must, therefore, not be referred
to a future council, but now they must be successfully stamped out,
covered up, and abolished forever by Your Imperial Majesty according
to the former decisions of the Church Councils.

This is, O Most Pious Emperor, Most Mighty Protector of the
Church and Defender of the Apostolic See, what we the humble and
devoted chaplains and insignificant servants of Your Majesty—not
by our own temerity, but by the commission given us—have thought
necessary, on account of the brevity of the time, to say and to write
reverently and obediently in answer to the confession signed by
those most illustrious princes and the two cities. We humbly pray
and supplicate that Your Imperial Majesty would graciously accept
it all in good part, and we certainly do not wish to have it confirmed,
not even the smallest iota, except as far as it will be approved by
the Most Holy Apostolic See and by Your Imperial Majesty. God,
the Best and Greatest, preserve Your Imperial Majesty safe and
sound always and grant that Your Imperial Majesty may bring
Germany, the country afflicted and most miserably troubled and
polluted by sects, back to its former soundness of faith and to
peace. Amen.

Christ lives and sits at the right hand, not of the Emperor (for
then should we have gone to destruction long ago), but at the right
hand of God. This is something incredibly great. But I am drawn
to this incredible truth, and am willing to die upon it, and why
should I not therefore also be willing to live upon it? Would God
that Philip would believe this least with my faith, if he has no
other. . . . Your Martin Luther.

Luther to Melanchthon, July 13: Doctor Martinus Luther, to the
faithful disciple and witness of Christ, M. Philipps Melanchthon,
his brother.

Grace and true peace of Christ! I believe, my dear Philipps,
that you in many ways now realize from experience that Belial can
in no manner be united with Christ, and that one can entertain
no hope of concord, so far as the doctrine is concerned. I wrote
about this to the princes that our cause cannot be left to the Emperor as judge. And now we perceive the purpose of the writing
that contains the so-gracious call. But, perhaps, the matter had
already progressed too far before my letter arrived. But at least
for myself I will not yield a hair's-breadth, nor allow that the matter be again brought into the former situation (restituti); I will
rather await all external danger, since they proceed so determinedly.

The Emperor may do what he can. But I wish to know what
you have done. . . I wish that you would not permit yourself to be disturbed on account of the victory and boastfulness of the enemies,
but that you would establish yourself against it through the power
and strength and might of Him Who raised Christ from the dead
and will quicken us with Him and raise us. . . Martin Luther.

48. CONFUTATIO PONTIFICIA, AUGUST 3, 1530[50]

As His Worshipful Imperial Majesty received several days since
a Confession of Faith presented by the Elector the duke of Saxony
and several princes and two cities, to which their names were affixed,
with his characteristic zeal for the glory of God, the salvation of
souls, Christian harmony and the public peace, he not only himself
read the Confession, but also, in order that in a matter of such moment he might proceed the more thoroughly and seasonably, he referred the aforesaid Confession to several learned, mature, approved
and honorable men of different nations for their inspection and examination, and earnestly directed and enjoined them to praise and ap-

prove what in the Confession was said aright and in accord with Catholic doctrine, but, on the other hand, to note that wherein it differed from the Catholic Church, and, together with their reply, to present and explain their judgment on each topic. 2. This commission was executed aright and according to order. For those learned men with all care and diligence examined the aforesaid Confession, and committed to writing what they thought on each topic, and thus presented a reply to His Imperial Majesty. 3. This reply His Worshipful Imperial Majesty, as becomes a Christian emperor, most accurately read and gave to the other electors, princes and estates of the Roman Empire for their perusal and examination, which they also approved as orthodox and in every respect harmonious with the Gospel and Holy Scripture. 4. For this reason, after a conference with the electors, princes and states above named, in order that all dissension concerning this our orthodox holy faith and religion may be removed, His Imperial Majesty has directed that a declaration be made at present as follows:

In reference to the matters presented to His Imperial Majesty by the Elector of Saxony and some princes and states of the Holy Roman Empire, on the subject and concerning causes pertaining to the Christian orthodox faith, the following Christian reply can be given:

PART I.

To Article I. Especially when in the first article they confess the unity of the divine essence in three persons according to the decree of the Council of Nice, their Confession must be accepted, since it agrees in all respects with the rule of faith and the Roman Church. 2. For the Council of Nice, convened under the Emperor Constantine the Great, has always been regarded inviolable, whereat three hundred and eighteen bishops eminent and venerable for holiness of life, martyrdom and learning, after investigating and diligently examining the Holy Scriptures, set forth this article which they here confess concerning the unity of the essence and the trinity of persons. 3. So too their condemnation of all heresies arising contrary to this article must be accepted—viz. the Manichaeans, Arians, Eunomians, Valentinians, Samosatanes, for the Holy Catholic Church has condemned these of old.

To Article II. In the second article we approve their Confession, in common with the Catholic Church, that the fault of origin is truly sin, condemning and bringing eternal death upon those who are not born again by baptism and the Holy Ghost. For in this they properly condemn the Pelagians, both modern and ancient, who have been long since condemned by the Church. 2. But the declaration of the article, that Original Sin is that men are born without the fear of God and without trust in God, is to be entirely rejected, since it is manifest to every Christian that to be without the fear of God and without trust in God is rather the actual guilt of an adult than the offence of a recently-born infant, which does not possess as yet the full use of reason, as the Lord says: "Your children which had no knowledge between good and evil," Deut. 1:39. 3. Moreover, the declaration is also rejected whereby they call the fault of origin concupiscence, if they mean thereby that concupiscence is a sin that remains sin in a child even after baptism. For the Apostolic See has already condemned two articles of Martin Luther concerning sin remaining in a child after baptism, and concerning the *fomes* of sin hindering a soul from entering the kingdom of heaven. 4. But if, according to the opinion of St. Augustine, they call the vice of origin concupiscence, which in baptism ceases to be sin, this ought to be accepted, since indeed, according to the declaration of St. Paul, we are all born children of wrath (Eph. 2:3), and in Adam we all have sinned (Rom. 5:12).

To Article III. In the third article there is nothing to offend, since the entire Confession agrees with the Apostles' Creed and the right rule of faith—viz. the Son of God became incarnate, assumed human nature into the unity of his person, was born of the Virgin Mary, truly suffered, was crucified, died, descended to hell, rose again on the third day, ascended to heaven, and sat down at the right hand of the Father.

To Article IV. In the fourth article the condemnation of the Pelagians, who thought that man can merit eternal life by his own powers without the grace of God, is accepted as Catholic and in accordance with the ancient councils, for the Holy Scriptures expressly testify to this. 2. John the Baptist says: "A man can receive nothing, except it be given him from heaven," John 3:27. "Every good gift and every perfect gift is from above, and cometh down from the Father of lights," James 1:17. Therefore "our sufficiency is of God," 2 Cor. 3:5. And Christ says: "No man can come to me, except the Father, which hath sent me, draw him," John 6:44. And Paul: "What hast thou that thou didst not receive?" 1 Cor. 4:7. 3. For if any one would intend to disapprove of the merits that men acquire by the assistance of divine grace, he would agree with the Manichacans rather than with the Catholic Church. For it is entirely contrary to Holy Scripture to deny that our works are meritorious. 4. For St. Paul says: "I have fought a good fight, I have finished my course, I have kept the faith; henceforth there is laid up for me a crown of righteousness, which the Lord, the righteous Judge, shall give me at that day," 2 Tim. 4:7,.8. And to the Corinthians he wrote: "We must all appear before the judgment-seat of Christ, that every one may receive the things done in his body, according to that he hath done, whether it be good or bad," 2 Cor. 5:10. For where there are wages there is merit. The Lord said to Abraham: "Fear not, Abraham, I am thy shield and thy exceeding great reward," Gen. 15:1. And Isaiah says: "Behold, his reward is with him, and his work before him," Isa. 40:10; and, chapter 58:7,8: "Deal they bread to the hungry, and thy righteousness shall go before thee; the glory of the Lord shall go before thee; the glory of the Lord shall gather thee up." So too the Lord to Cain: "If thou doest well, shalt thou not be accepted?" Gen. 4:7. 5. So the parable in the Gospel declares that we have been hired for the Lord's vineyard, who agrees with us for a penny a day, and says: "Call the laborers and give them their hire," Matt. 20:8. So Paul, knowing the mysteries of God, says: "Every man shall receive his own reward, according to his own labor," 1 Cor. 3:8. 6. Nevertheless, all Catholics confess that our works of themselves have no merit, but that God's grace makes them worthy of eternal life. Thus St. John says: "They shall walk with me in white; for they are worthy," Rev. 3:4. And St. Paul says to the Colossians, 1:12: "Giving thanks unto the Father, which hath made us meet to be partakers of the inheritance of the saints in light."

To Article V. In the fifth article the statement that the Holy Ghost is given by the Word and sacraments, as by instruments, is approved. For thus it is written, Acts 10:44: "While Peter yet spake these words, the Holy Ghost fell on all them which heard the word." And John 1:33: "The same is He which baptizeth with the Holy Ghost." 2. The mention, however, that they here make of faith is approved so far as not faith alone, which some incorrectly teach, but faith which worketh by love, is understood, as the apostle teaches aright in Gal. 5:3. For in baptism there is an infusion, not of faith alone, but also, at the same time, of hope and love, as Pope Alexander declares in the canon *Majores*, concerning baptism and its effect;

which John the Baptist also taught long before, saying, Luke 3:16: "He shall baptize you with the Holy Ghost and with fire."

To Article 11. Their Confession in the sixth article, that faith should bring forth good fruits, is acceptable and valid, since "faith without works is dead," James 2:17 and all Scripture invites us to works. For the wise man says: "Whatsoever thy hand findeth to do, do it with thy might," Eccles. 9:10. "And the Lord had respect to Abel and to his offering," Gen. 4:4. He saw that Abraham would "command his children and his household after him to keep the way of the Lord, and to do justice and judgment," Gen. 18:19. And: "By myself have I sworn, saith the Lord, for because thou hast done this thing, I will bless thee and multiply thy seed," Gen. 22:16. Thus he regarded the fast of the Ninevites, Jonah 3, and the lamentations and tears of King Hezekiah, 4:2; 2 Kings 20. 2. For this cause all the faithful should follow the advice of St. Paul: "As we have, therefore, opportunity, let us do good unto all men, especially unto them who are of the household of faith." Gal. 6:10. For Christ says: "The night cometh when no man can work," John 9:4.

3. But in the same article their ascription of justification to faith alone is diametrically opposite the truth of the Gospel, by which works are not excluded; because "glory, honor and peace to every man that worketh good," Rom. 2:10. Why? Because David, Ps. 62:12, Christ, Matt. 16:27, and Paul, Rom. 2:6 testify that God will render to every one according to his works. Besides, Christ says: "Not every one that saith unto me, Lord, Lord, shall enter into the kingdom of heaven; but he that doeth the will of my Father," Matt. 7:21. 4. Hence, however much one may believe, if he work not what is good, he is not a friend of God. "Ye are my friends," says Christ, "if ye do whatsoever I command you," John 15:14. 5. On this account their frequent ascription of justification to faith is not admitted, since it pertains to grace and love. For St. Paul says: "Though I have all faith, so that I could remove mountains, and have not charity, I am nothing," 1 Cor. 13:2. Here St. Paul certifies to the princes and the entire Church that faith alone does not justify. Accordingly, he teaches that love is the chief virtue, Col. 3:14: "Above all these things put on charity, which is the bond of perfectness." 6. Neither are they supported by the word of Christ: "When ye shall have done all these things, say, We are unprofitable servants," Luke 17:10. For if the doers ought to be called unprofitable, how much more fitting is it to say to those who only believe, When

ye shall have believed all things say, We are unprofitable servants!
This word of Christ, therefore, does not extol faith without works,
but teaches that our works bring no profit to God; that no one
can be puffed up by our works; that, when contrasted with the
divine reward, our works are of no account and nothing. 7. Thus
St. Paul says: "I reckon that the sufferings of this present time are
not worthy to be compared to the glory which shall be revealed in
us," Rom. 8:18. For faith and good works are gifts of God, whereby,
through God's mercy, eternal life is given. 8. So, too, the citation at
this point from Ambrose is in no way pertinent, since St. Ambrose
is here expressly declaring his opinion concerning legal works. For
he says: "Without the law," but, "Without the law of the Sabbath,
and of circumcision, and of revenge." And this he declares the more
clearly on Rom. 4, citing St. James concerning the justification of
Abraham without legal works before circumcision. For how could
Ambrose speak differently in his comments from St. Paul in the text
when he says: "Therefore by the deeds of the law there shall no
flesh be justified in his sight?" Therefore, finally, he does not exclude
faith absolutely, but says: "We conclude that a man is justified by
faith without the deeds of the law."

To Article VII. The seventh article of the Confession, wherein
it is affirmed that the Church is the congregation, of saints, <u>cannot
be admitted without prejudice to faith if by this definition the wicked
and sinners be separated from the Church.</u> 2. For in the Council
of Constance this article was condemned among the articles of John
Huss of cursed memory, and it plainly contradicts the Gospel. For
there we read that John the Baptist compared the Church to a
threshing-floor, which Christ will cleanse with his fan, and will
gather the wheat into his garner, but will burn the chaff with un-
quenchable fire, Matt. 3:12. 3. Wherefore this article of the Confession is in no way accepted, although we read in it their confession
that the Church is perpetual, since here the promise of Christ has
its place, who promises that the Spirit of truth will abide with it for
ever, John 14:16. And Christ himself promises that he will be with
the Church alway unto the end of the world. 4. They are praised
also in that they do not regard variety of rites as separating unity
of faith, if they speak of special rites. For to this effect Jerome says:
"Every province abounds in its own sense" (of propriety). But if
they extend this part of the Confession to universal Church rites,
this also must be utterly rejected, and we must say with St. Paul:

"We have no such custom," 1 Cor. 11:16. "For by all believers universal rites must be observed," St. Augustine, whose testimony they also use, well taught of Januarius; for we must presume that such rites were transmitted from the apostles.

To Article VIII. The eighth article of the Confession, concerning wicked ministers of the Church and hypocrites—viz. that their wickedness does not injure the sacraments and the Word—is accepted with the Holy Roman Church, and the princes commend it, condemning on this topic the Donatists and the ancient Origenists, who maintained that it was unlawful to use the ministry of the wicked in the Church —a heresy which the Waldenses and Poor of Lyons revived. Afterwards John Wicliff in England and John Huss in Bohemia adopted this.

To Article IX. The ninth article, concerning Baptism—viz. that it is necessary to salvation, and that children ought to be baptized— is approved and accepted, and they are right in condemning the Anabaptists, a most seditious class of men that ought to be banished far from the boundaries of the Roman Empire in order that illustrious Germany may not suffer again such a destructive and sanguinary commotion as she experienced five years ago in the slaughter of so many thousands.

To Article X. The tenth article gives no offence in its words. because they confess that in the Eucharist, after the consecration lawfully made, the Body and Blood of Christ are substantially and truly present, if only they believe that the entire Christ is present under each form, so that the Blood of Christ is no less present under the form of bread by concomitance than it is under the form of the wine, and the reverse. 2. Otherwise, in the Eucharist the Body of Christ is dead and bloodless, contrary to St. Paul, because "Christ, being raised from the dead, dieth no more," Rom. 6:9. 3. One matter is added as very necessary to the article of the Confession—viz. that they believe the Church, rather than some teaching otherwise and incorrectly, that by the almighty Word of God in the consecration of the Eucharist the substance of the bread is changed into the Body of Christ. For thus in a general council it has been determined, canon *Firmiter,* concerning the exalted Trinity, and the Catholic faith. 4. They are praised, therefore, for condemning the Capernaites, who deny the truth of the Body and Blood of our Lord Jesus Christ in the Eucharist.

To Article XI. In the eleventh article their acknowledgment that private absolution with confession should be retained in the

Church is accepted as catholic and in harmony with our faith, because absolution is supported by the word of Christ. For Christ says to his apostles, John 20:23: "Whosoever sins ye remit, they are remitted unto them." 2. Nevertheless, two things must here be required of them: one, that they compel an annual confession to be observed by their subjects, according to the constitution, canon *Omnis Utriusque,* concerning penance and remission and the custom of the Church universal. 3. *Another,* that through their preachers they cause their subjects to be faithfully admonished when they are about to confess that although they cannot state all their sins individually, nevertheless, a diligent examination of their conscience being made, they make an entire confession of their offences—viz. of all which occur to their memory in such investigation. But in regard to the rest that have been forgotten and have escaped our mind it is lawful to make a general confession, and to say with the Psalmist, Ps 19:12: "Cleanse me, Lord, from secret faults."

To Article XII. In the twelfth article their confession that such as have fallen may find remission of sins at the time when they are converted, and that the Church should give absolution unto such as return to repentance, is commended, since they most justly condemn the Novatians, who deny that repentance can be repeated, in opposition both to the prophet who promises grace to the sinner at whatever hour he shall mourn, Ezek. 18:21, and the merciful declaration of Christ our Saviour, replying to St. Peter, that not until seven times, but until seventy times seven in one day, he should forgive his brother sinning against him, Matt. 18:22.

2. But the second part of this article is utterly rejected. For when they ascribe only two parts to repentance, they antagonize the entire Church, which from the time of the apostles has held and believed that there are three parts of repentance—contrition, confession and satisfaction. Thus the ancient doctors, Origen, Cyprian, Chrysostom, Gregory, Augustine, taught in attestation of the Holy Scriptures, especially from 2 Kings 12, concerning David, 2 Chron. 33, concerning Manasseh. Ps. 31, 37, 50, 101, etc. 3. Therefore Pope Leo X. of happy memory justly condemned this article of Luther, who taught: "That there are three parts of repentance—viz. confession, contrition and satisfaction—has no foundation in Scripture or in holy Christian doctors." 4. This part of the article, therefore, can in no way be admitted; so, too, neither can that which asserts that faith is the second part of repentance, since it is known

to all that faith precedes repentance; for unless one believes he will
not repent. 5. Neither is that part admitted which makes light of
pontifical satisfactions, for it is contrary to the Gospel, contrary
to the apostles, contrary to the fathers, contrary to the councils, and
contrary to the universal Catholic Church. 6. John the Baptist cries:
"Bring forth fruits meet for repentance," Matt. 3:8. St. Paul teaches:
"As ye have yielded your members servants to uncleanness, even so
now yield your members servants to righteousness unto holiness,"
Rom. 6:19. He likewise preached to the Gentiles that they should
repent and be converted to God, bringing forth fruits meet for repentance, Acts 20:21. So Christ himself also began to teach and
preach repentance: "Repent, for the kingdom of heaven is at hand,"
Matt. 4:17. Afterward he commanded the apostles to pursue this
mode of preaching and teaching, Luke 24:47, and St. Peter faithfully
obeyed him in his first sermon, Acts 2:38. 7. So Augustine also
exhorts that "every one exercise toward himself severity, so that,
being judged of himself, he be not judged of the Lord," as St.
Paul says, 1 Cor. 11:31. Pope Leo, surnamed the Great, said: "The
Mediator between God and men, the man Christ Jesus, gave to those
set over the churches the authority to assign to those who confess
the doing of penance, and through the door of reconciliation to admit
to the communion of the sacraments those who have been cleansed
by a salutary satisfaction." Ambrose says: "The amount of the
penance must be adapted to the trouble of the conscience." Hence
diverse penitential canons were appointed in the holy Synod of Nice,
in accordance with the diversity of satisfactions. Jovinian the heretic,
thought, however, that all sins are equal, and accordingly did not
admit a diversity of satisfactions. 8. Moreover, satisfactions should
not be abolished in the Church, contrary to the express Gospel and
the decrees of councils and fathers, but those absolved by the priest
ought to perform the penance enjoined, following the declaration of
St. Paul: He "gave himself for us, to redeem us from all iniquity,
and purify unto himself a peculiar people, zealous of good works,"
Tit. 2:14. Christ thus made satisfaction for us, that we might be
zealous of good works, fulfilling the satisfaction enjoined.

     To Article XIII. The thirteenth article gives no offence, but is
accepted, while they say that the sacraments were instituted not only
to be marks of profession among men, but rather to be signs and
testimonies of God's will toward us; nevertheless, we must request
them that what they here ascribe to the sacraments in general they

confess also specifically concerning the seven sacraments of the Church and take measures for the observance of them by their subjects.

To Article XIV. When, in the fourteenth article, they confess that no one ought to administer in the Church the Word of God and the sacraments unless he be rightly called, it ought to be understood that he is rightly called who is called in accordance with the form of law and the ecclesiastical ordinances and decrees hitherto observed everywhere in the Christian world, and not according to a Jeroboitic (cf. 1 Kings 12:20) call, or a tumult or any other irregular intrusion of the people. Aaron was not thus called. 2. Therefore in this sense the Confession is received; nevertheless, they should be admonished to persevere therein, and to admit in their realms no one either as pastor or as preacher unless he be rightly called.

To Article XV. In the fifteenth article their confession that such ecclesiastical rites are to be observed as may be observed without sin and are profitable for tranquility and good order in the Church, is accepted, and they must be admonished that the princes and cities see to it that the ecclesiastical rites of the Church universal be observed in their dominions and districts, as well as those which have been kept devoutly and religiously in every province even to us, and if any of these have been intermitted that they restore them, and arrange, determine and effectually enjoin upon their subjects that all things be done in their churches according to the ancient form. 2. Nevertheless, the appendix to this article must be entirely removed, since it is false that human ordinances instituted to propitiate God and make satisfactions for sins are opposed to the Gospel, as will be more amply declared hereafter concerning vows, the choice of food and the like.

To Article XVI. The sixteenth article, concerning civil magistrates, is received with pleasure, as in harmony not only with civil law, but also with canonical law, the Gospel, the Holy Scriptures, and the universal norm of faith, since the apostle enjoins that "every soul be subject unto the higher powers. For there is no power but of God: the powers that be are ordained of God. Whosoever, therefore, resisteth the power, resisteth the ordinance of God, and they that resist shall receive to themselves damnation," Rom. 13:1, 2. And the princes are praised for condemning the Anabaptists, who overthrow all civil ordinances and prohibit Christians the use of the magistracy and other civil offices, without which no state is successfully administered.

To Article XVII. The confession of the seventeenth article is received, since from the Apostles' Creed and the Holy Scripture the entire Catholic Church knows that Christ will come at the last day to judge the quick and the dead. 2. Therefore they justly condemn here the Anabaptists, who think there will be an end of punishments to condemned men and devils, and imagine certain Jewish kingdoms of the godly, before the resurrection of the dead, in this present world, the wicked being everyhere suppressed.

To Article XVIII. In the eighteenth article they confess the power of the Free Will—viz. that it has the power to work a civil righteousness, but that it has not, without the Holy Ghost, the virtue to work the righteousness of God. This confession is received and approved. For it thus becomes Catholics to pursue the middle way, so as not, with the Pelagians, to ascribe too much to the free will, nor, with the godless Manichaeans, to deny it all liberty; for both are not without fault. 2. Thus Augustine says: "With sure faith we believe, and without doubt we preach, that a free will exists in men. For it is an inhuman error to deny the free will in man, which every one experiences in himself, and is so often asserted in the Holy Scriptures." 3. St. Paul says: "Having power over his own will." 1 Cor. 7:37. Of the righteous the wise man says: "Who might offend, and hath not offended? or done evil, and hath not done it?" Eccles. 31:10. God said to Cain: "If thou doest well, shalt thou not be accepted? and if thou doest not well, sin lieth at the door. And unto thee shall be his desire, and thou shalt rule over him," Gen. 4:7. Through the prophet Isaiah he says: "If ye be willing and obedient, ye shall eat the good of the land. But if ye refuse and rebel, ye shall be devoured with the sword." This also Jeremiah has briefly expressed: "Behold, thou hast spoken and done evil, as thou couldest," Jer. 3:5. We add also Ezek. 18:31f.: "Cast away from you all your transgressions whereby ye have transgressed; and make ye a new heart, and a new spirit; for why will ye die, O house of Israel? For I have no pleasure in the death of him that dieth, saith the Lord God; wherefore turn yourselves and live." Also St. Paul: "The spirits of the prophets are subject to the prophets," 1 Cor. 14:32. Likewise, 2 Cor. 9:7: "Every man according as he purposeth in his heart; not grudgingly or of necessity." 4. Finally, Christ overthrew all the Manichaeans with one word when he said: "Ye have the poor with you always, and whensoever ye will ye may do them good." Mark 14:7; and to Jerusalem Christ says: "How often would I have gathered thy children together, even as a hen gathereth her chickens under her wings, and ye would not!" Matt. 23:37.

To Article XIX. The nineteenth article is likewise approved and accepted. For God, the supremely good, is not the author of evils, but the rational and defectible will is the cause of sin; wherefore let no one impute his midsdeeds and crimes to God, but to himself, according to Jer. 2:19: "Thine own wickedness shall correct thee, and thy backslidings shall reprove thee;" and Hos. 13:9: "O Israel, thou hast destroyed thyself; but in me is thy help." And David in the spirit acknowledged that God is not one that hath pleasure in wickedness, Ps. 5:4.

To Article XX. In the twentieth article, which does not contain so much the confession of the princes and cities as the defence of the preachers, there is only one thing that pertains to the princes and cities—viz. concerning good works, that they do not merit the remission of sins, which, as it has been rejected and disapproved before, is also rejected and disapproved now. 2. For the passage in Daniel is very familiar: "Redeem thy sins with alms," Dan. 4:24; and the address of Tobit to his son: "Alms do deliver from death, and suffereth not to come into darkness," Tobit 4:10; and that of Christ: "Give alms of such things as ye have, and behold all things are clean unto you," Luke 11:41. 3. If works were not meritorious why would the wise man say: "God will render a reward of the labors of his saints"? Wisd. 10:17. Why would St. Peter so earnestly exhort to good works, saying: "Wherefore the rather, brethren, give diligence by good works to make your calling and election sure"? 2 Pet. 1:10. Why would St. Paul have said: "God is not unrighteous to forget your work and labor of love, which ye have showed towards his name"? Heb. 6:10. 4. Nor by this do we reject Christ's merit, but we know that our works are nothing and of no merit unless by virtue of Christ's passion. We know that Christ is "the way, the truth and the life,". John 14:6. But Christ, as the Good Shepherd, who "began to do and teach," Acts 1:1, has given us an example that as he has done we also should do, John 13:15. He also went through the desert by the way of good works, which all Christians ought to pursue, and according to his command bear the cross and follow him, Matt. 10:38; 16:24. He who bears not the cross, neither is nor can be Christ's disciple. That also is true which John says: "He that saith he abideth in him ought himself also so to walk, even as he walked," 1 John 2:6. Moreover, this opinion concerning good works was condemned and rejected more than a thousand years ago in the time of Augustine.

To Article XXI. In the last place, they present the twenty-first article, wherein they admit that the memory of saints may be set before us, that we may follow their faith and good works, but not that they be invoked and aid be sought of them. 2. It is certainly wonderful that the princes especially and the cities have allowed this error to be agitated in their dominions, which has been condemned so often before in the Church, since eleven hundred years ago St. Jerome vanquished in this area the heretic Vigilantius. Long after him arose the Albigenses, the Poor Men of Lyons, the Picards, the Cathari old and new; all of whom were condemned legitimately long ago. 3. Wherefore this article of the Confession, so frequently condemned, must be utterly rejected and in harmony with the entire universal Church be condemned; for in favor of the invocation of saints we have not only the authority of the Church universal, but also the agreement of the holy fathers, Augustine, Bernard, Jerome, Cyprian, Chrysostom, Basil, and this class of other Church teachers. 4. Neither is the authority of Holy Scripture absent from this Catholic assertion, for Christ taught that the saints should be honored: "If any man serve me, him will my Father honor," John 12:26. If, therefore, God honors saints, why do not we, insignificant men, honor them? Besides, the Lord was turned to repentance by Job when he prayed for his friends, Job 42:8. Why, therefore, would not God, the most pious, who gave assent to Job, do the same to the Blessed Virgin when she intercedes? 5. We read also in Baruch 3:4: "O Lord Almighty, thou God of Israel, hear now the prayers of the dead Israelites." Therefore the dead also pray for us. Thus did Onias and Jeremiah in the Old Testament. For Onias the high priest was seen by Judas Maccabaeus holding up his hands and praying for the whole body of the Jews. Afterwards another man appeared, remarkable both for his age and majesty, and of great beauty about him, concerning whom Onias replied: "This is a lover of the brethren and of the people Israel, who prayeth much for the people and for the Holy city—to wit, Jeremiah the prophet," 2 Macc. 15:12-14. 6. Besides, we know from the Holy Scriptures that the angels pray for us. Why, then, would we deny this of saints? "O Lord of hosts," said the angel, "how long wilt thou not have mercy on Jerusalem and on the cities of Judah, against which thou hast had indignation? And the Lord answered the angel that talked

with me comfortable words," Zech. 1:12,13. Job likewise testifies:
"If there be an angel with him speaking, one among a thousand,
to show unto man his uprightness, he will pity him and say, Deliver
him from going down to the pit," Job 33:23, 24. This is clear besides
from the words of that holy soul, John the Evangelist, when he
says: "The four beasts and the four and twenty elders fell down
before the Lamb, having each one of them harps and golden vials,
full of odors which are the prayers of saints," Rev. 5:8; and afterwards: "An angel stood at the altar, having a golden censer, and
there was given unto him much incense, that he should offer it with
the prayers of all saints upon the golden altar which was before
the throne. And the smoke of the incense, which came up with
the prayers of the saints, ascended up before God out of the angel's
hand." 7. Lastly, St. Cyprian the martyr more than twelve hundred
and fifty years ago wrote to Pope Cornelius, Book I Letter 1, asking
that "if any depart first, his prayer for our brethren and sisters may
not cease." For if this holy man had not ascertained that after this
life the saints pray for the living, he would have given exhortation
to no purpose. 8. Neither is their Confession strengthened by the
fact that there is one Mediator between God and men, 1 Tim. 2:5;
1 John 2:1. For although His Imperial Majesty, with the entire
Church, confesses that there is one Mediator of redemption, nevertheless the mediators of intercession are many. Thus Moses was both
mediator and agent between God and men, Deut. 5:31, for he prayed
for the children of Israel, Ex. 17:11; 32:11f. Thus St. Paul prayed
for those with whom he was sailing, Acts 27; so, too, he asked that
he be prayed for by the Romans, Rom. 15:30, by the Corinthians, 2
Cor. 1:11, and by the Colossians, Col. 4:3. So while Peter was kept
in prison prayer was made without ceasing of the Church unto God
for him, Acts 12:5. 9. Christ, therefore, is our chief Advocate, and
indeed the greatest: but since the saints are members of Christ, 1 Cor.
12:27 and Eph. 5:30, and conform their will to that of Christ, and
see that their Head, Christ, prays for us, who can doubt that the
saints do the very same thing which they see Christ doing? 10. With
all these things carefully considered, we must ask the princes and
the cities adhering to them that they reject this part of the Confession and agree with the holy universal and orthodox Church,
and believe and confess, concerning the worship and intercession of
saints, what the entire Christian world believes and confesses, and
was observed in all the churches in the time of Augustine. "A

Christian people," he says, "celebrates the memories of martyrs with religious observance, that it share in their merits and be aided by their prayers."

Part II. Reply to the Second Part of the Confession. I. Of Lay Communion under One Form. As in the Confession of the princes and cities they enumerate among the abuses that laymen commune only under one form, and as, therefore, in their dominions both forms are administered to laymen, we must reply, according to the custom of the Holy Church, that this is incorrectly enumerated among the abuses, but that, according to the sanctions and statutes of the same Church it is rather an abuse and disobedience to administer to laymen both forms. 2. For under the one form of bread the saints communed in the primitive Church, of whom Luke says: "They continued steadfastly in the apostles' doctrine and fellowship, and in breaking of bread." Acts 2:42. Here Luke mentions bread alone. Likewise Acts 20:7 says: "Upon the first day of the week, when the disciples came together to break bread." 3. Yea, Christ, the institutor of this most holy sacrament, rising again from the dead, administered the Eucharist only under one form to the disciples going to Emmaus, where he took bread and blessed it, and brake and gave to them, and they recognized him in the breaking of bread, Luke 24:30, 31; where indeed Augustine, Chrysostom, Theophylact and Bede some of whom many ages ago and not long after the times of the apostles affirm that it was the Eucharist. Christ also (John 6) very frequently mentions bread alone. 4. St. Ignatius, a disciple of St. John the Evangelist, in his Epistle to the Ephesians mentions the bread alone in the communion of the Eucharist. Ambrose does likewise in his books concerning the sacraments, speaking of the communion of Laymen. In the Council of Rheims, laymen were forbidden from bearing the sacrament of the Body to the sick, and no mention is there made of the form of wine. Hence it is understood that the *viaticum* was given the sick under only one form. 5. The ancient penitential canons approve of this. For the Council of Agde put a guilty priest into a monastery and granted him only lay communion. In the Council of Sardica, Hosius prohibits certain indiscreet persons from receiving even lay communion, unless they finally repent. There has always been a distinction in the Church between lay communion under one form and priestly communion under both forms. 6. This was beautifully predicted in the Old Testament concerning the descendants of Eli: "It shall come to pass," says God, 1 Kings 2 (1 Sam.

2:36), "that every one that is left in thine house shall come and
crouch to him for a piece of silver and a morsel of bread, and
shall say. Put me, I pray thee, into one of the priests' offices (Vulgate
reads: "Ad unam partem sacerdotalem."), that I may eat a piece of
bread." Here Holy Scripture clearly shows that the posterity of Eli,
when removed from the office of the priesthood, will seek to be admitted to one sacerdotal part, to a piece of bread. 7. So our laymen
also ought, therefore, to be content with one sacerdotal part, the
one form. For both the Roman pontiffs and cardinals and all bishops
and priests, save in the mass and in the extreme hour of life for a
viaticum, as it is called in the Council of Nice, are content with
taking one form, which they would not do if they thought that both
forms would be necessary for salvation. 8. Although, however, both
forms were of old administered in many churches to laymen (for
then it was free to commune under one or under both forms), yet
on account of many dangers the custom of administering both forms
has ceased. For when the multitude of the people is considered,
where there are old and young, tremulous and weak and inept, if
great care be not employed an injury is done the Sacrament by the
spilling of the liquid. Because of the great multitude there would
be difficulty also in giving the chalice cautiously for the form of
wine, which also when kept for a long time would sour and cause
nausea or vomition to those who would receive it; neither could
it be readily taken to the sick without danger of spilling. 9. For these
reasons and others the churches in which the custom had been to give
both forms to laymen were induced, undoubtedly by impulse of the
Holy Ghost, to give thereafter but one form, from the consideration
chiefly that the entire Christ is under each form, and is received no
less under one form than under two. In the Council of Constance,
of such honorable renown, a decree to this effect appeared, and
so too the Synod of Basle legitimately decreed. 10. And although
it was formerly a matter of freedom to use either one or both forms
in the Eucharist, nevertheless when the heresy arose which taught
that both forms were necessary, the Holy Church, which is directed
by the Holy Ghost, forbade both forms to laymen. For thus the
Church is sometimes wont to extinguish heresies by contrary institutions; as when some arose who maintained that the Eucharist is
properly celebrated only when unleavened bread is used, the Church
for a while commanded that it be administered with leavened bread;
and when Nestorius wished to establish that the perpetual Virgin

Mary was mother only of Christ, not of God, the Church for a time forbade her to be called Christotokos, mother of Christ. 11. Wherefore we must entreat the princes and cities not to permit this schism to be introduced into Germany, into the Roman Empire, or themselves to be separated from the custom of the Church universal. 2. Neither do the arguments adduced in this article avail, for while Christ indeed instituted both forms of the Sacrament, yet it is nowhere found in the Gospel that he enjoined that both forms be received by the laity. For what is said in Matt. 26:27: "Drink ye all of it," was said to the twelve apostles, who were priests, as is manifest from Mark 14:23, where it is said: "And they all drank of it." This certainly was not fulfilled hitherto with respect to laymen; whence the custom never existed throughout the entire Church that both forms were given to laymen, although it existed perhaps among the Corinthians and Carthaginians and some other churches. 13. As to their reference to Gelasius, Canon *Comperimus,* of Consecration. Dist. 2, if they examine the document they will find that Gelasius speaks of priests, and not of laymen. Hence their declaration that the custom of administering but one form is contrary to divine law must be rejected. 14. But most ·of all the appendix to the article must be rejected, that the procession with the Eucharist must be neglected or omitted, because the sacrament is thus divided. For they themselves know, or at least ought to know, that by the Christian faith Christ has not been divided, but that the entire Christ is under both forms, and that the Gospel nowhere forbids the division of the sacramental forms; as is done on Parasceve (Holy or Maundy Thursday) by the entire Church of the Catholics, although the consecration is made by the celebrant in both forms, who also ought to receive both. 15. Therefore the princes and cities should be admonished to pay customary reverence and due honor to Christ the Son of the living God, our Saviour and Glorifier, the Lord of heaven and earth, since they believe and acknowledge that he is truly present—a matter which they know has been most religiously observed by their ancestors, most Christian princes.

II. Of the Marriage of Priests. Their enumeration among abuses, in the second place, of the celibacy of the clergy, and the manner in which their priests marry and persuade others to marry, are verily matters worthy of astonishment, since they call sacerdotal celibacy an abuse, <u>when that which is directly contrary, the violation of celibacy and the illicit transition to marriage, deserves to be</u>

called the worst abuse in priests. 2. For that priests ought never
to marry Aurelius testifies in the second Council of Carthage, where
he says: "Because the apostles taught thus by example, and antiquity
itself has preserved it, let us also maintain it." And a little before
a canon to this effect is read: "Resolved, That the bishops, presbyters
and deacons, or those who administer the sacraments, abstain, as
guardians of chastity, from wives." From these words it is clear
that this tradition has been received from the apostles, and not
recently devised by the Church. 3. Augustine, following Aurelius
in the last question concerning the Old and New Testaments, writes
upon these words, and asks: "If perhaps it be said, if it is lawful
and good to marry, why are not priests permitted to have wives?"
4. Pope Calixtus, a holy man and a martyr, decided thirteen hundred
years ago that priests should not marry. The like is read also in
the holy Councils of Caesarea, Neocaesarea, Airica, Agde, Gironne,
Meaux, and Orleans. Thus the custom has been observed from the
time of the Gospel and the apostles that one who has been put into
the office of priests has never been permitted, according to law,
to marry. 5. It is indeed true that on account of lack of ministers
of God in the primitive Church married men were admitted to the
priesthood, as is clear from the Apostolic Canons and the reply of
Paphnutius in the Council of Nice; nevertheless, those who wished
to contract marriage were compelled to do so before receiving the
subdiaconate, as we read in the canon Si quis eorum Dist. 32. This
custom of the primitive Church the Greek Church has preserved and
retained to this day. 6. But when, by the grace of God, the Church
has increased so that there was no lack of ministers in the Church,
Pope Siricius, eleven hundred and forty years ago, undoubtedly not
without the Holy Ghost, enjoined absolute continence upon the priests,
Canon Plurimus, Dist. 82—an injunction which Popes Innocent I.,
Leo the Great and Gregory the Great approved and ratified, and
which the Latin Church has everywhere observed to this day. 7. From
these facts it is regarded sufficiently clear that the celibacy of the
clergy is not an abuse, and that it was approved by fathers so
holy at such a 'remote time, and was received by the entire Latin
Church.

8. Besides, the priests of the old law, as in the case of Zacharias,
were separated from their wives at times when they discharged their
office and ministered in the temple. But since the priest of the
new law ought always to be engaged in the ministry, it follows that

he ought always to be continent. 9. Furthermore, married persons should not defraud one the other of conjugal duties except for a time, that they may give themselves to prayer. 1 Cor. 7:5. But since a priest ought always to pray, he ought always to be continent. 10. Besides, St. Paul says: "But I would have you without carefulness. He that is unmarried careth for the things that belong to the Lord, that he may please the Lord. But he that is married careth for the things that are of the world, how he may please his wife," 1 Cor. 7:32,33. Therefore let the priest who should please God continually flee from anxiety for a wife, and not look back with Lot's wife, Gen. 19:26. 11. Moreover, sacerdotal continence was foreshadowed also in the Old Testament, for Moses commanded those who were to receive the law not to approach their wives until the third day, Ex. 19:15. Much less, therefore, should the priests, who are about to receive Christ as our Legislator, Lord and Saviour, approach wives. 12. Priests were commanded likewise to wear linen thigh-bandages, to cover the shame of the flesh (Ex. 28:42); which, says Beda, was a symbol of future continence among priests. 13. Also, when Ahimelech was about to give the blessed bread to the servants of David he asked first if they had kept themselves from women, and David replied that they had for three days. 1 Kings 21 (1 Sam. 21:4, 5). Therefore, they who take the living Bread which came down from heaven, John 6:32ff., should always be pure with respect to them. They who ate the passover had their loins girded, Ex. 12:11. Wherefore the priests, who frequently eat Christ our Passover, ought to gird their loins by continence and cleanliness, as the Lord commands them: "Be ye clean," he says, "that bear the vessels of the Lord," Isa. 52:11. "Ye shall be holy, for I am holy," Lev. 19:2. Therefore let priests serve God "in holiness and righteousness all their days," Luke 1:75. 14. Hence the holy martyr Cyprian testifies that it was revealed to him by the Lord, and he was most solemnly enjoined, to earnestly admonish the clergy not to occupy a domicile in common with women. 15. Hence, since sacerdotal continence has been commanded by the pontiffs and revealed by God, and promised to God, by the priest in a special vow, it must not be rejected. For this is required by the excellency of the sacrifice they offer, the frequency of prayer, and liberty and purity of spirit, that they care how to please God, according to the teaching of St. Paul. 16. And because this is manifestly the ancient heresy of Jovinian, which the Roman Church condemned and Jerome refuted in his writings, and

St. Augustine said that this heresy was immediately extinguished and did not attain to the corruption and abuse of priests, the princes ought not to tolerate it to the perpetual shame and disgrace of the Roman Empire, but should rather conform themselves to the Church universal, and not be influenced by those things which are suggested to them. 17. For as to what Paul says, 1 Cor. 7:2: "To avoid fornication, let every man have his own wife," Jerome replies that St. Paul is speaking of one who has not made a vow, as Athanasius and Vulgarius understand the declaration of St. Paul: "If a virgin marry, she hath not sinned" (1 Cor. 7:28), that here a virgin is meant who has not been consecrated to God. So in reference to: "It is better to marry than to burn" (1 Cor. 7:9), the pointed reply of Jerome against Jovinian is extant. For the same St. Paul says (1 Cor. 7:1): "It is good for a man not to touch a woman." For a priest has the intermediate position of neither marrying nor burning, but of restraining himself by the grace of God, which he obtains of God by devout prayer and chastising of the flesh, by fasting and vigils. 18. Furthermore, when they say that Christ taught that all men are not fit for celibacy, it is indeed true, and on this account not all are fit for the priesthood; but let the priest pray, and he will be able to receive Christ's word concerning continence, as St. Paul says: "I can do all things through Christ which strengtheneth me," Phil. 4:13. For continence is a gift of God, Wisd. 8:21. 19. Besides, when they allege that this is God's ordinance and command, Gen. 1:28, Jerome replied concerning these words a thousand years ago: "It was necessary first to plant the forest, and that it grow, in order that that might be which could afterwards be cut down." Then the command was given concerning the procreation of offspring, that the earth should be replenished, but since it has been replenished so that there is a pressure of nations, the commandment does not pertain in like manner upon those able to be continent. 20. In vain, too, do they boast of God's express order. Let them show, if they can where God has enjoined priests to marry. 21. Besides, we find in the divine law that vows once offered should be paid, Ps. 49 and 75; Eccles. 5 (Ps. 50:14; 76:11; Eccles. 5:4). Why, therefore, do they not observe this express divine law? 22. They also pervert St. Paul, as though he teaches that one who is to be chosen bishop should be married when he says: "Let a bishop be the husband of one wife"; which is not to be understood as though he ought to be married, for then Martin, Nicolaus, Titus, John the Evangelist, yea

Christ, would not have been bishops. Hence Jerome explains the words of St. Paul, "that a bishop be the husband of one wife," as meaning that he be not a bigamist. The truth of this exposition is clear, not only from the authority of Jerome, which ought be great with every Catholic, but also from St. Paul, who writes concerning the selection of widows: "Let not a widow be taken into the number under three score years, having been the wife of one man," 1 Tim. 5:9.

23. Lastly, the citation of what was done among the Germans is the statement of a fact, but not of a law. For while there was a contention between the Emperor Henry IV. and the Roman Pontiff, and also between his son and the nobles of the Empire, both divine and human laws were equally confused, so that at that time the laity rashly attempted to administer sacred things, to use filth instead of holy oil, to baptize, and to do much else foreign to the Christian religion. The clergy likewise went beyond their sphere—a precedent which cannot be cited as law. 24. Neither was it regarded unjust to dissolve sacrilegious marriages which had been contracted to no effect in opposition to vows and the sanction of fathers and councils; as even today the marriages of priests with their so-called wives are not valid. 25. In vain, therefore, do they complain that the world is growing old, and that as a remedy for infirmity rigor should be relaxed, for those who are consecrated to God have other remedies of infirmities; as, for instance, let them avoid the society of women, shun idleness, macerate the flesh by fasting and vigils, keep the outward senses, especially sight and hearing, from things forbidden, turn away their eyes from beholding vanity, and finally dash their little ones—i.e. their carnal thoughts— upon a rock (and Christ is the Rock), suppress their passions, and frequently and devoutly resort to God in prayer. These are undoubtedly the most effectual remedies for incontinence in ecclesiastics and servants of God. 26. St. Paul said aright that the doctrine of those who forbid marriage is a doctrine of demons. Such was the doctrine of Tatian and Marcion, whom Augustine and Jerome have mentioned. But the Church does not thus forbid marriage, as she even enumerates marriage among the seven sacraments; with which, however, it is consistent that on account of their superior ministry she should enjoin upon ecclesiastics superior purity. 27. For it is false that there is an express charge concerning contracting marriage, for then John the Evangelist, St. James, Laurentius, Titus, Martin, Catharine, Barbara, etc., would have sinned. Nor is Cyprian influenced

by these considerations to speak of a virgin who had made a solemn
vow, but of one who had determined to live continently, as the beginning of Letter XI. Book I. sufficiently shows. For the judgment
of St. Augustine is very explicit: "It is damnable for Virgins who
make a vow not only to marry, but even to wish to marry." Hence
the abuse of marriage and the breaking of vows in the clergy are
not to be tolerated.

III. Of the Mass. Whatever in this article is stated concerning
the most holy office of the mass that agrees with the Holy Roman
and Apostolic Church is approved, but whatever is added that is
contrary to the observance of the general and universal orthodox
Church is rejected, because it grievously offends God, injures Christian unity, and occasions dissensions, tumults and seditions in the
Holy Roman Empire. 2. Now, as to these things which they state
in the article: *First,* it is displeasing that, in opposition to the usage
of the entire Roman Church, they perform ecclesiastical rites not
in the Roman but in the German language, and this they pretend
that they do upon the authority of St. Paul, who taught that in the
Church a language should be used which is understood by the people,
1 Cor. 14:19. 3. But if this were the meaning of the words of St.
Paul, it would compel them to perform the entire mass in German,
which even they do not do. But since the priest is a person belonging
to the entire Church, and not only to his surroundings, it is not
wonderful that the priest celebrates the mass in the Latin language
in a Latin Church. 4. It is profitable to the hearer, however, if he
hear the mass in faith of the Church; and experience teaches that
among the Germans there has been greater devotion at mass in
Christ's believers who do not understand the Latin language than in
those who today hear the mass in German. 5. And if the words
of the apostle be pondered, it is sufficient that the one replying occupy
the place of the unlearned to say *Amen,* the very thing that the
canons prescribe. Neither is it necessary that he hear or understand
all the words of the mass, and even attend to it intelligently; for it
is better to understand and to attend to its end, because the mass is
celebrated in order that the Eucharist may be offered in memory
of Christ's passion. 6. And it is an argument in favor of this that,
according to the general opinion of the fathers, the apostles and
their successors until the times of the Emperor Hadrian celebrated
the mass in the Hebrew language alone, which was indeed unknown
to the Christians, especially the converted heathen. But even if

the mass had been celebrated in the primitive Church in a tongue understood by the people, nevertheless this would not be necessary now, for many were daily converted who were ignorant of the ceremonies and unacquainted with the mysteries; and hence it was of advantage for them to understand the words of the office; but now Catholics imbibe from their cradles the manners and customs of the Church, whence they readily know what should be done at every time in the Church. 7. Moreover, as to their complaints concerning the abuse of masses, there is none of those who think aright but does not earnestly desire that the abuses be corrected. But that they who wait at the altar live of the altar is not an abuse, but pertains equally to both divine and human law. "Who goeth a warfare any time at his own charge?" says Paul. "Do ye not know that they which minister about holy things live of the things of the temple? and they which wait at the altar are partakers with the altar?" 1 Cor. 9:7, 13. Christ says: "The laborer is worthy of his hire," Luke 10:7.

    8. But worthy of censure, above all things, is the discontinuance of the private mass in certain places, as though those having fixed and prescribed returns are sought no less than the public masses on account of gain. But by this abrogation of masses the worship of God is diminished, honor is withdrawn from the saints, the ultimate will of the founder is overthrown and defeated, the dead deprived of the rights due them, and the devotion of the living withdrawn and chilled. Therefore the abrogation of private masses cannot be conceded and tolerated. 9. Neither can their assumption be sufficiently understood that Christ by his passion has made satisfaction for original sin, and has instituted the mass for actual sin; for this has never been heard by Catholics, and very many who are now asked most constantly deny that they have so taught. For the mass does not abolish sins, which are destroyed by repentance as their peculiar medicine, but abolishes the punishment due sin, supplies satisfactions, and confers increase of grace and salutary protection of the living, and, lastly, brings the hope of divine consolation and aid to all our wants and necessities.

    10. Again, their insinuation that in the mass Christ is not offered must be altogether rejected, as condemned of old and excluded by the faithful. For Augustine says this was a very ancient heresy of the Arians, who denied that in the mass an oblation was made for the living and the dead. For this is opposed both to the Holy Scriptures and the entire Church. 11. For through Malachi the Lord

predicted the rejection of the Jews, the call of the Gentiles and the
sacrifice of the evangelical law: "I have no pleasure in you, he saith,
neither will I accept an offering at your hand. For from the rising
of the sun, even unto the going down of the same, my name shall
be great among the Gentiles, and in every place incense shall be
offered unto my name and a pure offering," Mal. 1:10, 11. But no pure
offering has already been offered to God in every place, except in the
sacrifice of the altar of the most pure Eucharist. This authority
St. Augustine and other Catholics have used in favor of the mass
against faithless Jews, and certainly with Catholic princes it should
have greater influence than all objections of the adversaries. 12. Besides, in speaking of the advent of the Messiah the same prophet says:
"And he shall purify the sons of Levi, and purge them as gold and
silver, that they may offer unto the Lord an offering in righteousness.
Then shall the offering of Judah and Jerusalem be pleasant unto the
Lord, as in the days of old and as in former years," Mal. 3:3, 4.
Here in the spirit the prophet foresaw the sons of Levi—i. e. evangelical priests, says Jerome—about to offer sacrifices, not in the
blood of goats, but in righteousness, as in the days of old. Hence
these words are repeated by the Church in the canon of the mass
under the influence of the same Spirit under whose influence they
were written by the prophet. 13. The angel also said to Daniel:
"Many shall be purified and made white and tried; but the wicked
shall do wickedly, and none of the wicked shall understand." And
again: "The wise shall understand; and from the time that the
daily sacrifices shall be taken away, and the abomination that maketh
desolate set up, there shall be a thousand two hundred and ninety
days," Dan. 12:10, 11. Christ testifies that this prophecy is to be
fulfilled, but that it has not been as yet fulfilled, Matt. 24:15. Therefore the daily sacrifice of Christ will cease universally at the advent
of the abomination—i.e. of Antichrist—just as it has already ceased,
particularly in some churches, and thus will be unemployed in the
place of desolation—viz. when the churches will be desolated, in
which the canonical hours will not be chanted or the masses celebrated
or the sacraments administered, and there will be no altars, no
images of saints, no candles, no furniture. 14. Therefore all princes
and faithful subjects of the Roman Empire ought to be encouraged
never to admit or pass over anything that may aid the preparers of
Antichrist in attaining such a degree of wickedness, when the woman
—i. e. the Catholic Church—as St. John saw in the Spirit, will flee

into the wilderness, where she will have a place prepared of God, that she may be nourished there twelve hundred and sixty days, Rev. 12:6. 15. Finally, St. Paul says, Heb. 5:1: "Every high priest taken from among men is ordained for men in things pertaining to God, that he may offer both gifts and sacrifices for sins." But since the external priesthood has not ceased in the new law, but has been changed to a better, therefore even today the high priest and the entire priesthood offer in the Church an external sacrifice, which is only one, the Eucharist. 16. To this topic that also is applicable which is read, according to the new translation, in Acts 13:1, 2: Barnabas, Simeon, Lucius of Cyrene, Manaen and Saul sacrificed—i.e. they offered an oblation, which can and ought justly to be understood not of an oblation made to idols, but of the mass, since it is called by the Greeks *liturgy*. 17. And that in the primitive Church the mass was a sacrifice the holy fathers copiously testify, and they support this opinion. For Ignatius, a pupil of St. John the Apostle, says: "It is not allowable without a bishop either to offer a sacrifice or to celebrate masses." And Irenaeus, a pupil of John, clearly testifies that "Christ taught the new oblation of the New Testament, which the Church, receiving from the apostles, offers to God throughout the entire world." This bishop, bordering upon the times of the apostles, testifies that the new evangelical sacrifice was offered trougout the entire world. Origen, Cyprian, Jerome, Chrysostom, Augustine, Basil, Hilary, etc., teach and testify the same, whose words for brevity's sake are omitted. 18. Since, therefore, the Catholic Church throughout the entire Christian world has always taught, held and observed as it today holds and observes, the same ought today to be held and observed inviolably. 19. Nor does St. Paul in Hebrews oppose the oblation of the mass when he says that by one offering we have once been justified through Christ. For St. Paul is speaking of the offering of a victim—i.e. of a bloody sacrifice, of a lamb slain, viz. upon the altar of the cross—which offering indeed once made whereby all sacraments, and even the sacrifice of the mass, have their efficacy. Therefore he was offered but once with the shedding of blood—viz. upon the cross; today he is offered in the mass as a peace making and sacramental victim. Then he was offered in a visible form capable of suffering; today he is offered in the mass veiled in mysteries, incapable of suffering, just as in the Old Testament he was sacrificed typically and under a figure. 20. Finally, the force of the word shows that the mass is a sacrifice, since "mass" is nothing but "oblation," and has received its name from the Hebrew word *misbeach,* altar—in Greek *thysiasterion,* on account of the oblation. 21. It has been sufficiently declared above that we are justified not properly by faith, but by love. But if any such statement be found in the Holy Scriptures, Catholics know that it is declared concerning *fides formata,* which works by love (Gal 5), and because justification is begun by faith, because it is the substance of things hoped for, Heb. 11:1. 22. Neither is it denied that the mass is a memorial of Christ's passion and God's benefits, since this is approved by the figure of the paschal lamb, that was at the same time a victim and a memorial, Ex. 12:13, 14, and is represented not only by the Word and sacraments, but also by holy postures and vestments in the Catholic Church; but to the memory of the victim the Church offers anew the Eucharist in the mysteries to God, the Father Almighty. 23. Therefore the princes and cities are not censured for retaining one common mass in the Church, provided they do this according to the sacred canon, as observed by all Catholics. But in abrogating all other masses they have done what the Christian profession does not allow.

24. Nor does any one censure the declaration that of old all who were present communed. Would that all were so disposed as to be prepared to partake of this bread worthily every day! But if they regard one mass advantageous, how much more advantageous would be a number of masses, of which they nevertheless have unjustly disapproved. 25. When all these things are properly considered we must ask them to altogether annul and repudiate this new form of celebrating the mass that has been devised, and has been already so frequently changed, and to resume the primitive form for celebrating it according to the ancient rite and custom of the churches of Germany and all Christendom, and to restore the abrogated masses according to the ultimate will of their founders; whereby they would gain advantage and honor for themselves and peace and tranquility for all Germany.

IV. Of Confession. As to confession, we must adhere to the reply and judgment given above in Article XI. For the support which they claim from Chrysostom is false, since they pervert to sacramental and sacerdotal confession what he says concerning public confession, as his words clearly indicate when in the beginning he says: "I do not tell thee to disclose thyself to the public or to accuse thyself before others." Thus Gratian and thus Peter Lombard replied three hundred years ago; and the explanation becomes still more manifest from others pasages of Chrysostom. 2. For in his twenty-ninth sermon he says of the penitent: "In his heart is contrition, in his mouth confession, in his entire work humility. This is perfect and fruitful repentance." Does not this most exactly display the three parts of repentance? 3. So in his tenth homily on Matthew, Chrysostom teaches of a fixed time for confession, and that after the wounds of crimes have been opened they should be healed, penance intervening. But how will crimes lie open if they are not disclosed to the priest by confession? Thus in several passages Chrysostom himself refutes this opinion, which Jerome also overthrows, saying: "If the serpent the devil have secretly bitten any one, and without the knowledge of another have infected him with the poison of sin, if he who has been struck be silent and do not repent, and be unwilling to confess his wound to his brother and instructor, the instructor, who has a tongue wherewith to cure him, will not readily be able to profit him. For if the sick man be ashamed to confess to the physician, the medicine is not adapted to that of which he is ignorant." 4. Let the princes and cities, therefore, believe these authors rather than a single gloss upon a decree questioned and rejected by those who are skilled in divine law. 5. Wherefore, since a full confession is, not to say, necessary for salvation, but becomes the nerve of Christian discipline and the entire obedience, they must be admonished to conform to the orthodox Church. For, according to the testimony of Jerome, this was the heresy of the Montanists, who were condemned over twelve hundred years ago because they were ashamed to confess their sins. It is not becoming, therefore, to adopt the error of the wicked Montanus, but rather the rite of the holy fathers and the entire Church—viz. that each one teach, according to the norm of the orthodox faith, that confession, the chief treasure in the Church, be made in conformity to the rite kept among them also in the Church.

V. Of the Distinction of Meats. What they afterwards assert concerning the distinction of meats and like traditions, of which they seem to make no account, must be rejected. 2. For we know from the apostle that all power is of God, and especially that ecclesiastical power has been given by God for edification; for this reason, from the Christian and devout heart of the holy Church the constitutions of the same holy, catholic and apostolic Church should be received as are useful to the Church, as well for promoting divine worship as for restraining the lust of the flesh, while they enable us the

more readily to keep the divine commands, and when well considered
are found in the Holy Scriptures; and he who despises or rashly
resists them grievously offends God, according to Christ's word:
"He that heareth you, heareth me; and he that despiseth you, despiseth
me; and he that despiseth me, despiseth Him that sent me," Luke
10:16. 3. A prelate, however, is despised when his statutes are
despised, according to St. Paul, not only when he says: "He that
despiseth, despiseth not man, but God, who hath also given unto
us his Holy Spirit." 1 Thess. 4:8, but also to the bishops: "Take
heed, therefore, unto yourselves and to all the flock over which the
Holy Ghost hath made you overseers, to rule (Vulgate) the Church
of God," Acts 20:28. 4. If prelates, therefore, have the power to rule,
they will have the power also to make statutes for the salutary
government of the Church and the growth of subjects. For the same
apostle enjoined upon the Corinthians that among them all things
should be done in order, 1 Cor. 14:40; but this cannot be done
without laws. 5. On that account he said to the Hebrews: "Obey
them that have the rule over you, and submit yourselves; for they
watch for your souls, as they that must give an account," Heb. 13:17.
Here St. Paul reckons not only obedience, but also the reason for
obedience. 6. We see that St. Paul exercised this power, as, in addition to the Gospel, he prescribed so many laws concerning the choice
of a bishop, concerning widows, concerning women, that they have
their heads veiled, that they be silent in the church, and concerning
even secular matters, 1 Thess. 4:1, 2, 6; concerning civil courts, 1
Cor. 6:1ff. And he says to the Corinthians very clearly: "But to
the rest speak I, not the Lord," 1 Cor. 7:12, and again he says elsewhere: "Stand fast and hold the traditions which ye have been
taught, whether by word or our epistle," 2 Thess. 2:15. 7. wherefore,
the princes and cities must be admonished to render obedience to
ecclesiastical statutes and constitutions, lest when they withdraw
obedience that is due God, obedience may be withdrawn also from
them by their subjects, as their subjects attempted in the recent civil
insurrection, not to allow themselves to be seduced by false doctrines.
8. Most false also is their declaration that the righteousness of faith
is obscured by such ordinances; nay, he is rather mad and insane
who would observe them without faith. For they are given to believers, and not to Turks or Ishmaelites. "For what have I to do
to judge them that are without?" 1 Cor. 5:12. 9. Moreover, in extol-
ling here faith above all things they antagonize St. Paul, as we have

said above, and do violence to St. Paul, whom they pervert to evangelical works when he speaks of legal works, as all these errors
have been above refuted.   10. False also is it that ecclesiastical
ordinances obscure God's commands, since they prepare man for
these, as fasts suppress the lust of the flesh and help him from falling
into luxury.   11. False also is it that it is impossible to observe ordinances, for the Church is not a cruel mother who makes no exceptions
in the celebration of festivals and in fasting and the like.   12. Furthermore, they falsely quote Augustine in reply to the inquiries of
Januarius, who is diametrically opposed to them.   For in this place
he most clearly states that what has been universally delivered by
the Church be also universally observed.   But in indifferent things,
and those whose observance and non-observance are free, the holy
father Augustine states that, according to the authority of St. Ambrose, the custom of each church should be observed.   "When I come
to Rome." he says, "I fast on the Sabbath, but when here I do not
fast."   13. Besides, they do violence to the Scriptures while they
endeavor to support their errors.   For Christ (Matt. 15) does not
absolutely disapprove of human ordinances, but of those only that
were opposed to the law of God, as is clearly acknowledged in Mark
7 :8, 9.   Here also Matt. 15:3 says: "Why do ye also transgress the
commandment of God by your tradition?"   So Paul (Col. 2) forbids
that any one be judged in meat or in drink, or in respect to the
Sabbath, after the Jewish manner; for when the Church forbids
meats it does not judge them to be unclean, as the Jews in the
Synagogue thought.   So the declaration of Christ concerning that
which goeth into the mouth (Matt. 15:11) is cited here without a
sure and true understanding of it, since its intention was to remove
the error of the Jews, who thought that food touched by unwashen
hands becomes unclean, and rendered one eating it unclean, as is
manifest from the context.   Nor does the Church bring back to
these observances Moses with his heavy hands.   14. In like manner
they do violence to St. Paul, for, 1 Tim. 4:1, 4. he calls that a doctrine of demons that forbids meats, as the Tatianites. Marcionites and
Manichaeans thought that meats were unclean, as is clear from the
words that follow, when St. Paul adds: "Every creature of God is
good."   But the Church does not forbid meats on the ground that
they are evil or unclean, but as an easier way to keep God's commandments; therefore the opposite arguments fail.   15. If they would
preach the cross and bodily discipline and fasts, that in this way

the body be reduced to subjection, their doctrine would be commend-
able; but their desire that these be free is condemned and rejected
as alien to the faith and discipline of the Church. 16. Nor does the
diversity of rites support them, for this is properly allowed in regard
to particular matters, in order that each individual province may
have its own taste satisfied, as Jerome says; but individual ecclesiastical rites should be universally observed, and special rites should
be observed each in their own province. 17. Also, they make no mention of Easter for the Roman pontiffs reduced the Asiatics to a uni-
form observance of Easter with the universal Church. In this way
Irenaeus must be understood, for without the loss of faith some
vigils of the apostles were not celebrated with fasting throughout
Gaul, which Germany nevertheless observes in fasts. 18. The princes
and cities must also be admonished to follow the decision of Pope
Gregory, for he enjoins that the custom of each province be observed
if it employs nothing contrary to the Catholic faith, Canon *Quoniam,*
Distinct. xii.   Hence we are not ignorant that there is a various
observance of dissimilar rites in unity of faith, which should be
observed in every province as it has been delivered and received
from the ancients, without injury, however, to the universal rites
of the entire Catholic Church.

VI. Of Monastic Vows. Although many and various matters have
been introduced in this article by the suggestion of certain persons
(Another text, *Cod. Pflug., reads* "Preachers"), nevertheless, when
all are taken into consideration with mature thought, since monastic
vows have their foundation in the Holy Scriptures of the Old and
New Testaments, and most holy men, renowned and admirable by
miracles, have lived in these religious orders with many thousand
thousands, and for so many centuries their ordinances and rules of
living have been received and approved throughout the entire Christian world by the Catholic Church, it is in no way to be tolerated that
vows are licentiously broken without any fear of God. 2. For, in the
Old Testament, God approved the vows of the Nazarenes, Num.
6:2ff. and the vows of the Rechabites, who neither drank wine or
ate grapes, Jer. 36:6, 19; while he strictly requires that the vow once
made be paid, Deut. 23:21f.; "It is ruin to a man after vows to
retract," Prov. 20:25; "The vows of the just are acceptable," Prov.
15:8. 3. God also teaches specifically through the prophet that monastic vows please him. For in Isa. 56:4, 5 it is read as follows: "Thus
saith the Lord unto the eunuchs that keep my Sabbath, and choose

the things that please me. and take hold of my covenant, Even unto them will I give in mine house and within my walls a place and a name better than that of sons and of daughters. I will give them an everlasting name that shall not be cut off." But to what eunuchs does God make these promises? To those, undoubtedly, whom Christ praises, "which have made themselves eunuchs for the kingdom of heaven's sake," Matt. 19:12; to those, undoubtedly, who, denying their own, come after Christ and deny themselves and follow him, Luke 9:23, so that they are governed no longer by their own will, but by that of their rule and superior. 4. In like manner, according to the testimony of the apostle, those virgins do better who, contemning the world and spurning its enticements, vow and maintain virginity in monasteries, than those who place their necks beneath the matrimonial burden. For thus St. Paul says, 1 Cor. 7:28: "He that giveth her in marriage doeth well; but he that giveth her not in marriage doeth better." Also, concerning a widow, he continues: "She is happier if she so abide, after my judgment." 5. No one is ignorant of the holiness of the hermit Paul, of Basil, Anthony, Benedict, Bernard, Dominic, Franciscus, William, Augustine, Clara, Bridget, and similar hermits, who indeed despised the entire realm of the world and all the splendor of the age on account of love to our Lord Jesus Christ. 6. Moreover, the heresy of the Lampetians was condemned in most ancient times, which the heretic Jovinian attempted in vain to revive at Rome. Therefore, all things must be rejected which in this article have been produced against monasticism—viz. that in the time of Augustine fraternities were free, that vows were added afterwards to monasteries; whereas the order was contrary—viz. that monasteries succeeded vows.

7. Of the nunneries it is sufficiently ascertained that, though pertaining to the weaker sex, how in most cloisters the holy nuns persevered far more constanly to vows once uttered, even under these princes and cities, than the majority of monks; even to this day it has been impossible to move them from their holy purpose by any prayers, blandishments, threats, terrors, difficulties or distresses. 8. Wherefore. those matters are not to be admitted which are interpreted unfavorably, since it has been expressly declared in the Holy Scriptures that the monastic life, when kept with proper observance, as may by the grace of God be rendered by any monks, merits eternal life; and indeed Christ has promised to them a much more bountiful reward. saying: "Every one that hath forsaken houses, or brethren,

or sisters, or father, or mother, or wife, or children or lands, for
my name's sake, shall receive an hundred-fold, and shall inherit
everlasting life," Matt. 19:29. 9. That monasteries, as they show,
were formerly literary schools, is not denied; nevertheless, there is
no ignorance of the fact that these were at first schools of virtues
and discipline, to which literature was afterwards added. 10. But
since no one putting his hand to the plough and looking back is
fit for the kingdom of heaven, Luke 9:62, all marriages and breaking
of vows by monks and nuns should be regarded as condemned, according to the tenor not only of the Holy Scriptures, but also of the
laws and canons, "having damnation, because they have cast off
their first faith," as St. Paul says, 1 Tim. 5:12. Moreover, that vows
are not contrary to the ordinance of God has been declared with
reference to the second article of the alleged abuses. 11. That they
attempt to defend themselves by dispensations of the Pope is of
no effect. For although the Pope has perhaps made a dispensation
for the king of Aragon, who, we read. returned to the monastery
after having had offspring, or for any other prince on account of
the peace of the entire kingdom or province, to prevent the exposure
of the entire kingdom or province to wars, carnage, pillage, debauch-
ery, conflagrations, murders,—nevertheless, in private persons who
abandon vows in apostasy such grounds for dispensations cannot be
urged. 12. For the assumption is repelled that the vow concerns a
matter that is impossible. For continence, which so many thousands
of men and virgins have maintained, is not impossible. For although
the wise man says (Wisd. 8:21): "I knew that I could not otherwise
be continent, unless God gave it me," nevertheless Christ promised
to give it. "Seek." he says, "and ye shall find," Luke 11:9; Matt.
18:28; and St. Paul says: "God is faithful, who will not suffer you
to be tempted above that ye are able, but will with the temptation
also make a way to escape, that ye may be able to bear it," 1 Cor.
10:13. 13. They are also poor defenders of their cause when they
admit that the violation of a vow is irreprehensible, and it must be
declared that by law such marriages are censured and should be
dissolved, C. Ut. Continentiae, xxvii. Q. 1., as also by the ancient
statutes of emperors. But when they allege in their favor C. Nup-
tiarum, they accomplish nothing, for it speaks of a simple not of a
religious vow, which the Church observes also to this day. The
marriages of monks, nuns, or priests, have therefore never been ratified. 14. Futile also is their statement that a votive life is an invention

of men, for it has been founded upon the Holy Scriptures, inspired
into the most holy fathers by the Holy Ghost. 15. Nor does it deny
honor to Christ, since monks observe all things for Christ's sake.
and imitate Christ. False, therefore, is the judgment whereby they
condemn monastic service as godless, whereas it is most Christian.
For the monks have not fallen from God's grace, as the Jews of
whom St. Paul speaks, Gal. 5:4, when they still sought justification
by the law of Moses; but the monks endeavor to live more nearly
to the Gospel, that they may merit eternal life. Therefore, the
allegations here made against monasticism are impious. 16. Moreover, the malicious charge that is still further added, that those in
religious orders claim to be in a state of perfection, has never been
heard of by them; for those in these orders claim not for themselves
a state of perfection, but only a state in which to acquire perfection—
because their regulations are instruments of perfection, and not perfection itself. In this manner Gerson must be received, who does
not deny that religious orders are states wherein to acquire perfection as he declares in his treatises, "Against the Proprietors of the
Rule of St. Augustine," "Of Evangelical Counsels," "Of Perfection
of Heart," and in other places. 17. For this reason the princes and
cities should be admonished to strive rather for the reformation of
the monasteries by their legitimate superiors than for their sub-
version—rather for the godly improvement of the monks than that
they be abolished; as their most religious ancestors, most Christian
princes, have done. 18. But if they will not believe holy and most
religious fathers defending monastic vows, let them hear at least
His Imperial Highness, the Emperor Justinian, in "Authentica,"
De Monachis, Coll. ii.

VII. Of Ecclesiastical Power. Although many things are introduced here in the topic of Ecclesiastical Power, with greater bitterness than is just, yet it must be declared that to most reverend bishops
and priests, and to the entire clergy, all ecclesiastical power is freely
conceded that belongs to them by law or custom. 2. Besides, it is
proper to preserve for them all immunities, privileges, preferments
and prerogatives granted them by Roman emperors and kings. Nor
can those things that have been granted ecclesiastics by imperial
munificence or gift be allowed to be infringed by any princes or any
other subject of the Roman Empire. 3. For it is most abundantly
proved that ecclesiastical power in spiritual things has been founded
upon divine right, of which St. Paul indeed says: "For though I

should boast somewhat more of our authority which the Lord hath given us for edification, and not for your destruction," 2 Cor. 10 :8, and afterwards : "Therefore I write these things being absent, lest being present I should use sharpness, according to the power which the Lord hath given me to edification, and not to destruction, 2 Cor. 13 :10. Paul also displays his coercitive disposition when he says : "What will ye? Shall I come unto you with a rod, or in love and in the spirit of meekness?" 1 Cor. 4 :21. And of judicial matters he writes to Timothy : "Against an elder receive not an accusation but before two or three witnesses," 1 Tim. 5 :19. 4. From these passages it is very clearly discerned that bishops have the power not only of the ministry of the Word of God, but also of ruling and coercitive correction in order to direct subjects to the goal of eternal blessedness. But for the power of ruling there is required the power to judge, to define, to discriminate and to decide what is expedient or conducive to the aforesaid goal. 5. In vain, therefore, and futile is all that is inserted in the present article in opposition to the immunity of churches and schools. Accordingly, all subjects of the Roman Empire must be forbidden from bringing the clergy before a civil tribunal, contrary to imperial privileges that have been conceded ; for Pope Clement the Martyr says : "If any of the presbyters have trouble with one another, let whatever it be adjusted before the presbyters of the Church." Hence Constantine the Great, the most Christian Emperor, was unwilling in the holy Council of Nice to give judgment even in secular cases. "Ye are gods," he says, "appointed by the true God. Go, settle the case among yourselves, because it is not proper that we judge gods." 6. As to what is further repeated concerning Church regulations has been sufficiently replied to above. Nor does Christian liberty, which they bring forth as an argument, avail them, since this is not liberty, but prodigious license, which, inculcated on the people, excites them to fatal and most dangerous sedition. 7. For Christian liberty is not opposed to ecclesiastical usages since they promote what is good, but it is opposed to the servitude of the Mosaic law and the servitude of sin. "Whosoever committeth sin is the servant of sin," says Christ, John 8 :34. 8. Hence their breaking fasts, their free partaking of meats, their neglect of canonical hours, their omission of confession—viz. at Easter—and their commission and omission of similar things, are not a use of liberty, but an abuse thereof, contrary to the warnings of St. Paul, who earnestly warned them, saying : "Brethren, ye have been called unto liberty; only use not, liberty for an occasion to the flesh, but by love serve one another," Gal. 5:13. Hence no one ought to conceal his crimes under the pretext of Gospel liberty, which St. Peter also forbade: "As free, and not using your liberty for a cloak of maliciousness, but as the servant of God," 1 Pet. 2:16. 9. As to what they have added concerning abuses, all the princes and estates of the Empire undoubtedly know that not even the least is approved either by His Imperial Majesty or by any princes or any Christian man, but that both the princes and the estates of the Empire desire to strive with a common purpose and agreement, in order that, the abuses being removed and reformed, the excesses of both estates may be either utterly abolished or reformed for the better, and that the ecclesiastical estate, which has been weakened in many ways, and the Christian religion, which has grown cold and relaxed in some, may be restored and renewed to its pristine glory and distinction. 10. To this, as is evident to all, His Imperial Majesty has thus far devoted the greatest care and labor, and kindly promises in the future to employ for this cause all his means and zeal.

Conclusion. From the foregoing—viz. the Confession and its Reply—since His Imperial Majesty perceives that the Elector, the princes and the cities agree on many points with the Catholic and Roman Church, and dissent from the godless dogmas that are disseminated all over Germany. and the pamphlets circulated everywhere, and that they disapprove of and condemn them,—His Holy Imperial Majesty is fully convinced, and hopes that the result will be, that when the Elector, princes and cities have heard and understood this Reply they will agree with united minds in regard to those matters also in which they perhaps have not agreed hitherto with the Roman Catholic Church, and that in all other things above mentioned they will obediently conform to the Catholic and Roman Church and the Christian faith and religion. 2. For such conduct on their part His Imperial Majesty will be peculiarly grateful, and will bestow his special favor upon them all in common, and also, as opportunity offers, upon them individually. For (which may God forbid) if this admonition, so Christian and indulgent, be unheeded, the Elector, princes and cities can judge that a necessary cause is afforded His Imperial Majesty that, as becometh a Roman Emperor and Christian Caesar and a defender and advocate of the Catholic and Christian

Church, he must care for such matters as the nature of the charge committed to him and his integrity of conscience require.

---

51. THE RECESS OF AUGSBURG, SEPTEMBER 22, 1530.[53]

WHEREAS His Imperial Majesty has convoked a general Imperial Diet at this city of Augsburg for the eighth day of April of this year for the purpose of disposing of various matters affecting the Holy Empire, all Christendom, and the German Nation, and especially for the purpose of considering ways and means of removing the errors and dissensions concerning the sacred faith and the Christian religion which now grievously afflict the Nation, in order so to bring it about, in better and sounder fashion, that divisions may be allayed, antipathies set aside, all past errors left to the judgment of Christ our Saviour, and every care taken to give a kind and charitable hearing to every man's opinions, thoughts, and notions, to understand them, to weigh them, to bring and reconcile men to a unity in Christian truth, to dispose of everything that has not been rightly explained or treated of on the one side or the other, to bring about the universal acceptance and preservation of the one true religion, to restore the unity of the Church in which we all live and battle under the one Lord Christ, and finally to resolve, prepare, restore, and preserve good unity, peace, and prosperity throughout the Holy Empire in these and similar matters— as was plainly and exhaustively stated in the Imperial summons to this Diet; and

WHEREAS His Imperial Majesty's Electors, Princes, and other Estates of the Holy Empire have obediently appeared in person before His Imperial Majesty and sent their plenipotentiaries to this Diet; and

WHEREAS His Imperial Majesty, together with said Electors, Princes, Prelates, Counts, Estates of the Holy Roman Empire and their ambassadors, has considered the various points and articles mentioned in the Imperial Summons, especially those which deal with the errors and dissensions in matters of the Christian faith, and in accordance with said Imperial Summons given a hearing to everyone who desired to speak concerning such dissensions, and especially to the Elector of Saxony, Margrave George of Brandenburg, the brothers Ernest and Francis Dukes of Lueneburg, Philip

Landgrave of Hesse, Wolfgang Duke of Anhalt, and the Delegates of the cities of Nuremberg, Reutlingen, Kempten, Heilbronn, Windsheim, and Weissenburg, graciously heard their opinion and their confession in the presence of the Electors, Princes, and Estates of the Holy Empire, given them much careful consideration, and thoroughly refuted them by means of the Gospels and other writings; and

WHEREAS so many painstaking efforts were devoted to this matter by His Imperial Majesty and the said Electors, Princes, and Estates in person, and by the committee of Electors, Princes, and others—first fourteen and subsequently six—that they arrived at an agreement with the other Elector, Princes, and Estates in reference to several articles of the faith although no such agreement was reached in regard to others of the articles,

THEREFORE His Imperial Majesty, for the benefit and prosperity of the Holy Empire, for the restoration of peace and unity, and for the purpose of manifesting His Majesty's leniency and special grace, has granted to the Elector of Saxony, the five Princes, and the six Cities a time of grace from now until the 15th day of April next year in which to consider whether or not they will confess the other articles together with the Christian Church, His Holiness the Pope, His Imperial Majesty, the other Electors, Princes, and Estates of the Holy Roman Empire, and other Christian rulers and the members of universal Christendom until a general council shall be convoked; and

His Imperial Majesty on His part will consider during the same interval what course of action it behooves Him to follow; and

The Elector of Saxony, the five Princes, and the six Cities shall prior to said 15th day of April officially inform His Imperial Majesty of their decision in this matter, whereupon His Imperial Majesty will likewise in writing disclose His intention; and

The Elector of Saxony, the five Princes, and the six Cities shall between now and said 15th day of April prohibit in their countries the printing, selling, and retailing of any new books dealing with religion, and it is His Majesty's earnest will and command that in the meantime all Electors, Princes, and Estates of the Holy Empire promote peace and unity in this respect; and

Neither the Elector of Saxony, the five Princes, the six Cities, nor their subjects shall make any attempt to induce or force the subjects of His Majesty and of the Holy Empire or those of the other

Electors, Princes, and Estates to join their sects; nor shall they in any way molest those—if any—in their lands, regardless of rank or station, who still wish to cling to the old Christian faith and usages; they shall not prevent them from attending church nor from worshipping God according to their old accustomed rituals; they shall introduce no innovations whatever; and they shall not hinder any members of religious orders, male or female, from celebrating the mass, from hearing or making confession, nor from offering or receiving the holy and blessed Sacrament; and

The said Elector, the five Princes, and the six Cities shall agree with His Imperial Majesty, the other Electors, Princes, and Estates in reference to a mode of procedure against those who reject the holy and blessed Sacrament and against the Anabaptists, and in no way separate from His Majesty and His own, but offer advice, counsel, and assistance as to how to proceed against them in accordance with the promise made by all the said Electors, Princes, and Estates, as was said above, so far as their own countries are concerned; and

Inasmuch as no general council has been held in the Christian Church for many years, although throughout Christendom, in all dominions and estates, secular as well as ecclesiastical, numerous abuses and errors may have taken root, His Imperial Majesty, for the purpose of a Christian reformation, has considered this matter with His Holiness the Pope, and resolved with all the Electors, Princes, and Estates here assembled at Augsburg, to use His influence in inducing His Holiness the Pope and all Christian kings and potentates to consent to the convocation of a general Christian council within six months of the conclusion of this Diet at a suitable place and to holding this council at the latest one year after convoking it, in the firm confidence and hope that thereby Christendom may be restored in spiritual and temporal matters to lasting peace and unity. Amen.

52. FIRST DRAFT OF MELANCHTHON'S APOLOGY, SEPTEMBER 22, 1530.[54]

In the Fourth and Sixth Articles a long disputation *de merito,* concerning merits, has been added, and yet there is no plain statement as to how far human works are meritorious. Whoever does not make this clear, by esteeming works too highly, obscures the blessed doctrine of faith and how faith justifies before God, which doctrine is most needful for an honest conscience and which as it is most essential, should occupy the chief place and be most zealously taught in the Christian Church.

It is a matter of surprise to see how cautiously they now speak of merits. In former times when they discussed the forgiveness of sins and justification they never took faith into account but only human works. Furthermore they said that works earned merit. *de congruo* without the aid of the Holy Ghost, and that afterwards, with grace added, works earned eternal life, *de condigne,* and so the whole Christian teaching was nothing but a philosophy of works and of worldly order, not of faith and divine operation, as they have indeed written with clear words: *Bonum opus sine gracia factum et bonum opus cum gracia factum esse ciusdem speciei: Cum gratia tantum adderet respectum meriti.* They attributed too much to the powers of human nature so that they thought the Holy Ghost was not necessary.

Some also doubted as to whether grace accomplished anything in sanctification and taught that man, by his own natural powers, could keep the commandments of God *quo ad substantiam actus, tametsi respectus meriti de esset.*

Wherefore do not the bishops condemn such sacrilege and open blasphemies as would have been their duty? Yea, they permitted such teachings and allowed them to be taught in the schools as holy tenets to the evident dishonor and disparagement of the merits and death of Christ. But when men began to grumble against the indulgence traffic and against the tyranny of the pope this was regarded as great and unbearable heresy, just as though they had been teaching nothing but precious holy truths up to this time. Some theologians, however, have now amended their ways and confess that too much, and more than is justifiable, has been imported into Holy Scripture out of human philosophy; they acknowledge that too much has been conceded to human powers; they confess that God's commandments not only direct how we are to be outwardly pious, for this can be accomplished to some degree by human reason, but that they are spiritual, demanding that the heart be clean, requiring faith, that we assuredly trust in God's help in every time of need, that we call upon God and that we put to death the flesh, which means all our fleshly lusts.

Now they are content to have faith added when they discuss justification and the forgiveness of sins, namely, that because of faith sins are not imputed to those who believe that they are for-given them for Christ's sake. Nevertheless they eke it out with the merit of works, although they admit that this is a very small part. They say that the works done in a state of grace earn eternal life, *sed minus principaliter*. They still retain this one little bit out of the dregs of previous false teaching.

Even if it were true, as is not, that works in some degree were meritorious, our article would still be framed in a proper and Christian manner, when we say that we must do good works because God has commanded them, but with the understanding that we do not rely on our own good works to become righteous before God but trust in the merits and promise of Christ. This our article teaches and it is beyond all doubt that all Christians must confess and teach likewise, for thus the prophet says in the Psalter: "Lord, enter not into judgment with thy servant: for in thy sight shall no man living be justified." And again: "If Thou, Lord, shouldest mark iniquities: O Lord, who shall stand?"

And Augustine says: "God leads us to eternal life not through our merits, but through His mercy." Accordingly our Article requires that we do good works because God has commanded and desires them, and still it condemns reliance on works since this reliance has always been condemned by all Christians and godly folk.

Our opponents have invented a little gloss on that statement of Christ which forbids such reliance on our own works, namely, "When ye shall have done all these things, say, We are unprofitable servants." They interpret unprofitable to mean that we are unprofit-able to God but profitable to ourselves. This is an appeal *ad hominem* but when this is put under inspection every intelligent person can readily see what will be said about it and it would be easy enough to ridicule this gloss, but we will obediently spare the Imperial Ma-jesty, our Most Gracious Lord, this business only those who have compiled this writing in the name of the Imperial Majesty should have been more discreet and careful not to make a jest of Scripture and God's Word in such all important matters.

St. Ambrose expounds this passage in a very different way, when he says: "It follows from this that no one should boast of his works, because we are in duty bound to serve God." And shortly after: "We should praise grace and not forget the weakness of nature." We wish briefly to prove that this saying of Christ condemns merits and our reliance upon them.

Christ is concerned in diverting us from an ungodly reliance on our own merits. He begins by using a parable to show us that we cannot make God our debtor, as though He owed us anything because of our merits, any more than a servant, who has done all that was required of him, can make demands upon his master and regard him as indebted to his servant for what he has done. So you likewise, says Christ, cannot make God your debtor, etc.

Because God is not indebted to us it follows that we cannot boast that our works are meritorious, for how can they be meritorious when God does not owe anything to our works?

Furthermore the statement is found in the text that Christ calls us unprofitable servants, which actually means as much as insufficient, because none has done as much as he should. For who loves God as he should? Who fears God as he should? Who bears all that God imposes on him as patiently as he should? Who loves his neighbor as it is his duty to do? Who, in all particulars, fulfils his calling as he should?

So it means *inutiles formaliter,* for we must use the language of the sophists in addressing them. So St. Paul also teaches that our works are impure when he says: "The good that I would I do not; but the evil which I would not, that I do." Again, "The flesh lusteth against the spirit," for in the flesh is nothing but sin, evil lusts, contempt of God, and little trust in God. That these sins hinder even the most saintly and defile all good works is the simplest and plainest interpretation of the words of Christ.

From this follows the inevitable conclusion that we cannot trust in the meritoriousness of our works, for if God is in no wise indebted to us and our works are insufficient, how can we boast of our works? As well might a servant boast that he had badly cultivated his master's field.

Finally: Even our opponents gloss is not against us, for if our works are not profitable to God, it follows that God is not indebted to them. If He is not indebted to our works how can we boast that the works merit something? But we will dismiss such a corrupt gloss because it is evident to everyone that Christ by this comparison desires to destroy and condemn all our boasting about works and merits.

Yet our opponents are so audacious that they venture to find a loop-hole in this clear text by the sophistical interpretation they have themselves invented. Therefore it is not necessary to dispute any longer for it is certain that Scripture everywhere forbids everyone to boast concerning anything, for what do we have that we have not received? Nor shall we again reckon on our own strength or powers or trust in them. Therefore we have correctly said that we must do good works because God has commanded them, and yet, at the same time, we must not trust in the works but alone in the merits of Christ.

But here! they say, Scripture uses the word *merces*, reward, therefore works are meritorious, for where there is reward there is also merit. They catch hold on the little word *merces* and think in this way, with one little word, to overturn all the other clear and comprehensive statements of Scripture, in which this matter is treated extensively and yet they do not understand the terminology of Scripture.

Reward is not called reward because of the worth of the work, but because of God's promise. This promise, however, as St. Paul teaches, is received by faith; not for the sake of our works, but because Christ has earned grace for us through His merit. For as the promise demands faith, according to St. Paul's statement, so the reward likewise requires faith, because a reward is something that God promises. *Et causa movens promittentem, non est dignitas operum nostrorum, sed meritum Christi.* If God promises anything He must have a cause which moves Him and which causes Him to do so. This cause is not the worth of our works but the merits of His dear Son Jesus Christ. This fact would be readily understood if St. Paul's teaching concerning the divine promises, concerning grace, justification, faith etc. had been taught and preached as diligently as these other useless teachings of sophistry. Therefore we have been satisfied, for the present, to limit ourselves to the consideration of these two points; that we must do good works because God has commanded them and that, at the same time, we must not rely on our good works nor trust in them, but only on the simple promise of Christ. For though *justicia legis* earns *praemia legis* it is certain that we do not earn grace and righteousness before God through our works, and whoever attributes such dignity to works disgraces and defames the honor of Christ, as Paul proves, when he says: If righteousness comes from the works which God Himself has commanded in His law, then Christ died in vain.

On the basis of this teaching we say that we are justified alone through faith, because faith lays hold on the grace and mercy of

God, and knows that God is gracious to us for the sake of Christ. This faith is accounted righteousness before God and, because faith receives the Holy Ghost, the Holy Ghost renews the hearts and produces in them a desire to do good, as is written in the Prophet: "I will put my law in their inward parts." Accordingly good works are the fruits of faith. So faith recognizes that we have a gracious God not because of our works but for the sake of Christ. Wherefore faith justifies and not our works, for faith looks to Christ and for His sake we are beloved. To all eternity men would never have any sure and certain assurance in the face of temptation and sin if we attained grace because of our works, for we perceive continually that we are unclean, but faith brings a certain consolation to our conscience when we are convinced that we have a gracious God, for Christs sake; in this no one can be deceived, let our works be as they may.

Our opponents almost maliciously delight themselves with the word *sola,* faith *alone,* and for that reason call us "Solarios." They intend that to be very biting, because we teach *sola fide justificari hominem,* man is justified by faith alone. and they shriek that the word *sola* is not found in Scripture and that the "soles" ought to be sent to the shoemaker.

They also complain that we exclude the Sacraments, but we maintain that man is justified by faith and not by preceding or succeeding works. This faith is awakened through Word and Sacrament and so we do not exclude the Sacraments but the meritoriousness of works. St. Paul does the same when he says: "It is the gift of God, not of works." This negative completely excludes works. Again, he often says that we become righteous through grace that is wholly free.

For *gratis* is also a *particula exclusiva* and is the same as when I say *sola fide justificamur,* we are saved by faith alone. In addition the word *donum* is also an *exclusiva particula,* which excludes merit.

Here the Imperial Majesty can see again that the fight over the word *sola* is forced upon us and that our opponents most violently twist the little word *sola* since all Christians and Christian teachers have always acknowledged that the forgiveness of sins is bestowed on us gratuitously. and our opponents themselves do not deny it. But they have been infatuated by sophistry and have not learned anything better, so they cannot refrain from controversies. But if this word *sola* troubles them so much, why do they not condemn the ancient teachers etc.? Why do they not erase it from their books? For we did not first discover this word nor are we the first who have used such language.

In our Confession we have cited the saying of Ambrose that God has so ordered it that whosoever believes in Christ shall be saved and shall gratuitously receive the forgiveness of sins without works, *sola fide,* through faith alone. So Hilary also says, Matt. 8, that the scribes were very much exercised that a man should forgive sins, for they could see in Christ nothing but a man and because that was forgiven which the law could not remit, *fides enim sola justificat,* for faith alone justifies. Now if this be wrong the sophists must erase the word *sola* from the books of the fathers, which have been read for so many centuries, but our opponents possess the great gift of not being ashamed of any calumnies. This whole matter as to how a man shall become godly and righteous in the sight of God is thoroughly discussed by Augustine in his work against the Pelagians, and by Ambrose in many passages, and although they know full well that we follow the opinion of these teachers, they seize on the one word and cavil with it so that they may appear to have something against us.

53. THE VARIATA OF 1540[55]

Part I. Chief Articles of Faith. Article IV. Of Justification. That we might obtain these benefits of Christ, namely, forgiveness of sins, justification and life everlasting, Christ hath given his Gospel, wherein these benefits are set forth unto us, as it is written in the last chapter of Luke: "That repentance and remission of sins should be preached, in his name, among all nations" (Luke 24:47). For since all men descended from one another after a natural manner, have sin and cannot truly satisfy the law of God, the Gospel convicteth us of sins, and showeth us Christ the Mediator, and so instructeth us concerning forgiveness of sins.

When the Gospel convicteth us of our sins, our terrified hearts ought to firmly hold that freely for Christ's sake forgiveness of sins and justification by faith are presented us; by which faith we ought to believe and confess that these things are given us for Christ's sake, who for us became a sacrifice, and appeased the Father. Although therefore the Gospel requireth repentance, nevertheless that the forgiveness of sins may be certain, it teacheth that this forgiveness is granted us freely; that is, that it doth not depend upon the condition of our own worthiness, nor is given for any works that go before, or for the worthiness of such as follow. For forgiveness would be uncertain if we would have to think that we obtain forgiveness of sins then only when we would deserve it by our preceding works, or our repentance were sufficiently worthy.

For in true alarm conscience findeth no work which it can oppose to God's wrath; and Christ hath been given and set forth unto us to be a propitiator. This honor of Christ ought not be transferred to our works. On this account, Paul saith: "By grace are ye saved (Eph. 2:8). Again: Therefore it is of faith, to the end that the promise might be sure." (Rom. (4:16), that is, forgiveness thus shall be certain, when we will know that it dependeth not upon the condition of our worthiness, but is given us for Christ's sake. This is a sure and necessary consolation to godly and terrified minds. And thus the holy fathers teach; and in Ambrose there is a notable and remarkable sentence in the following words: "This hath been appointed by God, viz. that he that believeth in Christ be saved without any work, by faith alone receiving freely the forgiveness of sins."

And the term *faith* signifieth not only a knowledge of the history of Christ, but also to believe and assent to this promise, which is peculiar to the Gospel, wherein forgiveness of sins, justification and life everlasting are promised unto us for Christ's sake. For this promise also doth pertain to the history concerning Christ, just as in the Creed there has been added to the history the article: "I believe the forgiveness of sins;" and to this article, the rest concerning the history of Christ ought to be referred. For this benefit is the design of the history. For on this account Christ suffered and rose, viz. that for his sake forgiveness of sins and everlasting life might be given us.

Article V. Of the Ministry of the Church. For this cause Christ hath appointed the ministry of teaching the Gospel, which preacheth repentance and forgiveness of sins. And the preaching of both of these is universal: it maketh known the sins of all men, and promiseth forgiveness of sins to all believers; to the end that forgiveness of sins may not be uncertain, but that all distressed minds may know that they ought to believe that forgiveness of sins is certainly granted us for Christ's sake, and not for our own merits or works.

And when in this manner we comfort ourselves with the promise or Gospel, and encourage ourselves by faith, we certainly obtain forgiveness of sins, and at the same time the Holy Spirit is given us. For the Holy Spirit is given, and is effectual, by the Word of God and by the sacraments. When we hear or meditate upon the Gospel, or use the sacraments, and comfort ourselves by faith, the Holy Spirit is at the same time efficacious, according to the declaration of Paul to the Galatians (3:22): "That the promise by faith of Jesus Christ might be given to them that believe; "and to the Corinthians (? Cor. 3:8). The Gospel is the ministration of the Spirit; and to the Romans (10:17): "Faith cometh by hearing." When therefore we comfort ourselves by faith, and are freed from the terrors of sin by the Holy Spirit, our hearts conceive other virtues, acknowledge truly the mercy of God, and conceive true love, true fear of God, trust, hope of divine help, prayer and similar fruits of the Spirit.

They therefore who teach nothing concerning this faith, whereby forgiveness of sins is received, but bid consciences doubt whether they obtain forgiveness of sins, and add that this doubt is not sin, are condemned. They also teach that men obtain forgiveness of sins on account of their own worthiness; they do not teach that we should believe that the forgiveness of sins is freely bestowed for Christ's sake. Also the fanatical spirits are condemned who feign that the Holy Ghost is given or is efficacious without the Word of God, and on this account contemn the ministry of the Gospel and sacraments. and seek illustrations without the Word of God, and besides the Gospel, and thus lead away minds from the Word of God to their own opinions,—which is most ruinous. Such were formerly the Manichees and Enthusiasts, and are now the Anabaptists. Such frenzies we constantly condemn. For they abolish the true use of God's Word, and falsely imagine that the Holy Spirit is received without the Word of God and relying upon their own opinions they invent godless dogmas and cause infinite separation.

Article VI. Of the New Obedience. Also they teach that, when we are reconciled by faith, the righteousness of good works which God hath commanded us ought necessarily to follow; even as Christ hath also enjoined: "If thou wilt enter into life, keep the commandments" (Matt. 19:17). But because the infirmity of man's nature is so great that no one can satisfy the law, it is needful to teach men not only that they must obey the law, but also how this obedience pleaseth, lest their consciences fall into despair when they understand that they do not satisfy the law.

This obedience therefore pleaseth, not because it satisfieth the law, but because the person that performeth it is reconciled by Christ through faith, and believeth that the remnants of sin are pardoned him. Therefore we must always hold that we obtain forgiveness of sins, and a person is pronounced righteous, i.e. is freely accepted, for Christ's sake, through faith; and afterwards, that this obedience towards the law doth also please, and is accounted a kind of righteousness, and merits rewards. For the conscience cannot set its own cleanness or worth over against the judgment of God; as Psalm 143: 2 testifieth: "Enter not into judgment with thy servant; for in thy sight shall no man living be justified." And John says (1 John 1:8, 9): "If we say that we have no sin, we deceive ourselves, and the truth is not in us. If we confess our sins, he is faithful and just to forgive us our sins, and to cleanse us from all unrighteousness." And Christ says (Luke 17:10): "When ye shall have done all those things . . . . say, We are unprofitable servants." But after the person is reconciled and righteous by faith, that is, accepted, his obedience both pleases and is accounted a sort of righteousness, as John saith (1 John 3:6): "Whoso abideth in him sinneth not," and (2 Cor. 1:12): "Our rejoicing is this, the testimony of our conscience."

This obedience ought to strive against evil desires, and continually by spiritual exercises become more pure, and to beware of committing anything contrary to conscience, according to the passage (1 Tim. 1:5): "The end of the commandment is charity out of a pure heart, and of a good conscience, and of faith unfeigned." But they who obey evil desires, and act contrary to conscience, live in mortal sins, and retain neither the righteousness of faith, nor the righteousness of good works, according to the declaration of Paul (Gal. 5:21): "They which do such things shall not inherit the kingdom of God."

Article IX. Of Baptism. Of Baptism they teach that it is necessary to salvation, as a ceremony instituted by Christ, and that by Baptism the grace of God is offered, and that infants, by Baptism commended unto God, are received into God's favor, and become children of God; as Christ testifieth, speaking of little children in the Church, in Matt. 18:14: "It is not the will of your Father which is in heaven, that one of these little ones should perish."

They condemn the Anabaptists, who allow not the Baptism of infants, and affirm that infants are saved without Baptism and outside of the Church.

Article X. Of the Lord's Supper. Of the Lord's Supper they teach that together with the bread and wine, the Body and Blood of Christ are truly tendered to those that eat in the Lord's Supper.

Article XI. Of Repentance. Touching repentance, they teach that such as have fallen after baptism may find remission of sins at what time they are converted, and that the Church should give absolution unto such as return to repentance.

Now repentance, that is, the conversion of the godless, properly consisteth of these two parts: One is contrition, that is, terrors stricken into the conscience through the acknowledgment of sin, wherein we both recognize the wrath of God, and grieve that we have sinned and abhor, and eschew sins, as Joel preacheth (2:13): "Rend your heart, and not your garments, and turn unto the Lord your God."

The other part is faith, which is conceived by the Gospel or absolution, and doth believe that for Christ's sake sins are certainly forgiven, and comforteth the conscience, and freeth it from terrors. Of which faith Paul speaketh when he saith: "Being justified by faith we have peace" (Rom. 5:1). Then should follow the good fruits of repentance, that is, obedience to God, according to the passage: "We are debtors not to the flesh, to live after the flesh. For if ye live after the flesh, ye shall die; but if ye, through the Spirit, do mortify the deeds of the body, ye shall live" (Rom. 8:12, 13).

They condemn the Novatians, who would not absolve such as, having fallen after Baptism, returned to repentance. They condemn also those that do not teach that forgiveness of sins is obtained freely by faith for Christ's sake, but labor to prove that forgiveness of sins is obtained on account of the worthiness of contrition, of love, or of other works, and command consciences in repentance to doubt whether they obtain forgiveness of sins, and affirm that this doubting is not sin. Likewise they condemn those who teach that canonical satisfactions are necessary to redeem eternal punishments or the punishments of purgatory; although we confess that present calamities are assuaged by good works, as Isaiah teacheth, chapter 58:10, 11: "Deal thy bread to the hungry," etc., "and the Lord will give thee rest always" (Vulgate for v. 11, in Eng. version: "Shall guide thee continually."). They reject also indulgences, which are presentations of imaginary satisfactions.

They condemn also the Anabaptists, who deny that those once justified can again lose the Holy Ghost. They condemn also those who contend that some men may attain to such perfection in this life that they even cannot sin any more.

Article XVII. Of Christ's Return to Judgment. Also they teach that in the consummation of the world Christ shall appear to judgment, and shall raise up all the dead and shall give unto godly men eternal life and everlasting joys; but ungodly men and the devils shall be condemned unto endless torments.

We condemn the Anabaptists, who now scatter Jewish opinions, and imagine that before the resurrection the godly shall occupy the kingdoms of the world, the wicked being everywhere destroyed or suppressed. For we know that, since the godly ought to obey the magistrates that now are, they must not seize their power from them or overthrow governments by sedition, because Paul enjoineth: "Let every soul be subject unto the higher powers" (Rom. 13:1). We know also that the Church in this life is subject to the cross, and shall not be glorified until after this life; as Paul saith (Rom. 8:29; 1 Cor. 15:49): We must be made like the image of the Son of God. Therefore we utterly condemn and detest the folly and dia-bolical madness of the Anabaptists.

We condemn also the Origenists, who have imagined that there will be an end of punishments to the devils and condemned.

Conclusion of the First Part. This is the sum of the doctrine which is propounded in our churches. And we regard it in harmony with the Prophetic and Apostolic Scriptures and the Catholic Church, and finally also with the Roman Church, so far as it is known from approved writers. We hope that all good and learned men will judge in like manner. For we do not despise harmony with the Catholic Church, nor is it our intention to introduce into the Church any dogma that is new and unknown to the holy Church, nor do we wish to advocate godless or seditious opinions which the Catholic Church has condemned. For not prompted by perverse party spirit, but compelled by the authority of the Word of God and of the ancient Church, we have embraced this doctrine, in order that God's glory might be the more manifest, and the interests of godly minds in the entire Church might be cared for. For it is manifest that very many abuses have crept into the Church which have need of cor-rection. Both for Christ's glory, and the salvation of all nations, we especially desire that, when these controversies have been care-fully examined, the Church may be cleansed and freed from those abuses which cannot be concealed; and for this reason all good men in all nations have long since been longing for a synod, some hope of which the most clement emperor showeth to all nations. Therefore the emperor will do what is most befitting his greatness and success, and what is greatly desired by the universal Church, if in a synod he will commit the judgment concerning matters of such importance not to those who bring self-interest to the deliberation, but will select godly and learned men who desire to consult for the glory of Christ and the welfare of the universal Church. This is the customary and lawful way to adjust dissensions, viz. by referring ecclesiastical controversies to synods. For the time of the apostles the Church hath preserved this mode. And the most distinguished emperors, Constantine and Theodosius, even in matters not very obscure and in regard to absurd dogmas, nevertheless were unwilling to decide anything without a synod, in order that they might preserve the liberty of the Church in decisions concerning dogmas. And it is very honorable to the emperor to imitate the example of those most excellent sovereigns, especially since we have changed nothing without the example of the ancient Church. And we hope that this so great happiness hath been divinely given the emperor for the amendment and welfare of the Church. Certainly God claimeth of him this service, viz. that he devote his power to commending the glory of Christ. to the peace of the Church, and to the prohibition of monstrous and most unjust cruelty, which with a certain wonderful rage is exercised in every direction against the members of Christ, against godly and innocent men. God hath entrusted the care of these very great matters to supreme sovereigns; on this account he exciteth monarchs to restrain unjust authority, as he excited Cyrus to deliver the people of the Jews from captivity, and Constantine to remove that infinite cruelty which, at that time, was being exercised against the Christians. Thus we desire that Caesar both undertake the care of the Church when reformed, and may restrain the unjust cruelty.

For our articles, which we have enumerated, bear witness with sufficient clearness that we neither teach nor approve of any dogma contrary to the Catholic Church, or of any godless or seditious opinion, yea even that certain prominent articles of Christian doctrine have been elucidated in a godly and useful way by our men. In external traditions some abuses have been changed, in regard to which even if there be some dissimilarity, provided only the doctrine and faith be pure, no one because of this dissimilarity of human traditions is to be regarded a heretic or a deserter from the Catholic Church. For the unity of the Catholic Church consisteth in agreement of doctrine and faith, not in human traditions, with respect to which there hath always been in the churches throughout the whole world great dissimilarity. Not indeed let His Imperial Majesty have confidence in those who, in order to enkindle hatred against us, are spreading abroad marvellous charges. They proclaim that all ceremonies, that all good customs in the churches, are abolished by us. These charges are clearly false. For we both preserve with the greatest devotion, the ceremonies that have been divinely instituted, and, in order to increase respect for them, we have only removed certain recent abuses, which contrary to the examples of the ancient Church, have, by the fault of the times, been received without any responsible authority. And to a great extent the ancient rites have been carefully preserved among us. Wherefore we ask His Imperial Majesty to hear us kindly, as to what is preserved in external rites, and what, for any reason, hath been changed.

 Part II. Articles Concerning Abuses Which Have Been Corrected in External Rites. Article I. Of the Mass. Our Churches are wrongfully accused to have abolished the mass. For the mass is still retained among us, and celebrated with great reverence; and almost all the ceremonies that are in use are preserved, saving that with the things sung in Latin we mingle certain things sung in German at various parts of the service, which have been added for the people's instruction. For on this very account we have need of ceremonies, that they may teach the unlearned, and that the preaching of God's Word may stir up some to the true fear and invocation of God. Not only did St. Paul command to use a tongue that the people understand (1 Cor. 14:9), but man's law also hath appointed it. We accustom the people to receive the Sacrament together, if so be any be found fit thereunto; and that is a thing that doth increase the reverence and due estimation of the public ceremonies. For none are admitted unless they be first proved. Besides, we put men in mind of the worthiness and use of the Sacrament, how great comfort it bringeth to those who repent, that men may learn both to fear God and to believe, and may practice invocation, and seek for and expect good things from him. This is the true worship of Christians; these services, fear, faith, prayer, hope, etc., God approveth. When, therefore, these services are performed in the use of ceremonies, then doth the use of the Sacrament please God.

When, therefore, the people are accustomed to the ceremony, and advised of its use, masses are said with us after a meet and godly manner; and all things are done in the Church with greater gravity and reverence than in times past.

It is not unknown that these many ages past there hath been public complaint made by good men of the profanation and abuse of masses. For it is easy to be seen how far this abuse hath spread itself in all churches; what kind of men they are that say the masses, contrary to the prohibition of the canons; also how shamefully they are turned to sacrilegious lucre; for there be very many that say masses without repentance, only for the belly's sake. These things are too well known to be passed by unnoticed. Neither from the beginning of the world doth any divine thing appear to be so commonly turned into gain as the mass. But St. Paul doth fearfully threaten them who deal unworthily with the sacrament, when he saith: "Whosoever shall eat this bread, or drink this cup of the Lord unworthily, shall be guilty of the body and blood of the Lord" (1 Cor. 11:27). And in the Decalogue it is written: "He that abuseth God's name shall not be unpunished" (Ex. 20:7). As, therefore the world hath oft at other times been punished for idolatry, so doubtless this enormous profaning of masses will be punished with most grievous penalties; and, perhaps chiefly for this reason, the Church, in these last times, is punished with blindness, discords, wars, and many other plagues. And these manifest abuses, the bishops, although they were not indeed ignorant of them, have thus far not only tolerated, but also mildly smiled at. Now too late they begin to complain of the calamities of the Church, although nothing else hath afforded occasion to the tumults of these times but the abuses themselves, which were already so manifest that they could no longer be tolerated by moderate men. Of what the bishops, in accordance with their office, had, before these times, restrained the avarice and impudence, whether of monks or of others, who, changing the manner of the ancient Church, have made the mass a money-matter!

But we will declare from what source these abuses have originated. The opinion hath been spread abroad in the Church that the Lord's Supper is a work which, celebrated by the priest, meriteth remission of sins, of the guilty and punishment, to him that doeth it and to others; and that, because of the work done, without any good affection of the one using it; also that when applied, on behalf of the dead, it is satisfactory, that is, it meriteth to them remission of the punishment of purgatory. Thus they interpret the word *sacrifice*, when they call the mass a sacrifice, viz. a work, which, when applied on behalf of others, meriteth for them remission of guilt and punishments, and that, because of the work done, without any good affection of the one using it. Thus they mean that offering is made for the living and the dead by the priest in the mass. And after this persuasion was once received, they taught men to seek forgiveness of sins, and good things of every kind, yea to free the dead from punishment by the benefit of the mass. Nor did it make any difference by what sort of men the masses were said, because they taught that they were available for others without good affection of the user. Afterwards a question arose, whether one mass said for many were as available as one said separately for a particular individual. This disputation infinitely increased both the number of masses and the gain; but we are not now disputing concerning the gain, we are only accusing their impiety. For our divines teach that this opinion of the merit and application of the mass is false and godless. This is the state of this controversy. And judgment concerning this case is easy to the godly, if any one will weigh the arguments that follow.

First. We have above shown that men obtain forgiveness of sins freely by faith, that is, by confidence in mercy for Christ's sake; therefore, it is impossible to obtain forgiveness of sins on account of the work of another, and that without a good affection; that is, without faith of one's own. This reason very clearly refuteth that monstrous and godless opinion concerning the merit and application of the mass.

Secondly. Christ's passion was an oblation and satisfaction, not only for the original fault, but for all other sins; as it is written in the Epistle to the Hebrews: "We are sanctified by the offering of Jesus Christ, once for all;" also: "By one offering he hath perfected for ever them that are sanctified" (Heb. 10:10, 14). In short, a good part of the Epistle to the Hebrews is devoted to confirming the position that only the sacrifice of Christ hath merited the forgiveness of sins or reconciliation for others. He saith that the Levitical sacrifices were ofttimes offered for the reason that they did not take away sins, but that by the sacrifice of Christ satisfaction hath been made for the sins of all. This honor of Christ's sacrifice ought not to be transferred to the work of a priest. For he saith expressly that, by one offering, the saints are made perfect. Besides, it is a godless thing to transfer to the work of a priest the confidence which ought to be placed in Christ's offering and intercession.

Thirdly. In the institution of the Lord's Supper, Christ doth not command the priests to offer for others, whether quick or dead. Upon what authority, then, was this worship instituted in the Church, without God's command, as an offering for sins? Much more absurd is it that the mass is applied to deliver the souls of the dead. For the mass was instituted for remembrance, that is, that those receiving the Lord's Supper should stir up and confirm their faith and comfort their distressed consciences by the remembrance of Christ's benefits. Neither is the mass a satisfaction for punishment, but it was instituted on account of the remission of the fault—namely, not that it should be a satisfaction for the fault, but that it might be a sacrament, by the use whereof we might be put in mind of the benefit of Christ and the forgiveness of the fault. Since, therefore, the application of the Lord's Supper for liberating the dead hath been received without warrant of Scripture, yea contrary to Scripture, it is to be condemned as a new and ungodly worship.   .

Fourthly. In the New Covenant a ceremony without faith meriteth nothing either for him that useth it or for others. For it is a dead work, according to the saying of Christ: "True worshippers shall worship the Father in spirit and in truth" (John 4:24). The eleventh chapter to the Hebrews throughout proveth the same: "By faith Abel offered a more excellent sacrifice" (v. 4). Also: "Without faith it is impossible to please him" (v. 6). Therefore the mass doth not merit remission of the fault, or of the punishment, for the work's sake performed. This reason doth evidently overthrow the merit, as they call it, which ariseth of the work that is done.

Fifthly. The applying of the benefit of Christ is by a man's own faith; as Paul witnesseth (Rom. 3:25): "Whom God hath set forth to be a propitiation through faith in his blood." And this applying is made freely. Therefore the application is not made by or on account of another man's work. For when we use the Sacrament the application is made by our own work and our own faith, and not by another man's work. For if the remission of sins would not become ours but by applying of the masses, it would be uncertain, and our confidence should be transferred from Christ to the work of a priest; and this has come to pass, as is manifest. Moreover, confidence placed in the work of a man hath been condemned. These arguments and many others testify that the opinion of the merit and applying of the mass for the quick and the dead was necessarily reproved. Now, if it will be considered how widely this error hath been spread, how the number of masses hath increased by this persuasion, how, by this sacrifice, remission of the fault and of the punishment hath been promised the quick and the dead, it will be apparent that, on account of this profanation, the Church hath been disfigured with dreadful sins. Never, O most worthy Emperor, hath a more important or more worthy case occurred concerning which learned and good men should carefully deliberate. It is the duty of all the godly to beseech God with most fervent prayers that the Church be delivered from these sins; and all kings and bishops should endeavor with all their might, that, when this entire matter hath been rightly explained, the Church may be cleansed.

Sixthly. The institution of the Sacrament conflicts with that abuse. For there is no injunction concerning an offering for the sins of the quick and the dead, but it is enjoined that the Body and Blood of the Lord be taken, and that this be done in remembrance of Christ's benefit. This remembrance signifieth, however, not a bare representation of the history, as it were in a show (as they dream who maintain that merit is gained from the work wrought), but it signifieth by faith to remember the promise and benefit, to comfort the conscience, and to render thanks for so great a benefit. For the principal cause of the institution is, that faith may be there excited and exercised when we receive this pledge of grace. Besides, the institution ordaineth that there be a communication, that is, that the ministers of the Church should offer to others also the Lord's Body and Blood. And that this custom was observed in the primitive Church, St. Paul heareth witness to the Corinthians, who commandeth also that one tarry for another (1 Cor. 11:33), that there may be a common partaking.

Therefore, since the abuses of private mass have been discovered, because they all for the most part were used on account of the application for the sins of others, and do not agree with the institution of Christ, they have ceased in our churches. Moreover, one common mass was appointed according to the institution of Christ, wherein pastors of churches consecrate, take and administer to others the Sacrament of the Body and Blood of Christ. Such mass is used on every holy day, and on other days also if any desire to use the Sacrament. Neither are any admitted to the communion, except they first be proved. Godly discourses also are added just as Christ has

commanded that there should be discourses when this ceremony is
employed. And in these discourses men are not only diligently
taught concerning other articles and precepts of the Gospel, but
also are admonished for what use the Sacrament was instituted—
to wit, not that this ceremony should merit for them remission of
sins by the bare work done, but that the Sacrament should be a testimony and a pledge, whereby Christ doth testify that he giveth the
things promised to us, and that this promises pertain to us; that
Christ tendereth to us his Body, to testify that he is efficacious in us.
as in his members; that he tendereth his Blood, to testify that we
are washed with his Blood. The Sacrament, therefore, doth profit
them who repent and seek comfort therein, and, being confirmed by
this testimony, believe that the forgiveness of sins is truly granted
them, and are thankful unto Christ for so great a benefit. Thus the
application of Christ's benefit is made, not on account of the work
of another, but by every man's own faith and his own use of the
Sacrament; for when we ourselves use it Christ's institution itself
testifieth that the benefit of the Gospel pertaineth to us.

Such a use of the Sacrament is godly and to be taught in the
churches, as it both illustrateth the doctrine of faith, and of spiritual
exercises, and of true worship, and bringeth to godly consciences
great comfort, and encourageth faith. Before these times the churches
were taught far otherwise concerning the use of the Sacrament. Nothing was propounded except this work was to be done; but no one
taught anything of faith or of the comfort of consciences. And consciences were racked with immoderate care in making confession.
This they thought to be the purity which the Gospel requireth, although
the Gospel requireth true fear and true trust, and comforteth
us by the use of this Sacrament, that they who repent may assuredly
believe that, for Christ's sake, God is propitious, even though nature
is frail and impure, and even though this inchoate obedience of ours
is far distant from the perfection of the law.

From all this it is sufficiently clear that the mass among us
agreeth with the instiution of Christ and the manner of the primitive
Church. Besides, it especially illustrates the true use of the Sacrament. Such a common mass was there in the Church of old time,
as Chrysostom testifieth, who saith that "the priest doth stand at
the altar, and call some unto the communion and put back others."
And by the Decrees of the Nicene Synod it is evident that some
one celebrated the Liturgy, as the Greeks call it, and did minister

the Body and Blood of the Lord to all the rest. For these are the words of the decree: "Let the deacons in their order, after the elders, receive the Holy Communion of a bishop or of an elder." Here it doth expressly say that the elders received the Sacrament from some one that ministered it. Neither is there any mention of a private mass before the times of Gregory; but as oft as the old writers speak of the mass it is evident that they speak of a mass that was common. Since, therefore, the rite of the mass among us hath the authority of Scripture and the example of the ancient Church, and only some intolerable abuses have been rejected, we hope that the custom of our churches be not disapproved. Other indifferent rites are, in great part, observed in the usual manner, but the number of masses is not alike. Neither in times past, in the churches whereunto was greatest resort, was the mass said daily, as the Tripartite History, lib. ix., cap. 38, testifieth: "Again, in Alexandria, every fourth and sixth day of the week, the Scriptures are read, and the doctors do interpret them; and all other things are done also, except only the celebration of the Eucharist."

54. REPETITIO CONFESSIONIS AUGUSTANAE, 1551[56]
(Confessio Saxonica)*

Of the Holy Supper of the Lord. Both Baptism and the Supper of the Lord are pledges and testimonies of grace, as was said before, which do admonish us of the promise and of our whole redemption and do show that the benefits of the Gospel do pertain to every one of those that use these ceremonies. But yet here is the difference: by baptism every one is ingrafted into the Church; but the Lord would have the Supper of the Lord to be also the sinew of the public congregation. God will have the ministry of His Gospel to be public, He will not have the voice of the Gospel to be shut up in corners only, but He will have it to be heard, He will have Himself to be known and invocated of all mankind. Therefore He would that there should be public and well ordered meetings, and in these He will have the voice of the Gospel to be heard; there He will be invocated and praised. Also He wills that these meetings should be witnesses of the confession and severing of the Church of God from

---

*The Confessio Saxonica and the Confessio Wuerttembergica were published in English in 1586; we give the strange English of this translation, modernizing only the spelling, not, however, the capitalization.

the sects and opinions of other nations. John assembled his flock
at Ephesus and taught the Gospel. And by the use of the sacraments
the whole company did declare that they embraced this doctrine and
did invocate this God who delivered the Gospel and that they were
separated from the worshippers of Diana, Jupiter and other idols.
For God will be seen, and have His Church heard in the world, and
have it distinguished by many public signs from other nations. So
no doubt the first fathers, Adam, Seth, Enoch, Noah, Shem, Abraham,
had their meetings; and afterward the civil government of Israel
had many rites, that their separation from the gentiles might be more
evident. Also God gave a peculiar promise to His congregation,
Matt. 18. "Wheresoever two or three are gathered together in my
name, there am I in the midst of them." Also, "Whatsoever they agree-
ing together shall desire, it shall be done to them." And in the 149th
Psalm, "His praise is in the congregation of saints." And the promises, wherein God does affirm that He will preserve His Church,
are so much the sweeter, because we know that He does preserve
and restore the public ministry in well ordered meetings; as also
in the very words of the Supper this promise is included. where He
commands that the death of the Lord should be shown forth, and
His Supper distributed till He come. That therefore we may use
this Sacrament with the greater reverence, let the true causes of
the institution thereof be well weighted, which pertain to the public
congregation, and to the comfort of every one. The first cause is
this: The Son of God will have the voice of His Gospel to sound
in a public congregation, and such a one as is of good behavior;
the bond of this congregation He will have this receiving to be, which
is to be done with great reverence, seeing that there a testimony
is given of the wonderful conjunction between the Lord and the
receivers; of which reverence Paul speaks, 1 Cor. 11, saying, "He
that receives unworthily shall be guilty of the body and blood of
the Lord." Secondly: God will have both the sermon and the ceremony itself to be profitable, both for the preservation and also for
the propagation of the memory of His Passion, resurrection and
benefits. Thirdly: He will have every receiver to be singularly confirmed by this testimony, that he may assure himself that the benefits of the Gospel do pertain to him, seeing that the sermon is common; and by this testimony and by this receiving He shows that
you are a member of His, and that you are washed in His blood,
and that He makes this covenant with you. John 15, "Abide in me,

and I in you." Also, "I in them and they in me." Fourthly: He will
have this public receiving to be a public confession whereby you may
show what kind of doctrine you do embrace and to what company
you do join yourself. Also He will have us give thanks publicly and
privately in this very ceremony to God the eternal Father, and to
the Son, and to the Holy Ghost, both for other benefits, and namely
for this infinite benefit of our redemption and salvation. Also He
wills that the members of the Church should have a bond of mutual
love among themselves. Thus we see that many ends do meet together. By the remembrance of these weighty causes, men are invited
to the reverence and use of the Sacrament; and we teach how the
use may be profitable. We do plainly condemn that monstrous error
of the monks, who have written that the receiving does deserve remission of sins, and that for the work's sake, without any good motion
of him that uses it. This Pharisaical imagination is contrary to
the saying, Hab. 2, "The just shall live by his faith." Therefore we
do thus instruct the Church, that they which will approach to the
Supper of the Lord, must repent or bring conversion with them,
and having their faith now kindled, they must here seek the confirmation of this faith in the consideration of the death and resurrection and benefits of the Son of God; because that in the use of
this Sacrament, there is a witness bearing which declares that the
benefits of the Son of God do pertain to you also; also there is a
testimony that He joins you as a member to Himself, and that He
is in you, as He said John 17, "I in them etc." Therefore we give
counsel that men do not think that their sins are forgiven them for
this work's sake, or for this obedience; but that in a sure confidence
they behold the death and merit of the Son of God and His resurrection, and assure themselves that their sins are forgiven for His
sake and that He will have this faith to be confirmed by this admonition and witness bearing; when as faith, comfort, the joy of conscience
and thanksgiving do after this sort increase, the receiving is profitable. Neither are any admitted to the Communion, except they be
first heard and absolved of the pastor or his fellow ministers. In
this trial the ruder sort are asked and oftentimes instructed touching
the whole doctrine and then is absolution published.

Also men are taught that sacraments are actions instituted of
God, and that without the use whereunto they are ordained the things
themselves are not to be accounted for a sacrament; but in the use
appointed, Christ is present in this communion, truly and substan-

tially, and the body and blood of Christ is indeed given to the receivers; that Christ does witness that He is in them and does make them His members and that He does wash them in His blood, as Hilary also says, "These things being eaten and drunk do cause both that we may be in Christ and that Christ may be in us." Moreover, in the ceremony itself we observe the usual order of the whole ancient Church, both Latin and Greek. We use no private masses, that is, such wherein the body and blood of Christ is not distributed; as also the ancient Church, for many years after the Apostles' times had no such masses, as the old descriptions which are to be found in Dionysius, Epiphanius, Ambrose, Augustine, and others do show. And Paul, 1 Cor. 11, does command that the Communion should be celebrated when many do meet together. Therefore in the public congregation and such as is of good behavior, prayers and the creed are rehearsed or sung and lessons appointed usually for holy days are read. After that there is a sermon of the benefits of the Son of God and of some part of doctrine, as the order of time does minister an argument. Then the pastor does rehearse a thanksgiving and a prayer for the whole Church, for them that are in authority, and as the present necessity requires; and he prays to God, that for His Son's sake whom He would have to be made a sacrifice for us, He would forgive us our sins and save us and gather and preserve a Church. Then He rehearses the words of Christ concerning the institution of the Supper, and he himself takes and distributes to the receivers the whole Sacrament, who come reverently thereunto, being before examined and absolved, and there they join theirs with the public prayers. In the end they do again give thanks. All men who are not altogether ignorant of antiquity, do know that this rite and this Communion do for the most part agree with the writings of the Apostles and with the custom of the ancient Church, even almost to Gregory's time; which thing being so, the custom of our church is to be approved, not to be disallowed. But our adversaries misliking our custom do defend many errors, come more foul and gross, others colored with new deceits.

Many heretofore have written that in the mass there is an oblation made for the quick and the dead, and that it does deserve remission of sins both for him that makes it and for others, even for the work's sake. And thus were most of them persuaded and as yet are like unto the Pharisees and the heathen. For after the same manner the Pharisees and the heathen did dream that they for the work's sake did deserve for themselves and for others remission of sins, peace and many other good things. Or, although those which were not so blind did speak more modestly and said that they did deserve, but not without the good intention of the sacrificer, yet they imagined that those sacrifices were merits and a ransom. By reason of this opinion there were a multitude of sacrifices and the crafty means of gain were increased. Such is the merchandise of masses and the profanation of the Lord's Supper almost throughout the whole world. But God will have corrupt kinds of worship to be reproved and abolished. Therefore we do simply and indeed propound the voice of God which does condemn those errors, and with all our heart we affirm before God and the whole Church in heaven and in earth that there was one only sacrifice propitiary, or whereby the wrath of the eternal Father against mankind is pacified, to wit, the whole obedience of the Son of God, our Lord Jesus Christ, who was crucified and raised up again. This is that only "Lamb which taketh away the sins of the world," John 1. Of this only sacrifice mention is made, Hebrews 10, "By one offering He hath perfected for ever them that are sanctified." And this sacrifice is applied to every one by their own faith when they hear the Gospel and use the sacraments, as Paul says, Rom. 3, "Whom God hath set forth to be a propitiation through faith in His blood." And Hab. 2, "The just shall live by his faith." And 1 Pet. 1, "Elect through sanctification of the Spirit unto obedience and sprinkling of the blood of Jesus Christ." Other sacraments in the Old Testament were typical, whereof we shall speak more at large in their place, and they did not deserve any remission of sins; and all the righteousness of holy men at all times were, are and shall be sacrifices of praise which do not deserve remission, either for them that did offer them, or for others. But they are services which every one ought to perform, and are acceptable to God for the Mediator's and our High Priest the Son of God's sake, as it is said, Heb. 13, "By Him let us offer the sacrifice of praise to God continually."

That this is an unchangeable and eternal truth is most manifest. And whereas certain fragments which they call the canons of the mass, are alleged against this so clear light of the truth, it is also manifest that the Greek and Latin canons are very unlike one to the other and that the Greek canons do disagree among themselves in a most weighty matter; and it appears that in the Latin canon many iagges and pecces were little by little patched together of ignorant authors. The ancient Church does use the names of sacrifice and oblation; but thereby it understands the whole action, prayers, a taking of it, a remembrance. faith, a confession and thanksgiving. This whole inward and outward action in every one that is turned to God and in the whole Church is indeed a sacrifice of praise or thanksgiving and a reasonable service. And when the Lord says, John 4, "The true worshippers shall worship the Father in spirit and in truth," He affirms that in the New Testament outward sacrifices are not commanded, which of necessity should be made, although there were no motions of the Holy Ghost in the heart, as in the Law it is necessary that the ceremony of the Passover should be kept. But touching the Supper of the Lord it is said, 1 Cor. 11, "Let every man examine himself, etc." So the Supper of the Lord does profit him that uses it when as he brings with him repentance and faith, and another man's work does not at all profit him.

Furthermore, concerning the dead, it is manifest that all this show is repugnant to the words of the institution of the Supper wherein it is said. "Take. eat. etc. This do in remembrance of me." What does this appertain to the dead or to those that are absent? And yet in a great part of Europe many masses are said for the dead; also a great number not knowing what they do, do read masses for a reward. But seeing that all these things are manifestly wicked, to wit, to offer, as they speak, to the end that they may deserve for the quick and the dead; or for a man to do he knows not what, they do horrible sin, that retain and defend these mischievous deeds. And seeing that this ceremony is not to be taken for a sacrament without the use whereunto it was ordained, what manner of idol worship is there used, let godly and learned men consider. Also it is a manifest profanation to carry about part of the Supper of the Lord and to worship it; where a part is utterly transferred to a use clean contrary to the first institution, whereas the text says, "Take, eat"; and this show is but a thing devised of late. To conclude, what are the manners of many priests and monks in all Europe who have no regard for this saying. 1 Cor. 11, "Let a man examine himself," also, "Whosoever shall eat and drink unworthily, shall be guilty of the body and the blood of the Lord." Every man of himself does know these things.

Now. although the chief bishops and hypocrites who seek delusions to establish these evils, do scoff at these complaints, yet it is most certain that God is grievously offended with these wicked

deeds, as He was angry with the people of Israel for their profanation
of the sacrifices. And we do see evident examples of wrath, to
wit the ruins of so many kingdoms, the spoil and waste that the
Turks do make in the world, the confusions of opinions, and many
most lamentable dissipations of churches. But O Son of God, Lord
Jesus Christ, who was crucified and raised up again for us. Thou
who art the High Priest of the Church, with true sighs we beseech
Thee, that for Thine and Thine eternal Father's glory, Thou wouldst take
away idols, errors and abominations, and; as Thou Thyself didst
pray, sanctify us with Thy truth, and kindle the light of Thy Gospel
and true invocations in the hearts of many, and bow our hearts to
true obedience, that we may thankfully praise Thee in all eternity.
The greatness of our sins, which the profanation of the Supper of
the Lord these many years hath brought forth doth surpass the elo-
quence of angels and men. We are herein the shorter, seeing that
no words can be devised sufficient to set out the greatness of this
thing, and in this great grief we beseech the Son of God that He
would amend these evils, and also for a further declaration we offer
ourselves to them that will hear it. But in this question we see that
to be chiefly done which Solomon says, "As vinegar upon nitre, so is he
that singeth songs to a wicked heart."

Our adversaries know that these persuasions of their sacrifice
are the sinews of their power and riches. therefore they will hear
nothing that is said against it. Some of them do now learn craftily
to mitigate these things, and therefore they say, the oblation is not
a merit, but an application. They deceive in words and retain still
the same abuses. But we said before that everybody does by faith
apply the sacrifice of Christ to himself, both when he hears the
Gospel and then also when he uses the sacraments; and it is written,
1 Cor. 11, "Let a man examine himself." Therefore Paul does not
mean that the ceremony does profit another that does not use it.
And the Son of God Himself did offer up Himself, going into the
holy of holies, that is, into the secret council of the Divinity, seeing
the will of the eternal Father, and bearing His great wrath, and
understanding the causes of this wonderful council; these weighty
things are meant when the text says, Heb. 9 "He offered Himself,"
and when Isaiah says, Chap. 53, "Thou shalt make His soul an
offering for sin." Now therefore what do the priests mean who say
that they offer up Christ? And yet antiquity never spoke after

418* Collection of Sources

this manner. But they do most grievously accuse us. They say that we do take away the continual sacrifice as did Antiochus who was a type of Antichrist. We answered before that we do retain the whole ceremony of the Apostolic Church; and this is the continual sacrifice, that the sincere doctrine of the Gospel should be heard, that God should be truly invocated; to conclude, as the Lord says, John 4, "Worship the Father in spirit and in truth." We do also herein comprehend the true use of the sacraments. Seeing that we retain all these things faithfully, we do with great reverence retail the continual sacrifice, they do abolish it who many ways do corrupt true invocation and the very Supper of the Lord, who command us to invocate dead men, who set out masses to sale, who boast that by their oblation they do merit for others, who do mingle many mischievous errors with the doctrine of repentance and remission of sins, who will men to doubt, when they repent, whether they are in favor, who defile the Church of God with filthy lusts and idols. These men are like unto Antiochus, and not we, who endeavor to obey the Son of God who says, John 14, "If a man love me, he will keep my words."

Of the use of the whole Sacrament. Let sophistry be removed from the judgments of the Church. All men know that the Supper of the Lord is so instituted that the whole Sacrament may be given to the people, as it is written, "Drink ye all of it." Also the custom of the ancient Church, both Greek and Latin is well known. Therefore we must confess that the forbidding of one part is an unjust thing. It is great injury to violate the lawful testaments of men; why then do the bishops violate the testament of the Son of God which he has sealed up with His own blood? But it is to be lamented that certain men should be so impudent as to feign sophistry against this so weighty an argument that they may establish their prohibition, the refutation of whom, the matter being so clear and evident, we do omit.

---

55. REPETITIO CONFESSIONIS AUGUSTANAE, 1551[57]
(Confessio Wuerttembergica)*

Of the Eucharist. We believe and confess that the Eucharist (for so it pleased our forefathers to call the Supper of the Lord)

---

*Compare note to No. 54.

is a sacrament instituted by Christ Himself, and that the use thereof
is commended to the Church, even to the latter end of the world.
But because the substance is one thing, and the use thereof another
thing, therefore we will speak of these in order. Touching the substance of the Eucharist, we thus think and teach, that the true
Body of Christ and His true Blood is distributed in the Eucharist;
and we refute them that say that the bread and wine of the Eucharist
are signs of the Body and Blood of Christ being only absent. Also
we believe that the omnipotence of God is so great, that in the
Eucharist He may either annihilate the substance of bread and wine,
or else change them into the Body and Blood of Christ; but that
God does exercise this His absolute omnipotence in the Eucharist,
is not shown by any clear statement of Scripture, and it is evident that
the ancient Church was altogether ignorant of it. For as in Ezek.
where it is of the City of Jerusalem, inscribed on the outside of a wall,
"This is Jerusalem," it was not necessary that the substance of
the wall should be changed into the substance of the City of Jerusalem; so when it is said of the bread, "This is my body," it is
not necessary that the substance of bread should be changed into
the substance of the Body of Christ; but for the truth of the Sacrament
it is sufficient that the Body of Christ is indeed present with the bread.
And indeed the very necessity of the truth of the Sacrament does
seem to require that true bread should remain with the true presence
of the Body of Christ. For as to the truth of the sacrament of Baptism it is necessary that in the use thereof there should be water
and that true water should remain, so it is necessary in the Lord's
Supper that there should be bread and the use thereof and that true
bread should remain; Whereas, if the substance of bread should be
changed, we should have no proof of the truth of the Sacrament.
Whereupon both Paul and also the ancient ecclesiastical writers
do call the bread of the Eucharist even after consecration, bread.
1 Cor. 11, "Let a man examine himself, and so let him eat of that
bread, etc." And, "Whosoever shall eat this bread, and drink this
cup of the Lord unworthily, etc." And Augustine in his sermon to
young children says, "That which you have seen, is the bread,
and the cup, the which thing also your eyes do witness unto you;
but that which your faith desires to learn is this: the bread is the
Body of Christ, the cup is His Blood."

Now, as touching the use of the Eucharist, *first,* although we
do not deny but that whole Christ is distributed as well in the

bread as in the wine of the Eucharist, yet we teach that the use of
either part ought to be common to the whole Church. For it is
evident that Christ being nothing at all terrified by any dangers,
which afterward human superstition invented, or by other devices,
gave unto His Church both parts to be used. Also it is evident that
the ancient Church did use both parts for many years. And certain
writers do clearly witness that "They which do receive bread alone,
do not receive the whole Sacrament sacramentally (for so they speak)
and that it is not possible to divide one and the self-same mystery
without great sacrilege." Wherefore we think that the use of both
parts is indeed Catholic and Apostolic, and that it is not lawful for
any man at his pleasure to change this institution of Christ, and
a ceremony of such continuance in the ancient and true Church, and
to take away from the laity, as they call them, one part of the
Eucharist. And it is to be marveled at that they who profess them
selves to defend the ceremonies of the ancient Church should so far
swerve from the ancient Church in this point. Moreover, seeing
that the word "sacrifice" is very large, and does generally signify
a holy worship, we do willingly grant that the true and lawful use
of the Eucharist may in this sense be called a sacrifice; howbeit
the Eucharist, according to the institution of Christ, is so celebrated
that therein the death of Christ is shown forth, and the Sacrament
of the Body and the Blood of Christ is distributed to the Church,
and so it is truly an applying of the merit of the Passion of Christ,
to wit, to them which receive the Sacrament.

Neither do we condemn godly lessons and prayers which use
to go before and to follow consecration, as they call it, and the
dispensation of the Eucharist. Yet in the meantime it is not lawful
for us to dissemble, or to allow of those errors which have been
added to this holy Sacrament rather by the ignorance of private men
than by any lawful consent of the true Catholic Church. One error
is this, that of the worship which ought to be common to the Church,
there is made a private action of one priest who as he does alone
to himself mumble up the words of the Lord's Supper, so also he
alone does receive the bread and wine. For Christ did institute
the Eucharist, not that it should be a private action of one man,
but that it should be a communion of the Church. Therefore to
the right action of the Eucharist two things at the least are requisite,
to wit, the minister of the Eucharist who blesses, and he to whom
the Sacrament of the Eucharist is dispensed. For when Christ did

institute this Sacrament, He did not eat thereof alone, but He did dispense it to His Church, which then was present with Him, saying, "Take, eat, etc." and "Drink ye all of it, etc." This institution of Christ the ancient and true Catholic Church did so severely observe that it excommunicated them which being present while this holy Sacrament was administered, would not communicate with the others. Anacletus in his first epistle says, "After that consecration is finished, let all communicate, except they had rather stand without the church doors." And he adds, "For so both the Apostles appointed, and the holy Church of Rome keeps it still." Also the Antiochian Council, chap. 2, says, "All those which come into the Church of God and hear the Holy Scriptures but do not communicate with the people in prayer and can not abide to receive the Sacrament of the Lord, according to a certain proper discipline, these men must be cast out of the Church." Dionysius in his book, "De Eccles. Hierarc." says, "The bishop when he has praised the divine gifts, then he makes the holy and most excellent mysteries and those things which before he had praised. being covered and hid under reverent signs, he brings into sight, and reverently showing forth the divine gifts, both he himself does turn to the holy participation thereof, and does exhort the others to participate them. To conclude, when the holy Communion is received and delivered to all, he rendering thanks, does make an end of these mysteries." Therefore we think it necessary to the retaining of the institution of Christ in the celebration of the Eucharist, and that we may follow the example of the ancient and true Catholic Church, that the private masses of the priests may be abrogated, and that the public communion of the Lord's Supper may be restored.

Another error is this, that the Eucharist is such a sacrifice, as ought to be offered daily in the Church for the purging of the sins of the quick and the dead and for the obtaining of other benefits, both corporal and spiritual. This error is evidently contrary to the Gospel of Christ which witnesses, "That Christ by one offering once only made. hath perfected for ever them that are sanctified." And because that Christ by His Passion and death has purchased remission of sins for us, which also is declared unto us by the Gospel in the New Testament. therefore it is not lawful to sacrifice any more for sin; for the Epistle to the Hebrews says, "Where there is remission of sins. there is no more offering for sin." And whereas Christ says, "This do in remembrance of me," He does not command to offer His body and blood in the Supper unto God, but to the Church that the Church by eating the body and drinking the blood of Christ and by showing forth the benefit of His death may be admonished of that oblation of the body and the blood of Christ which was made once only on the cross for the purging of our sins. For so Paul does interpret this saying of Christ, saying, "For so often as ye eat (he does not say, offer) this bread, and drink this cup, ye do show the Lord's death till He come." And truly we confess that the ancient ecclesiastical writers did call the Eucharist a "sacrifice," an oblation; but they expound themselves that by the name of sacrifice they mean a remembrance, a showing forth or a preaching of that sacrifice which Christ did once offer upon the cross; as also they called the memorial of the Passover and of Pentecost, the Passover and Pentecost itself.

The *third* error is this, that many do think that the Oblation (as they call it) of the Eucharist is not of itself a propitiation for sins, but that it does apply the propitiation and merit of Christ to the quick and the dead. But we have already shown that the Eucharist properly is not an oblation, but is so called, because it is a remembrance of the oblation which was once made on the cross. Moreover, the application of the merit of Christ is not made by any other outward instrument than by the preaching of the Gospel of Christ, and by dispensing those sacraments which Christ has instituted for this use; and the merit of Christ being offered and applied is not received but by faith, Mark 16, "Preach the Gospel to every creature." For by the ministry of the Gospel the benefits of Christ are offered and applied to creatures, that is, either to the Jews or to the gentiles. And it follows. "He that believeth and is baptized shall be saved"; because that by the receiving of the sacraments and by faith the benefits offered and applied are received. Rom. 1, "The Gospel is the power of God unto salvation to every one that believeth"; that is, the ministry of the Gospel is the instrument ordained of God, whereby God is able and effectual to save all those that believe the Gospel. Therefore the preaching of the Gospel does offer, or, if it likes any man so to speak, does apply salvation to all men, but faith does receive salvation offered and applied. Now in the private mass, bread and wine are so handled, that the priest does neither publicly declare the Gospel of Christ, but does softly mumble up to himself certain words, and especially the words of the Supper or of consecration; neither does he distribute bread and wine to others, but he alone takes them. Therefore there can be no applying of the merit of Christ in the private mass. This did our true Catholic elders well perceive, who, as we have declared before, did so severely require that they which were present at the mass and did not communicate should be excommunicated.

The *fourth* error is this, which we have already touched, in that they do require that the words of the Supper or of consecration may be rehearsed softly in the Eucharist, seeing that these words are a part of that Gospel, which according to the commandment of Christ is to be preached to all creatures. For although our ancestors did sometimes call the Eucharist "a mystery," yet they did not so call it with this purpose that they would not have the words of the Supper to be rehearsed before the Church in the Eucharist, publicly and in a tongue known, but because that in the Eucharist one thing is seen and another thing understood. For Christ Himself also is called "a mystery," who nevertheless is not to be hid, but to be preached to all creatures. And because that in the receiving of the Sacrament it is necessarily required that we should have faith, and "faith cometh by hearing, and hearing by the word of God," it is most necessary that in the Eucharist the word of the Supper, that is, the word of the Son of God should be publicly rehearsed; for this word is the preaching of the Gospel and the showing forth of the death of Christ. Therefore that the Church may understand what is done in the Eucharist and what offered unto her to be received, and that she may confirm her faith, it is necessary that in the Eucharist the words of the Lord's Supper should be rehearsed publicly.

The *fifth* error is this, that one part of the Eucharist is used in show of a singular worship of God to be carried about and to be laid up. But the Holy Ghost does forbid that any worship of God should be appointed without the express commandment of God. Deut. 12. "You shall not do every man whatsoever is right in his own eyes." And again, "What things soever I command you, observe to do it; thou shalt not add thereto nor diminish from it." And Matt. 15, "In vain do they worship me, teaching for doctrines the commandments of men." Clement in his second epistle to James and in three chapters, "De Consecr. Dist." 2 says, "Certainly so great burnt offerings are offered on the altar as may be sufficient for the people; if so be that anything remain till the next day, let them not be kept, but with fear and trembling, by the diligence of the clerks let them be consumed." We are not ignorant, how they use to delude these words of Clement by feigning a difference between the work of those that are ready to die and those that are ready to consecrate. But it is evident that the bread which used to be carried about and to be laid up to be adored is not reserved for those that are weak, but in the end is received of them that do consecrate. Cyril, or as others think, Origen, upon the seventh Chap. of Levit. says, "For the Lord concerning that bread which He gave to His disciples, said unto them, Take it and eat it, etc. He did not differ it, neither did He command it to be reserved till the next day, Peradventure there is this mystery also contained therein, that He does not command the bread to be carried in the high way, that you may always bring forth the fresh loaves of the words of God which you carry within you. etc."

56. CONFESSIO BOHEMICA, MAY 18, 1575[58]

Article I. Concerning the Word of God as Contained in the Sacred Writings of the Old and the New Testament. We heartily believe and openly confess, that the sacred writings of the Old and the New Testament, which treat of the one, true Godhead and of the three distinct Persons in the one Godhead, likewise of the perfect will of God, are, without exception, unalterably true, holy, trustworthy, and catholic, that is, ordained and given by God for the whole Church to believe and hold; furthermore, that in the two covenants of the Old and New Testament is fully contained everything needful for our salvation, not in obscure form, but clear and undiminished.

This, the Son of God, Himself, confirms in the word (John 5: 39, 40) . . . To this must be added another saying. According to the narrative of Luke, (24:44), Jesus. Himself, said to the two disciples whom He joined on the road from Jerusalem to Emmaus, that He was spoken of in the law and the prophets, and the scriptures. The Lord also says, (Luke 11:28) . . . Likewise, (John 8:47): . . . As is written in the Gospel of John and as Jesus, Himself, says; the fulnes of the Godhead dwells in everyone who keeps the word of the Son of God (John 14, 23). And St. Paul says, Romans 1:16) . . .

All other doctrines, therefore, must unquestionably give way before this Word of God and give place to it, for they are not of like value and may and dare not be cloaked with the same authority as the Word of God, which is like unto a two-edged and piercing sword. For God, the Heavenly Father, hath spoken from Heaven concerning His Son. (Matt. 3:17). And in the Fifth Book of Moses is written (4:2) . . .

Article 4. Concerning the Fall of the First Man and Original Sin. We also believe and confess, that the first man, Adam, was created in perfect holiness and innocence, that, however, at the instigation of the devil, he, wholly uncoerced and solely of his own will, by transgressing the divine command, turned away from God and thereby loaded upon himself and all his descendants and the entire human race both temporal and eternal death and all things from which this twofold death doth spring. For all men, begotten according to nature from sinful Adam, are mortally conceived and born with sin, that is, not only with the frailty and weakness of the flesh, but with inner corruption and perversion of the whole man and all his powers, so that, following the loss of his original health, innocence, and righteousness, man henceforth is turned away from the good and, devoid of fear of God and trust in Him, lies in subjection to sin and inherited concupiscence. This is original sin. Because it is and remains sin in truth, it also calls down upon everyone, not reborn through baptism and the Holy Ghost, the wrath of God and finally the other death and eternal damnation.

Article 5. Concerning the Free Will of Men. Concerning the free will of man we confess, that man's will undoubtedly has some liberty for living an outwardly honorable and orderly life in all things subject to the choice of reason. Thus if man, in works of this kind, uses his reason, judgment, and all will for a resolve at variance with the divine law, he cannot find an excuse before God. But without the Holy Ghost, he has no power to work the righteousness pleasing to God, that is, spiritual righteousness, for natural man receiveth not the things of the spirit of God; but this righteousness is wrought in the heart when the Holy Ghost is received through the Word.

Article 8. Concerning the Justification of Man before God. Then, we believe and confess, that the justification of man before God consists in this, that God regards and declares the repentant sinner to be innocent, holy and just; that men cannot be justified before God by their own strength, merit, or works, but are freely justified purely by divine grace, solely for Christ's sake through faith in His blood, whereby by grace of the Holy Ghost they heartily believe and in no wise doubt, that God according to His faithful promises, forgives all their sin and receives them into His favor for the sake

of the Redeemer and Saviour, Jesus Christ, Who by His holy, perfect obedience and His bitter, innocent death hath humbled Himself
and made satisfaction for the sins of the whole world. Even this
faith alone in the Lord Christ and His merit God imputeth to perfect righteousness in His sight, as St. Paul writes, Romans 3 and 4.
For he who believes, by his faith obtains part in Jesus Christ and
thereby is made partaker of the full holiness and righteousness which
the Lord Christ owned and wrought for him and his sake, and which
He imparts to Him as His member. Therefore, faith is imputed
and ascribed as perfect righteousness to every believer and by reason
of this perfect righteousness in Christ, he is granted eternal life, whose
pledge is the Holy Ghost. This the Lord Christ Himself confirms,
John 6:47.

For the attainment of this saving faith in Christ Jesus, the
office of the ministry was instituted, to teach and proclaim the
Holy Gospel and administer the Holy Sacraments. For through
the Word of God and the Sacraments, as through instruments divinely
ordained, the Holy Ghost is given, Who worketh saving faith, where
and when it pleaseth God. in them that hear the Gospel, which teaches
that God, not for our own merits, but wholly for Christ's sake, receiveth into grace all who believe on Christ, justifieth and sanctifieth
them through his holy Spirit unto life eternal.

Thus sanctification, renewal, and regeneration of man are wrought
through faith and the Holy Ghost, when by faith we participate in
the Lord Jesus Christ and all His merit, and in this manner are
made wholly just before God. Hereby also, through fellowship
with the Lord Christ, the Holy Ghost is poured out in us, living
members of Christ's body, Who sanctifies and renews us, so that
we begin to be holy, to die unto all fleshly sins and evil lusts, to
live unto God and day by day recover in increasing measure that
holiness once lost by Adam, which one day we shall perfectly attain in the life eternal.

But this, our holiness, which the Holy Ghost hath commenced
in us is not yet perfect in this life. There remain in us until death
many failings and much weakness, also many transgressions by reason
of which we pray unceasingly: "Forgive us our trespasses." Thus
we are not yet perfectly holy before God in the holiness begun in
us by the Holy Ghost, nor can we be, according to the word of the
Lord Christ in the Gospel of Luke, 17:10, and John 1:8. And David
prays (Ps. 143:2) : . . . .

Accordingly, as said above, our justification before God is based solely and entirely on the Lord Christ and is attained only through faith, which was also taught by the ancient teachers of Holy Church. For Ambrose writes: Thus it is ordained by God, that whosoever believeth on Christ is saved without works alone by faith, whereby he freely receiveth the forgiveness of sin.

Article 9. Concerning Faith. Concerning faith we confess, in accordance with the Word of God: Faith consists in this, that man not only believes that God is and that he not only holds everything to be true. which God, out of His grace, has proclaimed to us and promised in His Word—for this the devils also believe, and tremble—but that through the Holy Ghost he implicitly trusts that the gracious promises of God concerning the forgiveness of sin and eternal salvation are meant for everyone who believes on the Lord Christ, thus also for himself in particular, and that according to these promises the everlasting God is ready to forgive for Christ's sake not only the sins of other sinners, but also his own, to receive Him into grace, and sanctify him through the Holy Ghost unto eternal life. Leaning on the enduring promises founded on Christ, he seeks for himself the greatest possible assurance of his election to eternal life and of his salvation, pledged in Christ. Through such a cordial faith and trust in God, he conquers all temptations and wins a lively comfort and peace with God. To this faith he takes confident refuge and cries, Abba, dear Father, as written by the apostle Paul. Romans 5:1.

Because saving faith, when born in man through the Holy Ghost, be it mighty or weak, apprehends the Lord Christ and all His works for us—for only on the one condition that we believe on Him and trust Him with all our heart, does He come to us—and thereby obtains for the believer forgiveness of sin, reconciliation with God, justification, regeneration through the Holy Ghost, and eternal life; it, therefore, is not and cannot be lifeless in man, but must ever work new, eternal life subdue all of man's evil lusts, and engender in his heart love toward God and his neighbor. Thus through love faith effects divers good and holy works, by which, like the tree by its fruits, it is truly known. As little as there can be fire without warmth and the sun without light, so little can there be a true faith, which has any part in Christ, without renewal of life and love, thus, without many good and holy works.

Article 10. Concerning Good works. Concerning good works

we confess: Those are truly good and holy works which God requires in His Word, which come out of faith and are fruits of the Holy Spirit, Gal. 5:22, 23. For all things done by them who are not led by the Word of God and true faith in Christ, or who have been forsaken by the Holy Ghost, all such things, though good and beautiful in the eyes of men, are detestable and hateful in God's sight and must be accounted sin, according to the word of the apostle, Romans 14:24 and Hebrews 11:6.

Therefore, good works, in the true sense, are wrought only by the children of God, who through faith in Christ have obtained all His merit and full salvation, consequently justification and renewal of life, and who, moved by the Spirit of God, do and keep whatsoever God hath ordered and commanded in His Word, according to the Word of Ezekiel 20:11 and of Matt. 15:9.

Such good works are pleasing to God—not however, because of any excellence or perfection in themselves. For there are none such, according to the word of the prophet Isaiah, where he speaks of his own works and those of the whole Church (Is. 64:6), but such works are pleasing to God for Christ's sake only in those men, who have first been justified by Jesus Christ through faith in Him and been made acceptable to God...

Then, we believe and confess, that we ought and are obliged to do good works for the following reasons: First. By reason of our salvation in Christ and of our justification and sanctification. For whosoever is justified in Christ and regenerated and sanctified through the Holy Ghost cannot do other than good works, because he has become a new creature in Christ Jesus to the end that he perform good works, Eph. 2., even as the sun can do no other than shine, because created by God to that end. wherefore, if an unrepentant life and evil works be found in a Christian, God's work is certainly put to naught and such a man can nevermore be called a child of God, who shall be saved.

Secondly. We ought to do good works, because of the divine command and the obedience we owe, according to divine ordinance . . .

Thirdly. We ought to do good works in order to preserve faith and retain a quiet and untroubled conscience before God. For if we omit to do good and sin against conscience, the Holy Ghost is troubled and driven out. Thus faith is lost, together with true religion. . . .

Fourthly. We ought to do good works in order to escape the

temporal and eternal punishment in body and soul, which God, in His divine righteousness, hath ordained for those who transgress His commandments. . . .

Fifthly. We ought to do good works by reason of our high and sacred vocation in Christ, for we, who have come to faith in Christ, are members of His holy body and temples of Gods spirit (1 Cor. 6:15, 19) and, therefore, Gods dear children (1 John 1:12). We ought to be holy, even as our God is holy. . . .

Sixthly. We ought to do good works in order to obtain the great and abundant reward, which God hath promised our good works, not because of their innate excellence and perfection, but for the sake of the Lord Christ, Whose members we are. . . .

Article 11. Concerning the Church of God. We believe and confess, that one holy and universal Church now is and always will exist, and that in this world she is the visible congregation of believing saints, who everywhere hold fast to the true and pure doctrine of Christ as, laid down faithfully and truly, by the holy evangelists and apostles in Christ's holy Gospel, and who, also, in the bond of love, are guided in all things by the precept and ordinances of their only, King, Bishop, and Head, Jesus Christ, and who observe His mysteries, commonly called sacraments, as instituted by Christ and observed by the evangelists and apostles of the Lord Christ and bequeathed by them in the Holy Scriptures.

Now the Church properly is the Congregation of Saints, who through the ministration of the pure Word and the holy Sacraments, whereby they believe on Christ, have become one body with Him, and, in the communion of one faith, one love, and one spirit, lead a truly spiritual life. Nevertheless, since here on earth, are mingled with the saints many hypocrites, who confess the same truth and who, therefore, frequently cannot be distinguished from the believers and cast out from the Church, we understand under Church, in this life, the whole body of Christians, good and bad, who avow Christ and His law. The Church must be likened to the wheat, mixed with tares, and to the net which encloses both good and bad fish (Matt. 13).

However, this association of good and bad may be called the Catholic, Christian, and Holy Church only in consideration of the good fish and the wheat, that is the chosen children of God and the truly believing Christians, who are, without exception, holy by reason of the righteousness imputed to them in Christ and begun in them by the Holy Ghost. These only God calls His sheep. Their

community is in truth the Bride of Christ. the House of God, the
Pillar and Foundation of the Truth, the Mother of all Believers,
and the only Ark, outside of which there is no salvation. Those,
however, who merely adhere to the Church, especially all notorious
hypocrites and other evil and impious Christians, who continue in
the Church and generally make up the majority, these and their like
cannot be called the holy Church in the real sense, but merely her
dead members. Even though found in the Church of Christ, they
by no means, belong to the Church of His body.

Therefore, of all the true and infallible marks of Holy Church,
these are the most essential: First, the pure teaching and preaching
of God's Word and the Holy Gospel especially in respect to the
fundamentals and the principal articles of the Catholic Christian
faith. Secondly, the pure preservation, admonition, and observance
of the Lord's sacraments, as instituted by Himself. Thirdly, due
and meet obedience in the observance of all things, commanded by
the Holy Gospel and the precepts of Christ.

Beside these marks of God's Church are still others: brotherly
love, one toward the other, as members of Christ; much cross and
trial for truth's sake and God's kingdom, and, finally, the restraint
of open crime and sin against God, both, through friendly, brotherly
admonition and rebuke and also through the divinely appointed, orderly act of expulsion from the Christian Church, of those who would
not suffer themselves to be corrected by previous warning. This,
the holy fathers called church discipline.

However, the infallible marks of God's Church are not always
found in like evidence. At times they shine forth exceptionally
brightly, at times, however, they are so little discernible, that the
true Church can hardly be recognized. This is the case especially
then, when God thinks to chastise and purge the Church by taking
away the light of His Word and because of the Church's ingratitude
and contempt of His Word and benefits, by sending men, who lustily
disseminate error and reject the Word of the living God and build
the Church upon themselves and their traditions to their own glory.
Yet, the pious, even in such times of seduction and darkness in the
Church, cannot stray from her, if they will only look on the Head
of the Church, the Lord Christ; receive His Word in faith whereever
it is preached in truth and purity according to Holy Scriptures, and
deviate in no wise, either in doctrine or life, from His truth.

For wherever the Word of the Lord Christ is thus preached to the faithful and the Holy Sacraments are thus administered, there is certainly a part of His church. And in such a communion the Lord Christ is truly present and, through the ministry of His Word and the sacraments, works salvation in the hearts of the believing according to His establishment, even if at times, the servants of the Church, who administer the Word and the sacraments, are hypocrites and lifeless members of the Church. For the Word of God and the use of the sacraments are a power of God unto salvation for everyone who believes on them, not because of the merit of him who ministers, but because of their instiution by the Lord Christ, who is active in them by His real presence and the working of the Holy Ghost. For, as the worthiness of the servant can add nothing to the Word and sacraments of Christ. so his unworthiness and hypocrisy can nothing detract, according to the word of the Lord, Matt. 25 :2.

Nevertheless, it behooves the Church to remove from the ministry in the Church all, who lead an openly scandalous and unrepentant life and who will not be corrected by all proper means; furthermore, to strive. as much as possible, that in the Church of God doctrine and life be holy and blameless.

Article 14. Concerning Holy Baptism, the first Sacrament of Christ. Concerning Holy Baptism we confess and believe, that this sacrament, instituted by the Lord Christ Himself, is a washing of regeneration and . renewing of the Holy Ghost, which He shed on us abundantly through Jesus Christ, our Saviour, that being justified by His grace, we should be made heirs according to the hope of eternal life (Titus 3, 5ff). This baptism or washing of man with water together with the invocation of the Trinity, the Father, the Son, and the Holy Ghost, secures for him, who is thus implanted in the Church of Christ. forgiveness of sin and eternal life, as the Son of God said in the Gospel of Mark, 16:16.

We also confess, that little children should be baptized, since. according to the Lord's promise, the kingdom of God is theirs (Matt. 19 :14), and also that they, offered to God in prayer and baptism, are received into grace, according to many testimonies of Scripture.

Article 15. Concerning the Lord's Supper, the Other Sacrament of Christ. Concerning the Holy Sacrament of the Testament and the Last Supper, as it was instituted by Christ Himself before His Passion, we believe and confess, that the bread in the Supper is the true Body of our Lord Jesus Christ. offered for us, and that the wine in the chalice is the true Blood of our Lord Jesus Christ, shed for us, for the remission of sin. We believe that it is given to them, who receive it, for the purpose that they, when eating His Body and drinking His Blood, might do it for a remembrance of Him and a declaration of His innocent death, until He come, as the Lord Christ Himself, at His Last Supper and in His Testament, instituted and attested it with His own word, and as the holy evangelists and the apostle Paul clearly, teach, write, and confess: Matt. 26:26; Mark 14:22; Luke 22:19; 1 Cor. 11:24.

This Holy Sacrament was instituted: first for the awakening and strengthening of the faith, that we participate in the Lord Christ and all His benefits, in order that, when in the sacrament we receive spiritually and substantially, by faith and by mouth, the Body and Blood of our Lord Jesus Christ, we might never doubt, but firmly believe, that we truly are and, through such use, increasingly become living members of the Lord. Who in this manner incorporates His Body in us, that we as His members, might, like branches from out of the vine, take, as our only true food, from out of His body true nourishment for our souls, real enlightenment, joy, comfort, and all the benefits, which the Lord Christ graciously wrought for us by His death and perfect obedience and which, in His Gospel, He has promised to every penitent, namely, forgiveness of sin, reconciliation with God, justification, communication of the Holy Ghost, and the hope of eternal life.

Secondly, the Sacrament of the Lord's Supper was instituted, that we might render, in the public assembly of the congregation, most hearty thanks to God for all the good, He has wrought for us through Christ; and that we might, through the use of the Sacrament of the Lord's Body and Blood, be truly revived and strengthened so as to remain in the Body of Christ. For this purpose we are united with Him, that we might in Him die unto our many sins and evil lusts, arise unto righteousness, and, in conformity with all of God's laws, live unto God in all godliness and holiness, and through mutual, cordial love preserve the unity of Christ's Body, which is the Church. For we know, that all we, who, in this Sacrament eat of one bread, are united into one Body (as St. Paul says 1 Cor. 10:17), to the end that we, as common members of the one Lord Christ, might love one another with a cordial and sincere affection, in the certain conviction, that we cannot possibly despise or offend our neighbor without, at the same time, offending and despising in him the Lord Christ: and that we cannot love the

Lord Christ, except we love Him in our neighbor, as the Lord saith, Matt. 25:40.

61. THE "AMERICAN RECENSION OF THE AUGSBURG CONFESSION," 1855.

Article I.—Of God: Our churches with one accord teach, that the decree of the Council of Nice, concerning the unity of the Divine essence, and concerning the three persons, is true, and ought to be confidently believed, viz: that there is one divine essence, which is called and is God, eternal, incorporeal, indivisible, infinite in power, wisdom and goodness, the Creator and Preserver of all things visible and invisible; and yet, that there are three persons, who are of the same essence and power, and are co-eternal, the Father, the Son, and the Holy Spirit. And the term person they use in the same sense in which it is employed by ecclesiastical writers on this subject: to signify, not a part or quality of something else, but that which exists of itself.

Article II.—Of Natural Depravity: Our churches likewise teach, that since the fall of Adam, all men who are naturally engendered, are born with sin, that is, without the fear of God or confidence towards Him, and with sinful propensities; and that this disease, or natural depravity, is really sin, and still causes eternal death to those who are not born again. And they reject the opinion of those, who, in order that they may detract from the glory of the merits and benefits of Christ, allege that man may be justified before God by the powers of his own reason.

Article III.—Of the Son of God and His Mediatorial Work: They likewise teach, that the Word, that is, the Son of God, assumed human nature, in the womb of the blessed Virgin Mary. so that the two natures, human and divine, inseparably united in one person, constitute one Christ, who is true God and man, born of the Virgin Mary; who truly suffered, was crucified, died and was buried, that he might reconcile the Father to us, and be a sacrifice not only for original sin, but also for all the actual sins of men. Likewise that he descended into hell, (the place of departed spirits) and truly arose on the third day; then ascended to heaven, that he might sit at the right hand of the Father, might perpetually reign over all creatures, and might sanctify those who believe in him by sending into their hearts the Holy Spirit, who governs, consoles, quickens, and defends them against the devil and the power of sin. The same Christ will return again openly, that he may judge the living and the dead, etc., according to the Apostolic Creed.

Article IV.—Of Justification: They in like manner teach, that men cannot be justified before God by their own strength, merits, or works; but that they are justified gratuitously for Christ's sake, through faith; when they believe, that they are received into favor, and that their sins are remitted on account of Christ, who made satisfaction for our transgressions by his death. This faith God imputes to us as righteousness. Rom. 3, 4.

Article V.—Of the Ministerial Office: In order that we may obtain this faith, the ministerial office has been instituted, whose members are to teach the gospel, and administer the sacraments. For through the instrumentality of the word and sacraments, as means of grace. the Holy Spirit is given, who, in his own time and place, (or more literally, when and where it pleases God) produces faith in those who hear the gospel message, namely, that God. for Christ's sake. and not on account of any merit in us, justifies those who believe that on account of Christ they are received into (the divine) favor.

Article VI.—Concerning New Obedience (or a Christian Life): They likewise teach, that this faith must bring forth good fruits; and that it is our duty to perform those good works which God has commanded, because he has enjoined them, and not in the expectation of thereby meriting justification before him. For, remission of sins and justification are secured by faith; as the declaration of Christ himself implies: "When ye shall have done all those things, say, we are unprofitable servants."—The same thing is taught by the ancient ecclesiastical writers: for Ambrose says "this has been ordained by God, that he who believes in Christ is saved without works, receiving remission of sins gratuitously through faith alone."

Article VII.—Of the Church: They likewise teach, that there will always be one holy church. The church is the congregation of the saints. in which the gospel is correctly taught, and the sacraments are properly administered. And for the true unity of the church nothing more is required. than agreement concerning the doctrines of the gospel, and the administration of the sacraments. Nor is it necessary, that the same human traditions, that is, rites and ceremonies instituted by men, should be everywhere observed. As Paul says: "One Faith, one baptism, one God and Father of all," etc.

Article VIII.—What the Church is: Although the Church is properly a congregation of saints and true believers; yet in the present life, many hypocrites and wicked men are mingled with them.

Article IX.—Concerning Baptism: Concerning baptism, our

churches teach. that it is "a necessary ordinance," that is a means of grace, and ought to be administered also to children, who are thereby dedicated to God, and received into his favor.

Article X.—Of the Lord's Supper: In regard to the Lord's Supper they teach that Christ is present with the communicants in the Lord's Supper, "under the emblems of bread and wine."

Article XI.—Of Confessions: (As Private Confession and Absolution, which are inculcated in this Article, though in a modified form, have been universally rejected by the American Lutheran Church, the omission of this Article is demanded by the principle on which the American Recension of the Augsburg Confession is constructed; namely, to omit the several portions, which are rejected by the great mass of our churches in this country, and to add nothing in their stead.)

Article XII.—Of Repentance (after Backsliding): Concerning repentance they teach, that those who have relapsed into sin after baptism, may at any time obtain pardon, when they repent. But repentance properly consists of two parts. The one is contrition, or being struck with terrors of conscience, on account of acknowledged sin. The other is faith which is produced by the gospel; which believes that pardon for sin is bestowed for Christ's sake; which tranquilizes the conscience, and liberates it from fear. Such repentance must be succeeded by good works as its fruits.

Article XIII.—Of the Use of the Sacraments: Concerning the use of the sacraments our churches teach, that they were instituted not only as marks of a Christian profession amongst men; but rather as signs and evidences of the divine disposition towards us, tendered for the purpose of exciting and confirming the faith of those who use them. Hence the sacraments ought to be received with faith in the promises which are exhibited and proposed by them.—They therefore condemn the opinion of those who maintain, that the sacraments produce justification in their recipients as a matter of course, and who do not teach that faith is necessary, in the reception of the sacraments, to the remission of sins.

Article XIV.—Of Church Orders, (or the Ministry): Concerning church orders they teach, that "no person ought publicly to teach or preach," in the church, or to administer the sacraments, without a regular call.

Article XV.—Of Religious Ceremonies: Concerning ecclesiastical ceremonies they teach, that those ceremonies ought to be observed, which can be attended to without sin, and which promote peace and good order in the church, such as certain holy-days, festivals, etc. Concerning matters of this kind, however, men are cautioned, lest their consciences be burdened, as though such observances were necessary to salvation. They are also admonished that human traditionary observances, instituted with a view to appease God, and to merit his favor, and make satisfaction for sins, are contrary to the gospel and the doctrine of faith "in Christ." Wherefore vows and traditionary observances concerning meats, days, etc., instituted to merit grace and make satisfaction for sins, are useless, and contrary to the Gospel.

Article XVI.—Of Political Affairs: In regard to political affairs our churches teach that legitimate political enactments are good works of God; that it is lawful for Christians to hold civil offices, to pronounce judgment, and decide cases according to existing laws; to inflict just punishment, wage just wars, and serve in them; to make lawful contracts; hold property; to make oath required by the magistrate, to marry, and to be married.—Hence Christians ought necessarily to yield obedience to their civil officers and laws; unless they should command something sinful; in which case it is a duty to obey God rather than man. Acts 5, 29.

Article XVII.—Of Christ's Return to Judgment: Our churches also teach, that at the end of the world, Christ will appear for judgment; that he will raise all the dead; that he will bestow upon the pious and elect eternal life and endless joys, but will condemn wicked men and devils to be punished without end.

Article XVIII.—Of Free Will: Concerning free will our churches teach, that the human will possesses some liberty for the performance of civil duties, and for the choice of those things lying within the control of reason. But it does not possess the power, without the influence of the Holy Spirit, of being just before God, or yielding spiritual obedience: for the natural man receiveth not the things which are of the Spirit of God: but this is accomplished in the heart, when the Holy Spirit is received through the word.

The same is declared by Augustine in so many words: "We confess that all men have a free will, which possesses the judgment of reason, by which they cannot indeed, without the divine aid, either begin or certainly accomplish what is becoming in things relating to God; but only in "outward" works of the present life, as well good as evil. In good works, I say, which arise from our natural goodness, such as to choose to labor in the field, to eat and drink, to choose to have a friend, to have clothing, to build a house, to take a wife, to feed cattle, to learn various and useful arts, or to do any good thing relative to this life; all which things, however, do not exist without the divine government; yea, they exist and begin to be from Him through Him. And in evil works (men have a free will), such as to choose to worship an idol, to will to commit murder, etc."

It is not possible by the mere powers of nature, without the aid of the Holy Spirit, to love God above all things, and to do his commands according to their intrinsic design. For, although nature may be able, after a certain manner, to perform external actions, such as to abstain from theft, from murder, etc., yet it cannot perform the inner motions, such as the fear of God, faith in God, chastity, patience, etc.

Article XIX.—Of the Author of Sin: On this subject they teach, that although God is the Creator and Preserver of nature, the cause of sin must be sought in the depraved will of the devil and of wicked men, which, when destitute of divine aid, turns itself away from God: agreeably to the declaration of Christ, "When he speaketh a lie, he speaketh of his own."—John viii. 44.

Article XX.—Of Good works: Our writers are falsely accused of prohibiting good works. Their publications on the ten commandments, and other similar subjects, show, that they gave good instructions concerning all the different stations and duties of life, and explained what course of conduct, in any particular calling, is pleasing to God. Concerning these things, preachers formerly said very little, but urged the necessity of puerile and useless works, such as certain holy-days fasts, brotherhoods, pilgrimages, worship of saints, rosaries, monastic vows, etc. These useless things, our adversaries, having been admonished, now unlearn, and no longer teach as formerly. Moreover, they now begin to make mention of faith, about which they formerly observed a marvellous silence. They now teach, that we are not justified by works alone, but join faith to works, and maintain that we are justified by faith and works. This doctrine is more tolerable in their former belief, and calculated to impart more consolation to the mind. Inasmuch, then, as the doctrine concerning faith, which should be regarded as a principal one by the church, had so long been unknown; for all must confess, that concerning

the righteousness of faith, the most profound silence reigned in
their sermons, and the doctrine concerning works alone was discussed
in the churches; our divines have admonished the churches as follows :—

First, that our works cannot reconcile God, merit the remission
of sins, and grace, and justification : but this we can attain only
by faith, when we believe that we are received into favor, for Christ's
sake, who alone is appointed our mediator and propitiatory sacrifice,
by whom the Father can be reconciled. He, therefore, who expects
to merit grace by his works, casts contempt on the merits and grace
of Christ and is seeking the way to God, in his own strength, without
the Saviour; who nevertheless has told us, "I am the way, the truth,
and the life." This doctrine concerning faith, is incessantly inculcated
by the apostle Paul (Ephes. ii), "Ye are saved by grace, through faith,
and that not of yourselves, it is the gift of God," not of works, etc.
And lest any one should cavil at our interpretation, and charge it
with novelty, we state that this whole matter is supported by the
testimony of the fathers. For Augustin devotes many volumes to the
defence of grace, and the righteousness of faith, in opposition to the
merit of good works. And Ambrosius, on the calling of the Gentiles,
etc., inculcates the same doctrine. For thus he says, concerning the
calling of the Gentiles : "Redemption by the blood of Christ is of
little value, nor is the honor of human works subordinated to the
mercy of God, if justification, which is of grace, is supposed to be
merited by previous works, so as to be not the gift of him that
bestows it, but the reward of him that earned it." But although
this doctrine is despised by the inexperienced, the consciences of the
pious and timid find it a source of much consolation, for they cannot
attain peace in faith alone, when they entertain the confident belief
that, for Christ's sake, God is reconciled (Rom. v.), "Being justified
by faith, we have peace with God." This whole doctrine must be
referred to the conflict in the conscience of the alarmed sinner,
nor can it be otherwise understood. Hence the inexperienced and
worldly-minded are much mistaken, who vainly imagine that the
righteousness of the Christian is nothing else than what in common
life and in the language of philosophy is termed morality.

Formerly the consciences of men were harassed by the doctrine
of works, nor did they hear any consolation from the gospel. Some
conscience drove into deserts, and into monasteries, hoping there
to merit the divine favor by a monastic life. Others invented different

kinds of works, to merit grace, and make satisfaction for their sins. There was therefore the utmost necessity, that this doctrine concerning faith in Christ should be inculcated anew; in order that timid minds might find consolation, and know that justification and the remission of sins are obtained by faith in the Savior. The people are also now instructed, that faith does not signify a mere historical belief, such as wicked men and devils have; but that in addition to a historical belief, it includes an acquaintance with consequences of the history, such as remission of sins, by grace through Christ, righteousness, etc., etc.

Now he who knows that the Father is reconciled to him through Christ, possesses a true acquaintance with God, confides in his providence, and calls upon his name: and is therefore not without God as are the Gentiles. For the devil and wicked men cannot believe the article concerning the remission of sins. But they hate God as an enemy, do not call upon his name, nor expect anything good at his hands. Augustin, in speaking of the word faith, admonishes the reader that in Scripture this word does not signify mere knowledge, such as wicked men possess, but that confidence or trust, by which alarmed sinners are comforted and lifted up. We moreover teach, that the performance of good works is necessary, because it is commanded of God, and not because we expect to merit grace by them. Pardon of sins and grace are obtained only by faith. And because the Holy Spirit is received by faith, the heart of man is renovated, and new affections produced, that he may be able to perform good works. Accordingly Ambrosius states, faith is the source of holy volitions and upright life. For the faculties of man, unaided by the Holy Spirit, are replete with sinful propensities, and too feeble to perform works that are good in the sight of God. They are moreover under the influence of Satan, who urges men to various sins, and impious opinions, and open crimes; as may be seen in the examples of the philosophers who, though they endeavored to lead moral lives, failed to accomplish their designs, and were guilty of many notorious crimes. Such is the imbecility of man, when he undertakes to govern himself by his own strength without faith and the Holy Spirit.

From all this it is manifest, that our doctrine, instead of being charged with prohibiting good works, ought much rather to be applauded, for teaching the manner in which truly good works can be performed. For without faith, human nature is incapable of performing the duties either of the first or second table. Without it, man does not call upon God, nor expect anything from him, nor bear the cross: but seeks refuge amongst men, and reposes on human aid. Hence when faith and confidence in God are wanting, all evil desires and human schemes reign in the heart; wherefore Christ also says, "without me ye can do nothing" (John xv.); and the church responds, Without thy favor there is nothing good in man.

Article XXI.—Of the Invocation of Saints: Concerning the invocation of saints our churches teach, that the saints ought to be held in remembrance, in order that we may, each in his own calling, imitate the example of David, in carrying on war to expel the Turks from our country; for both are kings. But the sacred volume does not teach us to invoke saints or to seek aid from them. For it proposes Christ to us as our only mediator, propitiation, high priest, and intercessor. On his name we are to call, and he promises, that he will hear our prayers and highly approves of this worship viz.: that he should be called upon in every affliction (I John ii.): "If any one sin we have an advocate with the Father," etc.

This is about the substance of our doctrines, from which it is evident that they contain nothing inconsistent with the Scriptures. Under these circumstances, those certainly judge harshly, who would have us regarded as heretics. But the difference of opinion between us (and the Romanists) relates to certain abuses, which have crept into the (Romish) churches without any good authority; in regard to which, if we do differ, the bishops ought to treat us with lenity and tolerate us, on account of the confession which we have just made.

[The "American Recension of the Augsburg Confession" knows only of these 21 articles.]

NOTES TO THE COLLECTION OF SOURCES

1. Sehling, *Evangelische Kirchenordnungen des 16. Jahrhunderts,* I, 1 p. 149ff.—2. Luther's Works, Weimar Edition, 26, 499ff.—3. The genuine text will be published in the forthcoming volume of *Deutsche Reichstagsakten.*—4. Ney, *Geschichte des Reichstags zu Speyer,* p. 104ff.— —5. Ney, ibid, p. 129ff.—6. Ney, *Die Appellation und Protestation der evangelischen Stände auf dem Reichstag zu Speyer,* p. 50ff.— 7. H. v. Schubert, *Bekenntnisbildung und Religionspolitik,* 138ff.— 8. H. v. Schubert, *Bek. u. Rel.,* p. 61ff.—9. Luther, W. E. 30, III, 86ff. 10. H. v. Schubert, *Die Anfänge evangelischer Bekenntnisbildung,* p. 40.—11. Luther, W. E. 30, III, 160ff.—12. G. G. Weber, *Kritische Geschichte der Augsb. Confession, I, first supplement.*—13. H. v. Schubert, *Bek. u. Religionspolitik,* p. 169ff.—14. Schubert, *Bek. u. Rel.* p. 141ff.—15. Schubert, *Bek. u. Rel.,* p. 144ff.—16. J. J. Müller, *Historie von der Evangelischen Stände Protestation und Appellation* etc., p. 330ff. —17. Förstemann, *Urkundenbuch.* I, p. 1ff.—18. H. v. Schubert, *Bek. u. Rel.,* p. 245ff.—19. Gussmann, *Quellen und Forschungen,* II, p. 195f.— 20. Gussmann, *Quellen und Forschungen,* II, p. 196f.—21. Förstemann, *Urkundenbuch.* I, 68ff.—22. *Archiv für Reformationsgeschichte,* IX (1912), p. 251ff.—23. *Archiv f. Ref.* IX (1912), p. 332ff.—24. Gussmann, *Quellen und Forschungen,* II, p. 99ff.; compare Jacobs, *The Book of Concord, II,* 69ff.—25. Maurenbrecher, *Karl V. und die deutschen Protestanten,* Supplement One, 3ff.—26. Enders, *Luthers Briefwechsel,* VII, p. 327f.—27. Enders, VII, p. 330—28. Luther's Works, Erl. Ed., 54, p. 145.—29. Förstemann, *Urkundenbuch,* I, p. 87ff.—30. H. v. Schubert, *Bek. und Rel.,* p. 263ff.—31. Förstemann, *Urkundenbuch,* I, 220ff.—32. Förstemann, *Urkundenbuch.* I, p. 224ff.—33. Kolde, *Die älteste Redaktion der Augsb. Konfession,* p. 4ff.—34. *Archiv für Reformationsgeschichte,* IX (1912), p. 343ff.—35. Luther's Works, W. Ed., 30, II, p. 268ff.—36. Förstemann, *Urkundenbuch,* I, p. 283ff.— 37. Luther's Works, Erl. Ed., 54, p. 151ff.—38. Förstemann, *Urkundenbuch,* I, p. 375ff.—39. Kolde, *Aelteste Redaktion der Augsb. Konfession,* p. 11ff.—40. [Joh. Ficker] *Die Augsburgische Konfession in ihrer ersten Gestalt als gemeinsames Bekenntnis deutscher Reichsstände,* p. 4ff.—41. G. G. Weber, *Kritische Geschichte der Augsb. Confession,* I, Supplement 3.—42. *Corpus Reformatorum,* XXVI, p. 537ff. —43. Lanz, *Bibliothek des literarischen Vereins in Stuttgart,* XI, p. 45ff.—44. Jonas' letter to Luther: Enders VIII, p. 25ff. The Elector's letter to Luther. Enders VIII, p. 30ff. The letters of the representatives of Nürnberg; C. R. II, p. 127ff., 142ff.—45. Luther's letter to

Melanchthon, June 27; Enders VIII, p. 34ff. June 29; Enders VIII, p. 41ff. Letter to Brenz: Enders VIII, p. 59ff. Letter to Jonas: Enders VIII, p. 47ff. Letter to Melanchthon, June 30: Enders VIII, 50ff.— 46. Luther's Works, Erl. Ed., 54, p. 159ff.—47. Joh. Ficker, *Die Konfutation des Augsburger Bekenntnisses* p. 1ff.—48. Föerstemann, *Urkundenbuch*, II, p. 16ff.—49, Letter to the Elector: Luther's Works, Erl. Ed., 54, p. 169ff. To Jonas: Enders VIII, p. 93. To Melanchthon: Enders VIII, p. 99f.—50. Kolde, *Die Augsburgische Konfession*, p. 140ff.—51. To the Elector, Aug. 26: Luther's Works, Erl. Ed., 54. p. 188ff. To Melanchthon, Aug. 26: Enders VIII, p. 218ff. To Jonas: Enders VIII, p. 221ff. To Spalatin: Enders VIII, p. 217f. To Melanchthon, Aug. 28: Enders VIII, p. 234ff —52. *Corp. Ref.* II, p. 363ff.—53. Förstemann, *Urkundenbuch.* II, p. 474ff.—54. *Corp. Ref.* XXVII, p. 322ff.—55. Kolde, *Die Augsb. Konfession,* p. 170ff.— 56. Heppe, *Bekenntnisschriften der altprotest. Kirche,* p. 447ff.—57. *Heppe,* p. 514ff.—58. Eger. *Das Böhmische Glaubensbekenntnis von 1575,* p. 15ff.—59. *Gedenkbuch anlässlich der 400 jährigen Jahreswende der Confessio Augustana,* p. 33ff.; 51ff.; 60ff.—60. Teutsch, *Urkundenbuch,* II, p. 144ff.—61. Mentz, *Die Wittenberger Artikel von 1536,* p. 18ff. —62. Hardwick, *A History of the Articles of Religion,* p. 233ff.— 63. *Definite Platform, Doctrinal and Disciplinarian, for Ev. Lutheran District Synods* . . . 1855.